Rejuvenating
the
Humanities

Rejuvenating the Humanities

Edited by
Ray B. Browne
and
Marshall W. Fishwick

Bowling Green State University Popular Press
Bowling Green, Ohio 43403

Contents

Prologue

Ray B. Browne
and
Marshall W. Fishwick

Times have always been a-changing, and time changes all things. So does usage. All accounts of the past are unreliable approximations. History is not an account of the events of the past but biased and personalized renditions of what people want to believe happened. In a similar manner, recounting of the wisdom of the past in the words of the sages was to a certain extent culture-specific to the society in which it was operative. It may have been workable and useful in its original setting and to a certain extent to similar settings later on. We like to think that universals are as applicable out of time and out of original culture as they were in their original. To a certain degree perhaps they are, since human nature seems to remain constant through time and space. But there are significant differences.

In many ways the effort to apply the wisdom of the past to the culture of today is as impracticable as imposing the technology of the past upon that of today. In some instances it can be used; sometimes it must be taken into consideration. But in most cases the technology of long ago is mainly of historical interest, museum pieces which should not be brought out of their cases. Often we have great difficulty recognizing the extensions of this obvious fact. We are cautioned by historians that we must know the past or be forced to relive it. That maxim though perhaps accurate in broad outline is misleading in microcosmic understanding. It should read that unless the lessons of the past are fully *understood*, fully comprehended, we will be unable to free ourselves from the mistakes of our fathers and will therefore have to redo them again and again, never escaping from the cycle.

Mistakes—and proper decisions—were and remain culture-bound and time-specific. We are the culture we live in, and the culture is us. The culture of the past cannot be imposed upon that of today. Cultures have their organic dynamics, the powers that drive and control them. They constantly move away from their past. The actions, lessons and wisdom of the past cannot fit exactly into the present. Changing times equal changing culture. New imperatives create new necessities and new reactions, new problems and new solutions.

No one can deny, for example, that the recently heightened sensitivities about the rights of women, minorities, ethnic groups, lesbians and homosexuals have mandated broadened definitions of the way societies operate beneficially, how the Humanities must become more humane. Nor our necessary considerations

1

of the rights of other animals, the physical environment we live in and its increased susceptibility to the abuses of mankind.

So just as actions of the past must be modified, the inherited wisdom that we call the Humanities must be modernized, not necessarily discarded and destroyed but modernized surely. Shakespeare's observations that all the world's a stage surely means something quite different today than it did in *As You Like It*. Four hundred years of human motion have changed the setting. The world is bigger and more complex, the actors different.

As the world turns it may or may not be fated to wear out in a hundred million years. But in many ways its aging is manifest in most dramatic ways—in the exhausting of its natural, non-renewable resources. Humankind may finally have come to the point where they are slowing down the exhaustion of the natural resources, people may be living longer and less diseased lives through the discoveries of science. But science performs its miracles in the natural laws by reworking, rediscovering and modifying our knowledge used in the past. Not by defying the laws of nature but by discovering more accurately by fine-tuning those laws into our greater understanding. In so doing scientists are micro-understanding the natural laws and mankind's place in the world. As with our greater understanding of the laws of the physical universe, the time has come for us to micro-tune the Humanities and discover more accurately their dynamics.

If the Humanities are the essence of humankind's getting along in society and the world, then as our understanding society and our own nature and our relationship to physical nature changes, the Humanities also change.

Often the complicated electronic changes in the physical and social world occur so fast that they dazzle and confuse. Monumental changes are often completed around us before we realize that they are in the offing. Naturally they disconnect and disconcert us.

Such a fast pace is so dislocating that people often look to the past for understanding, comfort and stability. Doing so they place an unwarranted steadiness where it did not exist originally. The past was never so Edenic as it appears in the orange glow of nostalgia. In the past the wisdom of the time was felt to be tentative and equivocal, often makeshift, surely not destined to be the rock of ages of the future. The "basics" of life now so eagerly sought by the shortsighted and timid were not originally as basic and steady as they now seem. Lists of items we need to know to make us culturally literate and a return to the "good old days" and ways of imparting them are presumed facts in the night that will soon fade away. In other words, the security felt to have existed in the past was as uneasy as our times are to us today.

To confront the present—and the future—humankind desperately needs an open-minded awareness of the world that is in keeping with the reality of that world. In the Humanities this means an awareness that humankind's sensitivities, thinking, habits, reactions, life styles change over time and modify with the changing reality.

We need to become acutely aware that the Humanities are for the living, not memorials to the dead. The dead past must bury its dead. The Humanities are not headstones in the graveyard of history. They are living organisms for the use of living societies. They animate present-day cultures. Like all other aspects of life, the Humanities may grow threadbare and out of date. When they do they need to be reevaluated, patched, replaced as the need arises. Sometimes they must be put on permanent sabbatical. Often they are so out of touch with reality that they are dangerous. Nothing is immutable. So the imperfect Humanities, when they are found insufficient, should be abandoned and new ones, or new modifications, substituted.

The Humanities are perhaps the single most important and useful cultural philosphy driving societies and human actions. They oppose greed and lust and unbridled individual rapacity. They drive toward what is good in and necessary in society. To let the Humanities languish is to deprive life of the major beneficial living force in—or capable of being introduced into—society today.

This collection of essays is an effort to help modernize and make more useful some aspects of the Humanities which in the past seem to have been overlooked or underdeveloped. The papers reintroduce some of the missing parts of the Humanities puzzle back into our awareness, to add new parts and to level the table on which the game of scholarship is played.

Marshall Fishwick's initial essay is an alarm pistol in the night, awaking us to the present but demonstrating that we are, after all, very human and need the Humanities to make us continue to remain so. In the second essay Ray Browne and Michael Marsden tackle the problem of what people can do in their leisure-time and with their leisure-time to improve the human situation.

Folk cultures and their relationship—or vital role in—the Humanities are the subject of the third essay, by Ray Browne, in which he makes a special case for the importance of this large segment of any civilization, and argues that to ignore this importance is to pay no attention to the basis for all civilizations. In *"Homo Sum: Humani Nil Me Alienum Puto,"* Fred Schroeder demonstrates that popular material culture, increasingly coming into human awareness as important, in fact speaks very emphatically to us all. "The values of humanities are not intrinsic to a few rare objects," he says. "They are in the human meanings that we read into or out of things with thoughtful examination."

The role of art in human experience, its realities and pretentions, is faced squarely by Jon Huer in his essay "Of Art and Entertainment." In the growth of democracy and democratic rights, this examination is vital, and Huer's conclusions, though disquieting to many, necessary. In "Pornography, Obscenity, and the Humanities," William Brigman faces a vital question about definitions of art, the purposes those definitions—and the art—are put to and how in a democratic society people must be aware of and in opposition to the power grab of the privileged.

"Souls of Fire," by Susan Laubach, performs a valuable task in examining the Humanities in the real world: "I was having my Humanities test," she explains about her research, "in the place where Socrates and Plato thought it mattered most—out in the real world, in the market place, midst *humanitas,*" Surely she is right, the marketplace is the ideal laboratory for the Humanities.

Humankind is finally awaking to and admitting our inseparable role to other animals that exist on this globe and the realization that if human beings have natural and inalienable rights, so too do other animals. Michael Pettengell's essay, "Animal Rights and the Humanities," reveals some of the opportunities and obligations students of the Humanities must face. The role of the much maligned genre the comics is examined by Joseph Witek in his essay, "From Genre to Medium: Comics and Contemporary American Culture." His conclusions will come as no surprise to anybody but they will continue to be resisted. Prejudice dies hard and slow, especially among academics.

That no one seriously concerned with the continuation of the Humanities wants to guillotine them is evidenced in James Seaton's paper, "The Humanities and Cultural Criticism: The Example of Ralph Ellison." The past and present are always with us, constituting two lenses in our pair of glasses, allowing us to see both. Both visions are fundamental. Seaton's thesis is to a certain extent carried on in Joyce Pettis' essay on "Black Studies and the Humanities: An Alliance Forged Through Fire." Fire and the threat of fire seem to be the powers that galvanize people into action. Pettis points out the development and growth of Black Studies as areas of growth in the Humanities.

In our effort to rejuvenate the Humanities it is, of course, always vital that we look to our classrooms to see new approaches, new devices and new aids for better ways to teach. Jack Estes' paper, "Rejuvenating the Humanities— Learning Committees" sketches a new and vital approach. In "Go and Catch a Falling Star: The Humanities in a Post-Modern World," Marshall Fishwick suggests that in our society it is imperative that the broad world of popular culture be integrated into our consciousness, that is, popular culture in its broadest sense. His paper is an umbrella to the series of essays presented in this volume.

In "The Traveller and the Humanities," Ray Browne, Glenn Browne and Kevin Browne look at the role of the traveller, the place of travelling and the result of all this intermixing of humanities throughout the world. As the world gets smaller and smaller, societies get more and more mixed. Do we come more and more to recognize our likenesses and the imperatives of living together, or do we merely have easier access to the jugular of humanity and the underground flow of existence? Their argument is either we live together or we die together.

In our narrow vision we often think that the Humanities are Eurocentric and merely a Western tradition. Perhaps in the past this concept was understandable. But no more. Modern electronics have shrunk the world to the size of a large pumpkin—or beach ball. Television is providing a window on the world, as well as one of opportunity, that causes instant awareness of similarities and differences among all people. Television is also causing a crisis in the humanities, as Gary Burns points out in his essay "Television and the Crisis in the Humanities," and the imperative need for us to use this medium if we are to rejuvenate the humanities.

In the final essay in this volume, Marshall Fishwick brings us up short with the question "Can the Humanities Cross the Pacific?" An intriguing question. The answer has to be, of course, in the affirmative. From thousands of miles in the void of the universe, the Earth has no West or East, just a small, insignficant globe floating in a void. Huddled on that Earth can we afford to think of West and East, of Atlantic and Pacific, or is our home merely Earth? The answer seems obvious.

So these essays of expanding awareness of the various parts and forces in the Humanities attempt to broaden and intensify our knowledge of and reactions to the roles of the Humanities in our Culture. The examinations are not complete.

More minds must be applied to the problems. We hope, however, that these contributions will be helpful.

What's This? Another Crisis?

Marshall W. Fishwick

American culture is driven by reaction to crises. We do not dam a river until it has flooded the countryside dozens of times, we do not pass laws controlling Savings and Loans Institutions until after they have cost us billions of dollars. We do not check the space-worthiness of our spaceships until they are on the launching pad. The inspection is late—but at least it comes before repeated and repeated disasters. With the Humanities the inspection comes if at all only after they have virtually been worn out—like old tires with no thread left, slipping and sliding along the highways of life. In this caution about the Humanities, Marshall Fishwick traces the concept of the Humanities through history and suggests that it is time we reexamined their constituent parts and made repairs while repairs can be helpful.

The end draws near. We have closed the American Mind. We are cultural illiterates. The sky is falling in. Run for cover, Chicken Little!

Thus has it always been. The ancient Greeks—who invented what now goes under the label of "Humanities"—had their own Doom Boom. Socrates thought the young people were going to hell in a basket. Plato decided that democracy was the worst of all possible forms of government. The best Greek dramatists specialized in murder, rape and eye-gouging. Diogenes went around in a barrel, looking in vain for an honest man.

Centuries later, we find ourselves in the same predicament.

Born in the Great Depression, we struggled with the Dust Bowl, the empty soup bowl, Fascism and Communism—climaxing with Pearl Harbor. Then came global war, genocide, the Iron Curtain, the Korean War, Vietnam, Watergate, Iran-gate, a debt that wouldn't shrink, a budget that wouldn't budge, the Persian Gulf. Suddenly hundreds of thousands of Americans were in the desert. But we had been there, with the humanities, even earlier. The best poet of my generation, W.H. Auden had written:

> Come to our jolly desert,
> Where even the dolls go whoring
> Where cigarette ends become intimate friends
> And it's always three in the morning.

> Come to our well-run desert

Where anguish comes by cable
And the deadly sins can be bought in tins
With instructions on the label.

Dramatists (like Samuel Beckett, Tennessee Williams, Arthur Miller, Harold Pinter) struck the same ominous cord. At the same time historians and philosophers argued that the expansion of Europe had plunged the whole world into crisis; we had forced non-western cultures into confusion, demoralization, fanaticism and revenge. "Behind the bourgeois certainties," wrote Edmund Stillman in *The Politics of Hysteria: The Sources of 20th Century Conflict,* "there were sinister fantasies waiting to be acted out." Then our fantasies started turning up on the Six O'Clock Nightly News.

Who was to blame? The Left? The Right? The Center? Capitalism? Communism? Islam? How about secular humanism? The list of the accused was endless.[1]

As the century moved—or rather staggered—towards its end, and the year 2000 loomed on the horizon, the millenarians and fundamentalists sounded the alarm. As our millennium ended we faced Armageddon. Then Satan would be bound (see Revelations 20: 1-5) and Christ would reign on earth.

No wonder one of the major humanists of my generation—the late A.B. Giamatti, who was for several years president of Yale University, had this to say in 1978:

The vague but pressing conviction that things are not cohesive and obligations cannot be met seems to occur at the end of centuries. We are in the last part of the 20th century; we are at the very end of the second Christian millennium, and we are experiencing the sense of futility and the exaggerated regard of our worthlessness that attends periods which close major eras. The suggestion that the end is near and all is stained will grow around you and grow more insistent.[2]

Our task is to look at the Crisis of the 90s under what Aristotle called *sub specie aeternitatis* and to find in our past thinking roads to a new thinking. Two tried-and-true "isms" will, in my opinion, serve us well: utilitarianism and existentialism. And the wellspring from which they both flow is Aristotle. The place to start our crisis-control is with him.[3]

Born in 384 B.C., Aristotle laid the groundwork for science, the textbook of knowledge for over 2,000 years. In fact, he gave us much of the terminology of science and philosophy: words like faculty, mean, energy, actuality, category, motive, end, form, principle—these indispensable coins of modern thinking were minted in his mind.

Moreover, he invented a new science—logic. To that we must turn in times of crisis: the art and method of correct thinking. If ever we need to be logical, it is in our troubled time.

"If you wish to converse with me," Voltaire said centuries later, "define your terms." For him, and many others, the ideal life is like a proper syllogism.

Aristotle believed in solving problems by analyzing them. He loathed emotional excesses. Look always for the middle way, the golden mean. This is not an exact average of two precise calculations; it fluctuates with circumstances and is determined by what he calls "flexible reason." *Meden agan*—nothing in excess. Between cowardice and rashness is courage. Between stinginess and extravagance is liberality. Between sloth and greed is ambition. Between humility and pride is modesty. Between secrecy and loquacity is honesty; between moroseness and buffoonery, good humor; between quarrelsomeness and flattery, friendship; between Hamlet's indecisiveness and Quixote's impulsiveness is self-control. "Right," then, in ethics or conduct, is not different from "right" in mathematics or engineering; it means correct, fit, what works best to the best result.

This kind of thinking was still dominant in the life and work of John Stuart Mill (1806-1873), known as "the Aristotle of the Victorian Age." Mill was a liberal in politics, a modified laissez-faire thinker in economics, an empiricist in philosophy, and a secular humanist in religion. All this combined in an ethical pattern known as utilitarianism, on which much of our ethical thinking is based.

In his twenties, Mill underwent a psychological crisis brought on by his reading of romantic poets and philosophers. Exposed to their works, he rebelled against barren, calculating rationalism and adopted a more positive, and flexible point of view. While receptive to the romantic and democratic currents of mid-century European thought, Mill remained dedicated to objective, rational methods and never forsook his belief in individualism.

On Liberty (1859), Mill's greatest contribution to modern social thought, is an eloquent essay on "the nature and limits of the power which can be legitimately exercised by society over the individual," and it offers a reasoned defense of a balanced position between individual freedom and social necessity. For Mill, positive individual liberty is essential to both the personal happiness of self-realization and the advancement of the welfare of society.

The classic statement on Mill's philosophy appeared in his book *Utilitarianism* (1861). In it he sought to offer to the individual, as well as to society, a more secure moral foundation than existed in his time. He believed that the moral system of past centuries, based chiefly on divine revelation, had run its course. As for the future, moral principles based on intuition ("inner conviction") might serve individuals adequately—but the personal nature of such principles could not provide a common bonding for society. Utilitarianism seemed to offer what was needed: a moral system which would serve both the individual and society. Mill was certain that the well-spring of morality lay within each human being. Therefore, when faced with two choices, Mill believed that humans will give preference to the choice of higher value over that of lesser value. Consequently, the preference of the majority can normally be accepted and trusted as sound moral choices.

This is as clear and positive statement of the wedding of popular culture and ethics as one can find.

Of course it must be amended and expanded to meet new technologies and life patterns. As inner convictions change, so must outer manifestations. Talented new writers and thinkers, espousing popular causes, insist that women and other traditionally excluded groups be brought into discussions of philosophy. How can one claim to build a "crystal palace" (as Kierkegaard described Hegel's philosophy) if some individuals are not allowed residence inside it? One cannot write of ethics and rationality with context in which women and non-whites have been denied access to education and then assumed to be inferior. Similarly, Marxist philosophy denies that "the good" or "the true" exists independently of concrete historical and material circumstances. Marxism has argued that philosophy has tended to be a reactionary tool defending bourgeois culture and values.

Pragmatism, a philosophy whose origins and roots are mainly in America, has done much to explain our culture and re-define its ethics. Derived from the Greek word *pragma* (a thing done), this school emphasizes the immediate, actual and real; the validity of all concepts can be tested by the practical results. Truth, founder Charles Peirce insisted, is a process, and the "cash-value" of an idea. It is far better to speak of how ideas work than what truth is. Knowledge is a dynamic process rather than a static idea. The pragmatist John Dewey did much to re-shape the American educational system, and his ideas turn up in many aspects of popular culture.

Since World War II, two other major non-traditional schools have entered the field: phenomenology and existentialism.[4] Both have important messages for those concerned with ethics, actions and the communication process. Phenomenology's slogan—to the things themselves—is a mandate to explore being as it reveals itself to us without bias and presuppositions about "how it ought to be."

Phenomenologists have provided rich and insightful analyses of some of the more basic, everyday aspects of human experience, including play, leisure, sexuality, and loneliness. Phenomenologists, rather than doubt the reality of the world, tend to ignore that issue and instead look at how we see or feel or taste. Analyses of popular culture can provide similar insights, allowing ethical standards to emerge from the real world of experienced desires, so prevalent in many aspects of our electronic age.

Existentialism is one of the most powerful and controversial factors in our century, and the key to relating popular culture and ethics in our time. It became Europe's "popular" philosophy during and after World War II. Its motto: challenge. Scorners of abstractions, generalities, circumlocutions, and official values, its members are blunt to the point of brutality. With "blah blah words" they refuse to have anything to do. Inauthentic existence is another term for hell on earth. They will not stand by and see a person turned into a *thing*; or cog in the system of production and consumption. They reject the education of adjustment which presses everyone into a pattern and condones cultural brainwashing. Blandness and complacency can destroy us. We must ask hard questions:

Are we free? Have we *ever* been free? How, when, and where is creative freedom possible? Is guilt a permanent stain on the soul? Is free will a fact or an illusion? How can we choose not to choose? What does it mean to exist genuinely?

They dare to face meaninglessness as the answer to the question of meaning. They have the courage to be—or, if necessary, not to be.

Existentialism is a way of thinking about ultimate problems. This primordial concern is both its hallmark and its glory. Only when one realizes his plight and has the nerve to die can he find the strength to live.

Arguments about the founders of this doctrine abound. Some argue for the fifteenth-century French poet, Francois Villon, and after him Rabelais and Montaigne. Others stress the contributions of the early Greeks, still others nineteenth-century Germans. All those who have brought the struggle of heart vs. brain into the open can be included in the line of antecedents.

Soren Kierkegaard (1813-1855) played a pivotal role. To leave this great Dane out of the story is to watch the play minus Hamlet. Both father and son dealt constantly with ethical problems—were in fact obsessed by them. The son's writings mirror the struggle of a hypersensitive soul in an unethical world.

System-builders infuriated him. Kierkegaard felt that tight mental boxes confined rather than liberated the human spirit. He directed his critical attack against rationalism, which had dominated western thought from Descartes (1596-1650) through Hegel (1770-1831). This Danish rebel denied the possibility of public or objective solutions. We cannot deal effectively with truth as if it is something outside us. Truth is always personal and subjective. Built on each unique individual's existence, it reveals itself through involvement.

If ordinary people do not read Kierkegaard, they see his ideas expounded (often cheapened) in popular films, TV series, and best sellers. Horror movies, chillers and thrillers, and violent bombast have found a place in the popular imagination. Recent efforts to ban records, photographs, and pictures which seem to some obscene and puerile show growing resentment to excessive permissiveness and sexploitation. But who has a right to censor and condemn?

Ethics deal with people's psychic burden, which shifts over the centuries. The Ancients contended with fate, over which humans have no control. Fate culminates in death, as the Greek writers well knew. Medieval people wrestled with the problem of guilt, which culminated in condemnation. *Dies Irae* was heard throughout the land; the confession was the accepted avenue to redemption. For the modern world, guilt seems less overwhelming a problem than meaninglessness. Against this great emptiness modern man must struggle. Nothingness lies curled at the heart of being like a worm.

Modern existentialists have suggested various answers. Some favor sheer violent action. Malraux became a soldier of fortune. Saint Exupery flew over the Andes in a primitive plane, which could crash at any moment. Mauriac and Bernanos suggested that action might be moral rather than physical; the poor country priest might, in the drab routine of his work, come closest to reality.[5]

Jean-Paul Sartre insists that there are two kinds of being: *l'etre en soi* (being-in-itself) and *l'etre pour soi* (being-for-itself). The first is characterized by infinite density. A rock has no will, no choice, no intention. The second is characterized by mutability and desire. We have both will and intention. Project plus facility, we are haunted by the gnawing hopeless passion to thwart meaninglessness. Existentialism's first job is to make every one aware that the full responsibility rests on him or her. The five key propositions are:

1. Man exists—appears on the scene before he can be defined.
2. Man is indefinable because (at first) he is nothing. Being negativity, he can commit *all* errors.
3. He becomes something by making something of himself.

4. It is futile to speak of "human nature."

5. Hence man is only what he wills himself to be as he consciously moves upward toward authentic existence.

Sartre and his disciples see humans as a series of undertakings—an ensemble of relationships. Man is as he does. Action alone justifies life. Existence is action and involvement. The greatest sins are not those of commission or omission, but of *submission*. No one must allow himself to drift into and through oblivion. Avoid inner laziness—the tendency to give up; to sell out for phony security or position. Always we gravitate towards ruts, pigeonholes, and utopias. "Stop it!" the Existentialists cry. Only by struggling are you human. Social, physical, ethnic distinctions are not essential.

Simone de Beauvoir gives (in *The Ethics of Ambiguity*) her analysis of the types of modern men. She begins with Subman, that finite clod unmoved by a spark. He makes up the group, the herd, the "masses" as that term was used by Ortega y Gassett. Blind to life and desire, Subman clings to a dull insignificant world. His spiral points downward: the less he exists, the less reason there is for him to exist. Dangerous because he is a force for the clever to manipulate, Subman can be counted on when lynchings, pogroms, or any other dirty work arises.

Serious Man strives for permanent values by owning permanent objects. A child who never grows up, he accords ultimate meaning to the useful. Never does he ask, "*What* is this [or that] useful for?" His dishonesty comes from his obligation to renew the denial of his freedom. He abdicates his right to be truly human—in return for a bright feather to wear in his hat. The Adventurer, by contrast, doesn't try to justify himself. Interested in conquest, not consequences, he likes action for its own sake. He is a doer. Throwing himself into each new enterprise, he prefers to do or die than ask the reason why. Fulfilling himself by denying others' freedom, carrying within him the seed of the dictator, he is basically contemptuous of other men and women.

The Nihilist not only rejects his own existence, but also the existences that confirm it. "If I can't be anything, I'll be nothing." He rejects existence without being able to eliminate it. Like the playwright Samuel Beckett, he comes to the zero point—and zero times anything equals zero.

Passionate Man begins as Serious Man, but allows his passions to run away with him. The object of these passions he takes as an absolute; because it proves to be ephemeral, his "absolute" fades away. Burning ambitions are never fulfilled. All that is left is *angst*.

Simone de Beauvoir is describing not only ambiguity, but evil. She is putting into modern parlance what men have discovered, with tears and anguish, time and again. The serious man tends to err seriously. The adventurer sets out to save others, but ends up destroying himself. The passionate man makes an idol of his passions, and is enslaved by them. Thus the Existentialists are not, as critics have claimed, anti-religious, or atheistic. Instead they represent an ultimate religious concern. They see the general human predicament in every particular situation. They scorn "education of adjustment" which would press everyone into a single mold and the technological society which turns man into a thing.

In this, they are far more religious than many who turn out Sunday School literature or fill pulpits on Sunday morning.

They are also attuned to the general themes of disillusionment, pessimism, unrest, the lure of destruction. They know man is a disappointing actor, full of bad faith. All too often he refuses to face up to his freedom; hides behind banalities and abstractions; worships the trivial; indulges in racial and religious prejudice; dodges responsibilities on all levels. Like the dishonest dentist, he makes his living by disguising decay. Existentialists lament the lost innocence of men who try to raise morale by turning every day into a pseudo-Christmas.

German writers have been among the most successful interpreters of the Existentialist position. Karl Jaspers and Martin Heidegger exerted tremendous influence on formal philosophy. Heidegger's *Sein und Zeit* (1927) draws directly from Kierkegaard in stressing the mood of dread— "what anxiety is anxious about is 'being-in-the-world' itself." Terrified by the threat of nothingness, we retreat into anonymity. Life becomes like getting a bagful of second-class mail, sent to us without a name. We are lost in the lonely crowd. Somehow we must block our descent into hell, and achieve authentic existence.

Such thoughts Rainer Maria Rilke transmuted into poetry. Man the sojourner can never go home. Alienation saturates Rilke's poetry. In his special world even the quick-witted animals notice that we are "none too securely at home in the world that we know." We are lost not only in the world of space, but in the world of time, which draws us into the eternal void. Nothing highlights the ethical dilemma of popular culture more than this.

Existentialism has permeated our culture as dye permeates a jar of water. Even those who have never heard the word are haunted by the questions it raises. How can I exist genuinely? Should I be content to be a couch potato—to gaze among T.V.'s multiple channels, thinking I am being entertained? Overwhelmed by glitter and glitz, what can and do we believe? Existentialism insists that life is commitment. As we enter the final years of the twentieth century, what are we committed to?

Permeating much of western thought, such ideas have had great impact. The whole school has a strongly negative flavor. Theirs is a philosophy of flux and becoming. In it is no place for the fixed or stable. The ethical problems are often avoided. Is life livable (except on an animal level) without some structure? And does that not demand an ethic?

Existentialists are incurably individualistic. They ignore Aristotle's truism, "Man is a social animal." They also ignore the Hebraic truth contained in the notion of the covenant. God made this covenant with people, rather than a person—a consideration which has no validity in existentialism. The school is radically anthropocentric, often egocentric. Self is the alpha and omega of their concern.

Yet despite these shortcomings, existentialism is one of the most powerful weapons against explosive evil which has been devised. It isn't a theology, but a way of thinking about problems. While Existentialists raise critical questions, they do not purport to give final answers. Seeing a world advancing yet absurd, inescapable yet insufficient, they show us not only how to exist despite contradictions, but to hope despite tribulations. They are tough-minded thinkers for tragic times.

They are not, of course, popular with many people who watch NFL football play-offs, scream at game shows, and cry at soap operas. Elite writers have their effect indirectly, and in ways which many of the people affected never comprehend. Often there is a messenger who translates and popularizes such writings. A good example is Marshall McLuhan, an obscure English professor who became the Prince of Popthink, the carrier of the Existenial Word. Deejays who had never heard of Kierkegaard or Sartre were shouting, "Whatcha doin', Marshall McLuhan?" and pundits everywhere were announcing that "The Medium is the message."

Other writers and intellectuals were fascinated and bemused. "Suppose McLuhan is what he sounds like," Tom Wolfe wrote in a popular magazine, "the most important thinker since Newton?" Frenchmen began praising "le McLuhanism." The man and his works provide a critical link between popular culture and ethics in our time.

"I am an investigator," McLuhan said time and again. "I make probes. I have no point of view. I do not stay in one position, I talk back to media and set off an adventure of exploration." He has consciously assumed the role of gadfly. The deeper his bite, the more bitter the resentment. Gadflies are never easy to live with. Look what the Greeks did to Socrates.

With impressive academic credentials (graduate of Trinity College, Cambridge, positions in leading universities) he produced articles, books, disciples, and detractors in a steady stream.

For McLuhan it was Gutenberg's movable type—not Petrarch, Copernicus, or Columbus—who created the modern world views with its special outlook. His observations had quirk, a hook; a special angle that turned the conventional world into something startling and strange. His was a surrealism of words rather than images. No one who has heard or read him will ever see the world in quite the same way again.

We have all come to realize that the media have been changing *what* is being communicated, not merely *how*. The media change our perception of the outside world, but they do much more: they change how we see ourselves and what we see in ourselves.

Neither the "medium" nor the "message" determines the other, but each shapes the other. McLuhan's greatest insight is not "The medium is the message" but "Technology is an extension of man—" not just a tool. (Drucker, *Adventures of a Bystander*, 66). Technology does not master us, but changes our personalities, just as much as it changes what we can do. The ethical implications are profound and far-reaching.

Like Buckminster Fuller, another popularizer of ideas, McLuhan tried to show that new approaches to our culture require that we deal with technology as "human" and "cultural," not purely "technical." In this sense, they are two prophets for our age.

Starting in the 1960s, McLuhan began his re-evaluation of mass communications and public ethics. He began to reconceive history as a pageant whose inner meaning is our metamorphosis through media. He sees an age dominated not by political or military leaders, but money ("The Poor Man's Credit Card"), photographs ("Brothels Without Walls"), and movies ("The Reel World"). Electronic media have created a global village in which all information can be shared, simultaneously, by everyone. Walls between people, nations, art, and thought come tumbling down. And McLuhan's popular culture status zoomed upward. Based on a survey of "Articles in Popular American Magazines by and about Selected Figures in 1967," he came in just behind Pope Paul IV and ahead of Martin Luther King.

Since then his pop rating has declined but certain significant results are his legacy:

1. McLuhanism moved into the very marrow of the bones that make up mass communication theory. Even those critics who violently disagree with or berate him have to acknowledge his impact.
2. The very students he so captivated are the instructors and writers from whom a whole new generation of students learn.
3. His strong moralistic stands (both in his personal life and academic analyses) had an appeal in the 80s that was ignored in the 60s and 70s.
4. McLuhan's linking elite and popular culture built a bridge between the two over which many of us now cross.

Because he dreamed of a new protean mythology—and he knew he must attack the old before he could reconstruct the new—McLuhan irritated many with maddening slogans, paradoxes, and puns. What he wrote and said sounded to some like utter nonsense. But as Alfred North Whitehead pointed out, "The nonsense of today is the sense of tomorrow."

What then might we conclude? Is all the crisis talk nonsense? Or are we doomed always to go through yet another crisis, only to discover later on (in the words of Gilbert and Sullivan) that "things are seldom what they seem?"

The answer, I venture to say, is yes. Because we know little of the past, life is an ever-receding present, and see the future through a glass darkly, we must face crisis after crisis, generation after generation. Finding a pattern for the humanities is an eternal desire. Each of us hopes that he or she will solve the mystery, find the answer.

So we mix pride with prejudice, fact with fiction, hype with hunch, and invoke history. Like old man river, history just keeps rolling along. If the humanities can roll along, they will not only survive but flourish. They are, after all, what makes us human.

Notes

[1]Two of the best books dealing with these matters are Richard Hofstadter, *Paranoid Style in American Politics* (New York: Knopf, 1965); and Seymour Lipset and Earl Raab, *Politics of Unreason: Right-Wing Extremism in America, 1790-1970* (New York: Harper's, 1979). Some of the material in this essay appeared earlier in my chapter on "The Ethics of Popular Culture," in Robert Denton, editor, *Ethical Dimensions of Political Communication* (New York, Praeger, 1991).

[2]Giamatti's article was published in the November 1978 edition of the *Yale Alumni Magazine.*

[3]One of the most comprehensive summaries of Aristotle can still be found in chapter II of Will Durant's *The Story of Philosophy* (New York: Simon & Schuster, 1961). Scores of more recent books deal with multiple aspects of this fascinating genius.

[4]I attempt to summarize the impact of existentialism on Western thought in *Faust Revisited: Some Thoughts of Satan* (New York: Seabury P, 1963). See the Bibliographical note, 179 f.

[5]Since much existential writing originated in France, one can learn of its eventual effects on the humanities in John Ardagh, *France in the 1980s* (London: Penguin Books, 1985).

[6]See Philip Marchand, *Marshall McLuhan: The Medium and the Messenger* (New York: Knopf, 1989).

Additional Reading

Arendt, Hannah. *The Human Condition*. Chicago: U of Chicago P, 1958.

Biagi, Shirley. *Media/Impact*. Belmont, Ca.: Wadsworth, 1990.

Bigsby, C. W. E., ed. *Approaches to Popular Culture*. Bowling Green: Popular Press, 1984.

Browne, Ray B. *Against Academia*. Bowling Green: Popular Press, 1990.

Burke, Peter. *Popular Culture in Early Modern Europe*. New York: Harper, 1978.

Christians, Clifford, Mark Fackler, and Kim Rotzell. *Media Ethics*. New York: Longman, 1987.

Denton, Robert E., Jr. *The Primetime Presidency of Ronald Reagan* New York: Praeger, 1988.

Druker, Peter. *Adventures of a Bystander*. New York: Harper & Row, 1979.

Dundes, Alan. *The Study of Folklore*. Englewood Cliffs, N.J.: Prentice-Hall, 1965.

Fishwick, Marshall W. *Parameters of Popular Culture*. Bowling Green: Popular Press, 1977.

Fishwick, Marshall W. *Seven Pillars of Popular Culture*. Westport: Greenwood, 1985.

Hirschfield, Charles. *The Modern World*. New York: Harcourt Brace Jovanovich, 1980.

Holsinger, Ralph L. *Media Law*. New York: Random House, 1987.

Hulteng, John. *The Messenger's Motives: Ethical Problems of the News Media*. Englewood Cliffs, N.J.: 1985.

Knoebel, Edgar, ed. *Classics of Western Thought—The Modern World*. New York: Harcourt Brace Jovanovich, 1988.

Luedtke, Luther S. *The Study of American Culture: Contemporary Conflicts*. Deland, FL: Everett Edwards, 1977.

Marchand, Philip. *Marshall McLuhan: The Medium and the Messenger*. New York: Knopf, 1989.

Rooney, Andy. "The Journalist's Code of Ethics," *Pieces of My Mind*. New York: Atheneum, 1984.

Rotzell, Kim, James Haefner, and Charles Sandage. *Advertising in Contemporary Society*. Cincinnati: South-Western, 1986.

Schickel, Richard. "Misunderstanding McLuhan," *More* 3.8 (1978).

Smith, Anthony. *Goodbye Gutenburg*. New York: Oxford UP, 1980.

Susman, Warren I. *Culture as History*. New York: Pantheon Books, 1984.

Weiner, Norbert. *The Human Use of Human Beings*. New York: Doubleday, 1960.

Non-Work Time and the Humanities

Ray B. Browne
and
Michael T. Marsden

The time we have which is not devoted to support of life—our "leisure time"—can be a blessing or a curse. Often it is both. We work ourselves to death in order to acquire leisure time only to discover that it might bore us to death. Whatever non-work time's role in life, most of us work no more than eight hours a day, leaving us with at least sixteen hours out of every twenty-four to cope with. Though we give up working for the period, we must continue to face the problems and potentials of life and society. We thus have a lot of time to utilize the Humanities as fundamental elements of human existence if we are aware of their importance and potentials. The following essay by Ray Browne and Michael Marsden points out some of those elements and their inseparability from other aspects of our lives.

As technology frees people from what they perceive as the slavery of work, it becomes imperative that individuals and society fully realize what they are giving up—the joy of having a purpose in life, though it can be sacramentalized with a lot of effort—and what they are getting in return—leisure to do what they like or can, and possibly the frustration and despair of purposelessness in life. Despite the fact that most participants applaud and many theoreticians explain the virtues of leisure and leisure-time activities, there are many areas, both physical and emotional, that need to be filled in concerning leisure and recreation. Many people, for example, are made nervous by the realization that the freedom of retirement for individuals over sixty brings with it the necessity of finding fulfilling ways to use their full-time leisure. The highly touted golden years can become quickly tarnished and rusty. One of the important and helpful subjects that can be brought to bear on making the most of leisure time is the humanities. The humanities can help explain the role of leisure activities in life, place them in historical and cultural perspectives and forge an understanding that should be useful in this very important personal and cultural segment of human existence. The humanities prepare one for a life-long fulfilling experience with leisure.

The humanities are those elements in culture which respond to the basic human needs in all of us; they are the common threads in all individuals and all societies, the ties that bind us all together as *homo sapiens*. The humanities are a people's inheritance, their history. They are also the totality of the present

16

as well as of the past. The humanities are what the tribe's sages teach by word of mouth and example, by book, television or any other medium, and what everybody sees on the streets of his or her daily existence. The present-day humanities are, as they have always been, the popular culture of everyday life—the mass media, entertainments, diversions, heroes, icons, rituals, psychology, religion—the whole swirl of a nation's various mixes of attitudes and actions. Popular culture, serving the basic drive of the humanities, has always tried to democratize society, to make all people equal participants in life and in the culture it generates. "The mass of mankind has not been born with saddles on their backs, nor a favored few booted and spurred," observed Thomas Jefferson.

In popular culture the rule "one person—one equal participant" tried to prevail. Increasingly it has come to be recognized that the popular culture is the "new humanities," the present voice of the humanities. Concerning them, Robert Coles, psychologist and Pulitzer Prize winning author, summed up the role of the humanities in any society, but especially our own, this way: "The humanities belong to no one kind of person; they are part of the lives of ordinary people, who have their own various ways of struggling for coherence, for a compelling faith, for social vision, for an ethical position, for a sense of historical perspective," for a meaning—a *raison d'etre*, a rationale—in life.

Leslie Fiedler, outstanding literary critic of our time, pushes Cole's concept one step further toward its logical conclusion because he believes that popular culture can achieve mankind's greatest challenge, that of bringing all people together into the community which must have existed before people became separated by class, education, interests and desires. While the humanities are part of everyday life, they also help to shape the future by making it possible for us to remember the past. The agricultural fair, for example, continues to be a popular entertainment and informational form because it not only reflects the everyday life of rural culture, but it also displays new agricultural technology while preserving and lovingly displaying the skills and arts of the past.

Throughout history mankind in general has hated his fate of being tied to the staff of labor. To escape it, at least via creative imagination, he created the Garden of Eden, Christendom's first theme park, as a place where food was plentiful, rest was assured, the living was comfortable and recreation, at least of certain types, was everywhere. The concept of the Garden as mankind's ultimate goal in life continues to drive people's highest ambition, at least in America, for what would in fact be all play and no work. Mankind apparently burns not for a classless society but a workless one, a land of eternal summertime, where in the words of George Gershwin's immortal "Summertime," "The livin' is easy." Given the option, the choice is irreversible. According to the popular song of 1941, "Easy Street," "life is sweet for those who live on Easy Street," where one "don't want no job today, so please go 'way." Leisure time is the Great Equalizer. Consider the contemporary Gardens of Eden—the retirement village, the country club, the exotic vacation packages—the playground of the rich and the poor.

Throughout the thousands of years that the human race has had to grub out an existence, generally falling victim to poverty, disease and overwork, people have looked upon the favored few who were comparatively better off and have felt that their lifestyle—their use of time and artifacts—was what everyone desired.

Now with the development of a technology that at least promises to do all necessary work—at least if the technicians can keep the technology working—human beings will be granted their desires. However, they will be faced with the question of how to utilize their non-working time. Human beings are imbued with the realization of their own mortality—with the brevity of the average life span and the uncertainty of the death-span—and therefore want to make of life all they can. One of the desires is making the most of the temporal existence by being fully alive and sensually engaged. One leading author on the subject suggests that the desire "to be healthy, to be free, to discover ourselves, to be wanted, to be useful, and to find ourselves in the universe" leads to "the enjoyment of living, to a kind of happiness" (Brightbill 18).

To discover these pleasures, a growing consensus is, we must have leisure. The word *leisure* is from the Latin *licere*, which means "to be permitted," and is defined in the modern dictionary as "free, unoccupied time during which a person may indulge in rest, recreation, etc." The term for leisure parallels the Latin *schola* (Greek *skole*) which means not school but leisure, despite its closeness to our word school. Historically it has been clearly felt that without free time unoccupied with the work of surviving there would be less likelihood of schooling and pleasure. But the careful reader of definitions will find in the dictionary definition of *leisure* the word *indulge*, and to some the thought of *indulgence* does not promise great learning.

It should be remembered, however, that vocabulary and usage follow political situations. The Greeks found their leisure on the backs of their slaves, and the Romans at the end of their short swords. But Socrates insisted on the leisurely approach of his students to knowledge as the most effective, though he may have been mainly justifying his own teaching methods. And the so-called "life of the mind," favored by many academics today who might be trying to avoid the treadmill of work, seems to be the goal of many intellectuals. A case might be made that without the freedom of leisure there cannot be the freedom of thinking, though such an attitude contravenes the pragmatic wisdom of the old American attitude that necessity is as much the mother of learning as is invention.

History is replete with the comments of people on the necessity of non-work time. The Bible commands, "Have leisure and know that I am God." Socrates observed, "Leisure is the best of all possessions." Cicero commented, "Leisure with dignity is the supremely desirable object of all sane and good men." Bertrand Russell, one of yesterday's leading philosophers, observed, "To be able to fill leisure intelligently is the last product of civilization." (Brightbill 27).

The burden of all these observations is well-used, filled and fruitful leisure. Without proper use, leisure becomes idleness, and we all know that the idle mind is the Devil's workshop. The occupied mind, on the contrary, is God's school. "The idle mind knows not what it wants," observed Quintus Ennius, two hundred years before Christ (*Iphigenia*, Chorus). "Idleness and lack of occupation are the best things in the world to ruin the foolish," observed Dio Chrysostrom (*Tenth Discourse on Servants*, Ch. 7) in a back-jerking paradox.

Therefore, the purpose of contemporary *homo sapiens* is to find some way to profitably employ the leisure that technology promises for the 21st century. With the supercharger of God's mandate, this proper use of leisure (recreation) becomes the great democratizer and twin to religion. In fact, recreation becomes muscular Christianity, or Christianity in action. If man is God writ small and fallible, as most religions assert, the frail vessel of God's divine dispensation, then whatever man does to glorify himself is glorification of God. Dr. Roger Bannister, the man who first ran the mile in less than four minutes, when asked why he ran, answered: "We run not because we think it is doing us good, but because we enjoy it and cannot help ourselves.... It gives a man the chance to bring out the power that might otherwise remain locked away inside himself. The urge to struggle lies latent in everyone. The more restricted our society and work become, the more necessary it will be to find some outlet for this craving for freedom" (Brightbill 36).

In searching for an "outlet for this craving for freedom," we should perhaps not make leisure too virtuous. People seek leisure activities for their intrinsic value, of course, but they also seek the pleasure of leisure activities out of envy, because other people and especially those of the "leisure" class engage in them. People are apt to make such activities too important and too self-justifying, something like a self-fulfilling prophecy. Sociologist Charles Brightbill uses freedom-activities as an index into characters: "Tell me what you do when you are free to do as you wish and I will tell you what kind of person you are" (*Education for Leisure*, 1966). Such smiling approval of leisure as the desired end of existence simply overlooks a sterner and perhaps more realistic glance at existence in Henry David Thoreau's feeling that we all lead lives of quiet desperation. And it is the desire to escape desperation that drives us into all forms of non-work activities.

Man finds many ways to use his non-working hours. One is in giving up the individual freedom for the larger pool of organized rituals as in sports, church attendance, parades, communal meals, etc., and in organized activities in certain designated places such as race tracks, casinos, malls, theme parks, etc., where the concepts and activities are regularized and made routine with overlying dynamics of some power beyond the individual will. Rituals are public reenactments and therefore celebrations through the prescribed use of duly designated artifacts and objects. Ritual is the actions of individuals or groups in celebration of some extrinsic and supposedly higher form of intent and purpose. "Celebration," according to anthropologist Frank Manning, "is a 'text,' a vivid aesthetic creation that reflexively depicts, interprets and informs its social context" (6).

Ritual is the engine that propels celebration, because in ritual the objects involved become alive with meaning. "Objects certainly 'speak,' that is they directly communicate a message through visible and tangible qualities such as form, color, texture, size and so forth," observes Victor Turner (15). But the objects remain "mute" until decoded and understood, that is, brought alive in the experience of the people engaged in the ritual.

Thus some of the most fundamental and important aspects of life, especially in the life of leisure and non-work, remain mere dumb-shows, shadows, until they are understood. Understanding and full participation comes when the keys to unlocking the meaning, and thereby allowing full participation, are found and the locks opened. The keys are symbols because symbols are the reflected meaning—the spiritual element—which gives soul to the artifacts. In order to comprehend, the audience must understand the symbols and artifacts in the context of their setting and in the context of the action, i.e., the original and developing meaning as it unfolds in its context. The symbols, the action, the artifacts, must be understood in relation to one another as they interact, but also they must be understood in relation to those gone before and those that will follow. In other words, there is a narrative to the ritual which must be understood.

A community festival, for example, is rich with meaning for the trained observer who looks for the objects associated with work which are transformed into magical symbols of fullness and completeness, often harvest symbols. Festival organizers may choose a fruit or vegetable which pays tribute to a local specialty. Thus the Melon Festival, the Strawberry Festival and the Popcorn Festival celebrate the harvest and the richness of life, while at the same time they also celebrate the significance of place through time. The theme gives focus to other events of the festival from beauty pageants and craft displays to games and food concessions.

Mere participation in ritual does not guarantee understanding. There are, in fact, three levels of participation. The first is the mere routinized stereotypical participation, done with half a mind and half a commitment. The second is the emotional commitment and participation, as when someone cheers on their favorite sports team. The third, and by far the most profound, is when the routinized participation is carried on in its international, intercultural, timeless profoundity—spaceless and timeless. In this action, on the level of what Jung called the collective unconscious, the individual player in the ritual becomes not a participant but in a sacred manner becomes the ritual. In other words, in taking the sacrament, the participants become to all intents and purposes the sacrament.

In searching for the meaning of ritual we need to go into transdisciplinary as well as interdisciplinary investigation. We need to have the ritual turned on its axis from north and south to east and west, from the physical to the spiritual, and from the time-bound to the timeless. As we search for the wholistic meaning of ritual and celebration we need to use the approach of the humanities, for they tie all back together into our total existence. The humanities are the various rivers of life—the history, philosophy, explanations, icons, rituals, everyday meaning, etc.—flowing separately but, if properly understood, merging into the large stream of understanding.

In order to help provide the answers about mankind's proper use of non-work time, the humanities must first question all the assumptions about the importance of leisure. In causing us to question the givens, the humanities will perhaps deepen our appreciation and work toward somewhat more correct answers.

Harry Overstreet, in *A Guide To Civilized Loafing* (146), states that recreation and leisure allow us to base our philosophies upon the three gateways to a happy life: "living in the past, exploring the present, and visualizing the future." An observer deep in understanding of the humanities must look askance at these assumptions, at least as commonly understood. No person can really make any sense out of living in the past. Even archeologists use the past in order to understand the present. Anthropologist M.K. Shuman, for example, studies the ancient Maya culture by studying contemporary Mayan cultures. The past is prologue to the present, as Shakespeare observed. Longfellow wrote in his poem "Psalm of Life" that we should let the dead Past bury its dead. Any thoughtful individual must think, as Jefferson did, that it is wiser to live in the present than in the past. "The earth belongs to the living, not the dead," (1813) he observed. The past should be mined for use in the present, for what it can teach us so that we will not, because of ignorance of the past, be condemned to relive it. But, in the words of Winston Churchill, "If we open a quarrel between the past and the present, we shall find that we have lost the future: (Speech, June 18, 1940). The wound need not be opened. The past should be a text that is required reading for all, but a text that spurs to action and understanding of the present and the future. Understanding the present is more urgent, more compelling, than understanding the past, because the present is the problem. Though the prudent should have one eye on the past, the other must be kept on the present with peripheral vision sweeping the future.

Full understanding of the present through the humanities is realized if it is understood that the humanities are the popular culture, the great democratizer of society, the power which through the poll and the purse directs culture. The lesson is not easily learned and at times it is even more difficult to accept. As Jefferson observed, the conflict is longlasting: "Men by their constitutions are naturally divided into two parties: 1. those who fear and distrust the people, and wish to draw all powers from them into the hands of the higher classes; 2. those who identify themselves with the people, have confidence in them, cherish and consider them as the most honest and safe, although not the most wise depository of the public interest" (1824). But the people are overwhelming. To paraphrase Emerson's fear of material things driving culture, leisure is in the saddle and drives culture, especially for the baby boomers. To fail to understand the cultural power of any group, but especially of the 77+ million baby boomers born between 1946 and 1964, is to fail to understand the cultural directions the leisure pursuits of these millions will establish. The people have always determined their cultural priorities, even though it seemed as if the culture brokers were really in control. There will be no such allusions about cultural power as this large demographic "blip" moves into the 21st century with its leisure priorities intact and in control.

Failure to understand these clear truths imposes a static time-stopper on comprehension and appreciation of the flow of life and in so doing falsifies both the present and the past. For example, elite humanists read the past through the graves of the powerful and self-proclaimed important. Thus the artifacts of King Tutankhamen's (fl. c. 1350 b.c.) tomb became the voice of the world in which he lived, the key to unlocking the meaning of his age. This is viewing science through the wrong lens. Tut was not the spirit of his age but the picture of its corruption. Though there is a great deal to be learned from viewing this booty ground by the tyrant from the skins of his subjects, there is a great deal more to be learned from examination of the contents of hundreds of graves of the commoners who were forced to serve Tut.

An excellent example of the value of examining the commonplace items of an era in reality is sought in the eleven-hour series on PBS in 1990 called *The Civil War*, an effort to picture the total America during that conflict. In many ways the South's society was similar to Tut's, slavery and very few people on the top of privilege, but a lot of people with work power and the weakness to be manipulated. Their voices, though weak, eventually shaped the course of history.

Perhaps even a reevaluation of Tut's intentions in burying his treasures might lead the scholar to suspect that Tut, and all the other tyrants of his period, did not bury his artifacts so that he could have them in his next life so much as so that his successors could not enjoy them in this life without having to work for them. The desire to will one's riches to his successors is a recent sophistication in man's realization of the limitations of death and the baggage many check for the river trip into the future.

Even a superficial noticing of the comparative sizes of pyramids suggest that every Pharoah was trying to outdo his predecessor in size of pyramid and burial chamber. Since each inherited nothing from his predecessor, there was little chance he was going to grub for treasures that he would leave to his successor. The business of grinding treasures from one's subjects was far too problematical for him to start a Foundation for the betterment of his followers.

Some of this information can be gained from properly reading the burial places of the commoners littering the desert around the pyramids. Alan Gowans, a thoughtful and provocative art historian, says that a work of art—or any artifact—when properly understood can be a rosetta stone from which one can read a whole culture. In the graves of the commoners are simple artifacts from a simple life which when fully understood tell us more about the age of the Pharaohs than the Pharaoh's treasures tell. Here, again, the tale of the people is told by the people—in their popular culture, *their* language.

The humanities are by definition the record as complete as it can be, the full inventory, of mankind's journey on this earth. Mankind's thinking, dreams, goals, ideals, actions. They range from the profoundest and most abstruse to the simplest. From the noblest purposes to the most selfish. From the most spiritual to the most fleshly. They consist not of a short shelf in a hidden library but a total library of thoughts, insights, sounds, smells, actions, intentions, unforeseen results. The total picture. At least up to this date. The calendar of man's foolishness and possible wisdom.

For thousands of years people have anatomized the human body in an effort to understand the bones, the muscles, the chemistry. Locating and naming the parts has been a desperate game of survival. The New Humanities extend that chart to the body of culture, again with a desperate need and urge to understand it. The contemporary person who would comprehend the body must read the whole picture and put all the pieces together. The reader must understand that the total that exceeds the sum of the parts may fall short. The lump sum is relatively unimportant. The knowledge is vital, the need urgent. It would be a tragedy now that we have leisure to learn and enjoy if mankind failed to read and preserve the text of knowledge and leisure in its full potential and ramification. Life would have been robbed of many of its possibilities.

Works Cited

Brightbill, Charles K. *Man and Leisure: A Philosophy of Recreation.* Greenwich: Greenwood, 1961.

Brightbill, Charles K. *Education for Leisure-Centered Living.* New York: Wiley, 1977.

Manning, Frank E. *The Celebration of Society: Perspectives on Contemporary Cultural Performances.* Bowling Green: Popular Press, 1983.

Overstreet, Harry. *A Guide to Civilized Loafing.* New York: W.W. Norton, c. 1934.

Turner, Victor. *Celebration: Studies in Festivity and Ritual.* Washington: Smithsonian Institution Press, 1982.

Folk Cultures and the Humanities

Ray B. Browne

The folk, for better or worse, some elitists might say, are always with us; the elitists, surely for the worse, many folk might say, always plague us. Regardless of the point of view and the prejudice, folk cultures with the assertion of individual, ethnic and national rights will be with us for ages to come. Since there are so many of these "folk" communities and they are so varied in background and eventual development, they are sure to impact all the cultures of the world for many years to come. These folk carry with them many currents of the humanities which elite and popular societies should be aware of, for they ignore the folk humanities at their peril. In the following essay Ray Browne points out the interrelatedness of the folk humanities with others in society and their importance.

The study of folklore or folk cultures, now often called folkloristics, offers an excellent field for people interested in the popular and elite humanities to broaden and enrich their understanding of the total picture of their subject. Folk cultures are the conscious and unconscious patterns of life in one large segment of a community. Folk cultures, in other words, are the life styles of both individuals and groups of people in a large section of society, and as such, to paraphrase a definition of the proverb, represent the collective wisdom of the group. As such folk cultures embody the humanities of an element of a total society's way of life, the timeless and world-wide comparative attitudes toward the problems of life and those people's way of adjusting to and coping with those problems.

It is therefore proper, indeed urgent, that students of the humanities, both popular and elite, recognize the value of the folk humanities and extract from them immediately the important elements for the benefit of all society, just as people interested in the problems of environment and endangered plant and animal species now call upon folk wisdom wherever possible to assist them in their efforts to understand the total world problems before the possibilities of answers disappear. Not that folk cultures will disappear. But the traditional elements continually modify and change under the stress of electronic media and other modernizing forces acting on society, and many important elements are bound to metamorphose into new forms and statements, considerably altering the face and perhaps the content of folk cultures. We have already lost irretrievable treasures. We should not lose more by failing to act now.

Though folk cultures obviously are deeply influential parts of the humanities in general, most students of popular and elite humanities apparently disregard them. Yet is is clearly imperative that students of the conventional humanities supplement their knowledge by getting to know what the folk cultures can contribute to the larger context of the humanities in general.

If folk cultures, though shot through with ignorance and lack of understanding on many topics, have sufficed to nurture and carry peoples and societies through history, they must have contained elements which were sufficient for their needs and which might be of value today, both for contemporary culture and for the future. Those nurturing and sustaining elements were the folk humanities.

What are the humanities that people can and need to find alive and well in folk cultures?

The humanities are those elements in culture which respond to the basic human needs in all of us; they are the common threads in all individuals and societies, the ties that bind us all together as *homo sapiens*. The humanities are a people's inheritance, their history. They are also the totality of the present as well as of the past. The humanities are what the tribe's sages teach by word of mouth and example, by book, television or any other medium, and what everybody sees on the streets of his or her daily existence. Folk humanities are, as they have always been, the whole swirl of a nation's various mixes and attitudes and actions—the entertainments, diversions, heroes, icons, rituals, psychology, religion, what the individuals and groups get from other members of the society and in turn pass on to others. The folk humanities of a group are those elements which at the same time set them off from other groups yet tie them, perhaps subtly and unconsciously, to the world at large. The folk humanities of the past were those elements which, despite not having the speed of electronics which Marshall McLuhan predicted would soon convert all isolated groups on earth into a global village, in fact tied all people into an extended folk community. This umbrella is both comprehensive and complicated.

Most folklorists try to be comprehensive in their studies, including all aspects of folk life. According to one leading scholar, Jan Brunvand, "Modern folkloristics embraces oral, customary, and material aspects of tradition equally, and it makes eclectic use of theoretical and methodological approaches from anthropology, linguistics, communications, psychology and other relevant areas. The hope is to develop a viable approach to studying the whole phenomenon that is known as 'folklore' (behavior, tests, performances, effects, etc.) whenever and wherever it occurs and from a point of view that is uniquely 'folkloristic'."

But toward what end are folk cultures to be studied? What is to be gained of value to humanity and the humanities from a study of "the whole phenomenon" that is known as "folklore"? What is to be gained of value to humanity from the isolating and studying of phenomena associated with particular, distinguishable sets of people as isolated by academics and intellectuals? The subject is not settled. There is more to be gained from the study of folk cultures than is generally included in the conventional approach to the field. Folk culture studies are too important to leave to the conventional approach, just as the study of the humanities in general is far too vital to human society to leave in the hands of the so-called humanists—especially elite humanists—alone.

Some folklorists are interested in the broader outreach of their studies. Alan Dundes, for example, one of today's leading theoreticians and innovators in folkculture studies, looks toward the broader and more humanistically useful study of his field. He thinks that folklorists by analyzing folklore "can discover general patterns of culture." In his eyes, "Folklore as a mirror of culture provides unique raw materials for those eager to better understand themselves and others." But Dundes unfortunately stops short of the full thrust of his implications. Folk cultures may be raw materials to outsiders but to the folk community they are smooth, finished and comprehensive and provide answers to the problems that society faces.

True, folklorists and we can better comprehend their subject by more fully understanding a portion of society, and these understandings can lead to generalizations of patterns of culture that benefit people interested in the humanities. But the folklorist who is content to stop without these benefits to the humanities to be gained from the study of folkcultures leaves two areas insufficiently explored which benefit from folkculture studies. One might be the people themselves, and Dundes makes a jab at evaluating this. "Folk should be put back into folklore," he says (x). "Folklore represents a people's image of themselves," he asserts (x). "The image may be distorted but at least the distortion comes from the people, not from some outside observer armed with a range of *a priori* premises" (x).

Folklorists and general students of culture should realize that though the immediate reason for studying folkcultures might well be so that we can better understand a portion of society in its context, this is not the ultimate purpose of knowledge of the subject, nor of knowledge of the folk. The real reason for the scholar, especially the student in the humanities and social sciences, to study folkcultures should be in order to tie them in with the world cultures that have existed through the ages and continue to live today.

In other words, the study of folkcultures offers a range of the universality and depth of those cultures which tie them in with cultures around the world. This tie-in with elite, popular and other folk cultures, gives a dignity, truth and importance to folkcultures which they have not been accorded so far. It is a serious mistake to restrict the significance of folk cultures short of the general humanities and even to the folk humanities themselves, though this is an extension ordinarily denied to folk cultures. This needed extension is achieved through the study of humanities *and* folkcultures and the humanities *in* folkcultures. Such inclusion requires considerable effort on the part of the student. These humanities, or the knowledge of them, cannot necessarily be achieved through the individual approaches to the study of folk cultures through literature, history, anthropology, sociology, linguistics, communications, psychology, architecture, entertainments—but far more effectively through the study of the humanities *in* and *of* folk cultures. In other words, the study of folk cultures through literature, anthropology and the other disciplines provides the script of the humanities but they are not the humanities. The humanities are far more than the individual parts. Like elite and popular culture, folk cultures are far more than the sum of their parts. And far more significant.

To a large extent the proposal here is that the study of folk culture be restored to what it was before academics began separating it from the generalities in which it properly belongs. Throughout history folk cultures have participated in whatever smaller or larger cultures existed around them and have been recognized as integral aspects of the cultures people lived in and close to. Peter Burke has demonstrated how Europeans of the 15th-16th centuries were essentially folk civilizations moving toward becoming urban—that is less folk-communities. In England, Shakespeare's world was essentially a folk world, no matter if many individuals like himself, Ben Jonson, Queen Elizabeth and their associates were hardly exemplifications of the folk. England, with its uniquely English determination to remain a country of isolated villages and linguistic groups, was perhaps in many ways more of a folk nation than others in Europe. What was true of England and Europe has been paralleled throughout the world to one degree or another at one time or another.

As cultures throughout the world have tended to move beyond conventional folk societies, scholarship on folk cultures has moved into the process of separating the study of folklore into a separate discipline, for political, fiscal and perhaps scholarly needs. Though these moves may have assisted in the short run, and may in fact be proper on a continuing basis, in the development of the humanities in folk cultures—surely one of the ultimate goals of folklorists and presumably one of the goals of humanities scholars in general—it is time that at least one branch of folk culture scholars and humanities scholars in general start generalizing again and search out the humanities *in* and *of* folk cultures.

Great effort should be made, if not by folkculture specialists then by humanities generalists, to place the study of folkcultures back in the humanistic tradition and to associate the folk humanities with the elite and popular traditions. To do so is to extend and enrich, as it were, concurrently the folk, the popular and elite humanities, and in so doing discover just how much value there is in the folk humanities as general humanities. These folk humanities feed a wisdom and universality that exceeds the individual folk communities. For the observer they shed a great deal of light on the human condition and ways best to deal with it. It is therefore time to put the humanities back into folk cultures and folk humanities back into the humanities.

The folk humanities are an integral part of the total humanities of the world. They fit into the larger unit of humanities. They constitute a culture that is worldwide and timeless, as Stith Thompson's *Motif Index* demonstrates, as he shows how certain motifs—which are the smallest units in a setting which generate action—are worldwide. The stick-fast motif, found in Joal Chandler Harris' lovely story of the tar baby and Brer Rabbit, for example, is found in numerous countries throughout the world, even in countries that have no tar or resin. This motif represents one element of the humanities.

But there are far more important elements of the humanities represented by local folk cultures that are tied into the universal. For example, service and benefit to humanity, traditionally tied in with the culture hero, can be seen in, among hundreds of other examples, the legend of Johnny Appleseed. Appleseed roamed throughout the Midwest during the last half of the 19th century distributing knowledge in the forms of book chapters and other publications he carried from one person to another, practical assistance in the form of appleseed that people planted and benefited from, and through both activities gave a knowledge of the value of empathy, sympathy and community assistance on the American frontier—and by implication on any exposed flank of society. Davy Crockett through the legends about his life and death gave clear evidence of the value of selflessness in a growing nation. One who loves a nation enough to die for it demonstrates one of the more heroic and valuable elements in the humanities. Animal tales always speak to the human condition, as this folk story with the storyteller's introductory comment from Alabama demonstrates:

The Frog that wanted to be big

Dis one I always tells to de little chillun in Sunday School.—

De mother frog want her children to think dey was de biggest people in de worl'. And dey did. One day dey was walkin' down de road and saw uh turkle. Dey saw dat de turkle was biggern dey was. So dey rushed home and ask dere ma if de turkle wasn't biggern dey was. Ma frog started swellin' and swellin', tryin' to show dat she was biggern de turkle, and she swell up till she busted.

An' de moral of dat story is: Don't go 'roun' tryin' to be biggern other people.

After I tole em dat story de little chillun go 'roun' playin' like dey is swellin' up bigger 'n bigger and shoutin' "Boom!" (Browne 95)

Folktales also demonstrate how country people deal with the shortage of food, the goodness of country folk (and the therapeutic value of a sense of humor), as this blending of two Alabama folktales demonstrates:

Mountain folks is the best folks in the world. They don't often have much, but they are awful free with what they do have. One time a stranger came up to a mountain cabin about dinner time. Well, the father of the house asked the stranger to come in and have dinner. All they had to eat was boiled taters served on bark. The man was rather shy about taking many taters when he saw that that was all they had. So he just took a couple of little ones. The husband said: "Go ahead, take some more taters." The man took one more. The husband said: "Take some more taters. Just take a damn lot of taters."

Another time another stranger came to this same mountain family and asked to spend the night. All they had to eat that night was taters. Taters fried; boiled taters; baked taters. Cause he was hungry, the stranger ate a pretty good bait of taters. Well, later on that night, he woke up sick at his stomach. He went outside the house and vomited. While he was out there the woman of the house heard him and came out to see what she could do. When she found out that he was sick at his stomach she said: 'well, we ain't got no medicine in the house, but I'll be glad to make you some tater tea'."

Humor does help to grease the rough road of life. The humanities in action in the folk community can be seen in the numerous ballads and folksongs which permeate nearly all folk communities. Songs are in many ways extremely useful carriers of the cultures in which they thrive because being music they are therefore an "art," and as such they allow a certain impersonal impunity to the songs, so that nearly any subject can be covered, especially if it can be disguised, and because people tend to pour a lot of sentiment and conviction into the freedom and license given them in song. It is of course dangerous for people to impose cultural and political standards and interpretations on moments in history because to avoid anachronistic misinterpretation one needs to completely understand the cultural milieu surrounding an event—or a song—in order not to pervert and misinterpret the artifact. But songs undoubtedly float certain universals and timeless aspects of humanity. With caution in interpretation they can be useful today in helping us understand the cultures of the singers as well as our own culture.

There are thousands of ballads and folksongs that would be usefully illustrative. "Lord Randall," famous from the 17th century on and still widely sung under several names, gives us a picture of a man poisoned by his lady-love by putting the potion in eels or eel-broth (a common device in 13th century Italy). His hatred for her deed and curse placed upon her apparently was favored by society. The concluding stanza voices the curse (called in this version Lord Donald):

> What will ye leave to your true-love, Lord Donald, my son?
> What will ye leave to your true-love, my jollie young man?
> The tow and the halter, for to hang on yon tree,
> And lat her hang there for the poysoning o me.

Another poignant ballad, "Barbara Allen," has through the centuries pictured a hard-hearted woman who, having been slighted for some reason by her lover, when summoned to his dying bedside refused to go, leaving him dying unconsoled and apparently without love. When she learned of his death, however, she was stricken with remorse and immediately died of a broken heart. From their graves grew flowers to symbolize their eternal love. Her remorse and the developing symbols are revealed in the final two stanzas:

> Oh, father, father! dig my grave,
>   And dig it deep and narrow;
> For a young man died for me to-day,
>   I'll die for him to-morrow:
>
> On the one was buried a red rose bud,
>   On the other, a sweet briar;
> And they grew and they grew to the church-steeple top,
>   Till they could grow no higher.
> There they twined in a true-lover's knot,
>   For all true lovers to admire."

The power of this ballad, as it protests hard-hearted cruelty of one human being for another, even with persons who cannot possibly have any connection with such behavior except through the long line of human compassion, is great today. Singers, especially women, still shed tears and lament the indifference, the lack of compassion of one human being for another, of "hard-hearted Barbara Allen," who refused love and attention at life's final act, the man's dying.

Perhaps no song is more dramatic and pregnant with meaning than the fifteenth century British ballad "Sir Patrick Spence," which although now virtually forgotten among the folk speaks a volume on life and culture in the fifteenth and sixteenth centuries.

Sir Patrick Spens

The king sits in Dumferling toune,
  Drinking the blude-reid wine:
"O whar will I get guid sailor,
  To sail this schip of mine?"
Up and spak an eldern knicht,
  Sat at the kings richt kne:
"Sir Patrick Spens is the best sailor
  That sails upon the se."
The king has written a braid letter,
  and signd it with his hand,
And sent it to Sir Patrick Spens,
  Was walking on the sand.
The first line that Sir Patrick red,
  A loud lauch lauched he;
The next line that Sir Patrick red,
  The teir blinded his ee.
"O who has done this deid,
  This ill died don to me,
To send me out his time o' the year,
  To sail upon the se!
"Mak hast, mak hast, my mirry men all,
  Our guid schip sails the morn."
"O say na sae, my master dier,
  For I feir a deadlie storme.
"Late, late yestreen I saw the new moone,
  Wi the auld moone in hir arme,
And I feir, I feir, my deir master
  That we will cum to harme."
O our Scots nobles were richt laith
  To weet their cork-heild schoone;
Bot lang owre a' the play were played,
  Thair hats they swam aboone.
O lang, lang may their ladies sit,
  Wi their fans into their hand,
Or eir they see Sir Patrick Spens
  Cum sailing to the land.
O lang, lang, may the ladies stand,
  Wit thair gold kems in their hair,
Waiting for thair ain deir lords,
  For they'll see thame na mair.
Haf owre, haf owre to Aberdour,
  It's fiftie fadom deip,
And thair lies guid Sir Patrick Spens,
  Wi the Scots lords at his feit.

This song is pregnant with innuendoes of treachery, loyalty, indifference to man and to compassion to women. It condenses a whole culture.

Among folk culture's many artifacts—and visual representations of artifacts—there are many which indicate the folks' reactions to the challenges and problems of life. Architecture, for example, reveals how men and women have tried to design their structures, and rooms within the structures, to make them less uncomfortable, less subject to the vagaries of outside weather, and to ease the physical discomforts of living under potentially restricting and hostile conditions. Art and photo representations of these aspects of life demonstrate how people have shaped their art according to their attitudes and reactions of life.

All these efforts to face up to and stare down the various aspects of life have the essence of the humanities just as much as do the utterances of the popular and elite sages of culture. Nineteenth century British poet and essayist Matthew Arnold's dictum about the definition of culture—"Culture, the acquainting ourselves with the best that has been known and said in the world"—is easily translated into folk wisdom: "The most useful aspect of life most helpfully said." Robert Cole's comments about what are the real humanities is also pertinent: "The humanities," he said, "belong to no one kind of person; they are part of the lives of ordinary people, who have their own various ways of struggling for coherence, for a compelling faith, for social vision, for an ethical position, for a sense of historical perspective." Translated into folkspeech Cole's words become something like: "Everybody has their problems. We don't know where we came from or where we're going, so all we can do is hope." Out of sheer necessity hope springs eternal in the folk breast. And from the individual melds into the collective breast.

Marshall McLuhan felt that the popular humanities as transmitted through television are creating a global village, in which, as Leslie Fielder sees it, there can be a real sense of community similar to that which existed in folk communities before people were separated by class, interests, goals and ambitions. In some folk cultures—Japan, for example—television is perpetuating regional and village cultures at least temporarily. But folk cultures, despite temporary aberrations, tend to drive, at least verbally, toward brotherhood and sisterhood. Those are the traits of the humanities.

Often it takes intellectuals, driven astray by their misguiding intellects, many centuries to relearn what their folk predecessors knew and took for granted. For example, historian of art Alan Gowans believes that in order to understand art one must know what purpose it was created for and serves. "In order to know art, one must know why it was created," he feels. Folk wisdom has always known that the primary question one asks about art is, "Why did you do it?" Gowans felt that every artifact if properly understood can mirror the culture in which it was created and circulated. In the folk mind the question might well be, "I wonder why he did that. What's he going to do with it?"

Frank Lloyd Wright's philosophy about the imperatives of architecture which enlightened the architectural world, about the need for architecture to grow out of the land on which it rested, was the working necessity of people for thousands of years in their folk housebuilding in the form of caves, log houses, igloos, grass sheds, sod shanties, rain forest pygmy leaf huts, bungalows, lean-to's, all of which had to utilize the building materials available and to modify the structure to suit the terrain on which it was built. What is so new about that which is thousands of years old? Only the short-sightedness of the people doing the looking.

In fact all elite culture, as nearly everybody knows, stands neck deep in popular and folk cultures. Elite culture is like a classical mythological animal, with folk feet, popular culture body and elite eyes and nose. The three are equal and inseparable. The same nutrients feed all. The head cannot exist without the body, the body without the feet, though among intellectuals the talking head is a symbol and fact of futility. The talking head is also an important part of popular and folk cultures. But in folkculture actions speak louder than words, so results are more important than hypotheses. The finished act or product is more important than the plan or blueprint. That is not to say that folk cultures are not filled with dreams. In fact dreams are the very spirit of folk cultures— as mythologies, marchen, animal stories, horror stories, witches' tales testify. Nearly all the dreams and fantasies of elite cultures today have been at one time or another a part of folk cultures, have pulsated through popular culture and, despite the feeling among elitists that their culture is the origin of all which is good and which trickles down, have moved on to energize elite culture.

It is indeed time to put the folk back into folklore, as Alan Dundes says, and into culture also. To examine a folksong, tale, practice, artifact without realizing that it is an important aspect of folk life, and of culture, is to underevaluate, underappreciate, folk cultures, and to deprive cultures of important ingredients. The folk humanities are the very heart of folk cultures, and the foundation of all cultures and humanities. Folk humanities, like popular and elite humanities, drive toward generalizations that are needed in a world that has for too long driven towards specializations, separations into castes based on origins, finances, education and accomplishments. The humanities address the commonality in us all.

Nowadays when elitists speak of the humanities they seldom mention the folk humanities. Lynne Cheney, Chairman of the National Endowment for the Humanities, in her NEH Report *Humanities in America* mentions all the buzz names for the conventional evaluations of the humanities. She talks about Western civilization and even hints that there might be room for the intellectual study of popular culture as being within the realm of the humanities. Bloom in his best-selling study *The Closing of the American Mind* already had his closed against folk cultures. E.M. Hirsh in his book *Cultural Literacy* includes the word folklore in his 5000 items needed to allow one to call himself/herself literate but he uses the old fashioned word "folklore" when "folk cultures" is the more appropriate term. Cheney, Bloom, and to a certain extent Hirsh, are canon-conscious and folk-blind, when folk literature in all the media pulsates all around them, on such subjects as Johnny Appleseed, Paul Bunyan, the Erie Canal, the great song "Shenandoah," on Daniel Boone, jump-rope rhymes, on how to build a boat and a fishing net, on how to choose the proper mate for marriage— all speak with the voice of the humanities. These subjects address themselves to the problems of living, of being human.

In writing about them the various forms of folk literature are perhaps more vitally a part of the humanities than other forms of literature. They do not use Matthew Arnold's precious literary phraseology, nor Lynne Cheney's. But they do use Abraham Lincoln's. Carl Sandburg's, the cowboy's, the workman's,

Emma Lazarus's, the working woman's. Like the canonized humanities among other people, the folk humanities include every aspect of life from the domestic to the spiritual, from the physical sweat to the dream, from reality to fantasy. Though written in a different dialect for a differently educated group, the folk humanities reflect Robert Cole's listing of everybody's dreams of survival and happiness.

And they obviously are comprehensive and all-permeating. To paraphrase Lincoln's comment about God surely loving the poor because he made so many of them, God must approve of the folk humanities because He made so many of them. Like old leather they wear long and well. They are unlike the theories of intellectuality of the intelligentsia (like premodernism, modernism, postmoderism, structuralism, destructuralism, constructionism, deconstruction-ism, marxism, stalinism, perhaps Gorbyism and post-Gorbyism, ethnicism, regionacism, etc.). They are not concerned with such precious arguments or on the basis of the great scientific disagreement in the late 1980s, published in various media, over whether coffee is beneficial or detrimental to drinkers' health. Perhaps we will have, in imitation of the 18th century Swiftean conflict over Big Endians and Little Endians, the Big Cupist and Little Cupist theories. Even post-Cupism when the conflict has run its course. There is simply no pretentious intellectual fad that is too silly for the intellectual, especially if it has been discredited, as for example continuing to espouse marxism in the 1990s in the face of the total collapse of the Marxist theories in action in the Soviet Union.

Academics like to sail their yachts down the gentle current of so-called intellectuality and come to anchor at some small island which represents the latest fad in theory-making. But the flotsam soon passes, the theory fades, and it is time to weigh anchor and drift to the next island. The thin one-crop unproductive soil of these islands is revealed if one looks back upstream at the long line of now-abandoned stopovers with their pathetic shredded flags limp and listless in the breeze. But the academic yachts have too small intellectual power to drive toward new ideas or to create new thoughts. So scholarship in the elite humanities essentially consists of drifting from one seemingly promising theory-fad to the next, with no rich soil in the offing. Ponce de Leon could not find a fountain of youth. Intellectuals cannot find rich soil for their cultivation because their plows are too shallow. Lincoln's observation about not being able to fool all the people all the time apparently does not hold for intellectuals. Throughout academia people are dedicated to fooling most of themselves most of the time. *Plus ça change, plus c'est la même chose.* The more things change, the more they stay the same.

But the folk humanities do not pass with every yearly floodstage. They were there yesteryear, are here today and will be here tomorrow. The folk wisdom of the American humorist Josh Billings perhaps hits closest home in connection with the folk and their humanities vis-à-vis the canonical humanities: "It ain't the things that we know that makes such fools of us, but a whole lot of things that we know that ain't so," he said. That the folk humanities may be closer to the mark of truth than the elite humanities is demonstrated by the fact that the folk don't have to change theirs as often as the elite do. The folk humanities endure. With the folk humanities, the question "What's new?" is almost certain to be answered with, "Not much," whereas the same question to a conventional elite canonical humanist is likely to elicit the naming of the latest intellectual fad that buys great mileage today on the elite superhighway but will be discredited tomorrow. Folk wisdom has always had its versions of Shakespeare's observation, "What fools [academics] be," and a large portion of those versions is laced with four and three letter words. *Plus c'est la même chose, plus ça change.*

The change now as we look toward a needed rejuvenation and revitalization of the humanities should be the assurance that there is much to be learned from the realization that the folk humanities should be, must be, a vital part of our search for the value of the full potential of the humanities. An old universal riddle supposedly asked by the Sphinx of all passersby is germane to us all: "What walks on four feet in the morning, two at noon and three at night?" Humankind, the answer, needs to include the realization that we need the folk, popular and elite humanities to help us struggle along. Without all, our picture cannot be complete.

Works Cited

Brunvand, Jan, *The Study of American Folklore.* New York, Norton, 2nd Ed. 1978.
Dundes, Alan, *Interpreting Folklore.* Bloomington, IN, Indiana UP, 1980.

Homo Sum: Humani Nihil a Me Alienum Puto: Popular Material Culture and the Humanities

Fred E.H. Schroeder

All aspects of life, Fred Schroeder reminds us in the following essay, originally had humble beginnings. Nothing humbler, he reminds us, than the material objects of life—those things which support our "spiritual" and "superior" life, the material culture which we use to sustain life and then cast away with contempt. Now, of course, for one reason or another, many of us are saving, collecting, archiving, museuming the everyday, vernacular objects of life. Are we merely saving because of nostalgia, financial gain, ego gratification or are we finally recognizing that the material culture around us speaks in many rich and important voices about the Humanities? Schroeder suggests that "the values of humanities are not intrinsic to a few rare objects" but are instead "in the human meanings that we read into or out of things with thoughtful examination." To read the objects we must have them accessible. But in order to take advantage of their accessibility we must, as Schroeder points out, recognize their importance.

Nineteen-ninety was the year of Dick Tracy hype, and the *Chicago Tribune* proudly displayed the great profile in the street-level windows on Michigan Avenue, proclaiming that this is the Home of Dick Tracy. Let us take this as emblematic of the usual conception of popular culture—mediated mass entertainment of twentieth-century America. But the Tribune Tower also provides emblems of historical popular *material* culture that relate directly to the humanities, for its walls are studded with souvenir stones, souvenirs of the Great Wall of China, the Parthenon, Hamlet's castle at Elsinore, Westminster Abbey, the Alamo, Injun Joe's cave and many other places equally rich in literary, political, architectural and heroic associations. These are solid pieces of stone, brick, adobe, terracotta, about as *material* as one can get. Few of them have any intrinsic value, indeed some are unworked fragments of geology that gain meaning and value only from the incised identifier, such as "Kentucky Mammoth Cave." Nevertheless, the historical associations makes them all objects of *culture*. They are *popular* as well, in two senses, first that they are as recognizable to the general public as Dick Tracy's profile, and second, that they are souvenirs, cousins germane to miniature Statues of Liberty, centennial spoons, 49er pennants, and Hard Rock Cafe t-shirts.

But are these objects of popular material culture also worthy of being labelled as *humanities*? Unfortunately, there's a double difficulty about relating popular material culture to the humanities. One, of course, is shared with all aspects

1. Warren Beatty's 1990 film *Dick Tracy* prompted this proud popular culture exhibit on Chicago's Michigan Avenue.

2. A final efflorescence of the popular Gothic Revival style, the Tribune Tower (1925) has its walls imbedded with souvenir stones, redolent of historic and cultural associations.

of popular culture. The humanities' regular stock-in-trade is masterworks; stuff that yields more value the deeper we probe, things that can yield up fresh meanings to each new generation, human lives that defined their times and continue to inspire us today. Humanists like to believe that they are known by the company they keep, and better to be with Aristotle than Dick Tracy. This belief can contribute to a stance of resistance of incorporating popular culture into the humanities that is bald-faced prejudicial snobbery. Nevertheless there also are legitimate questions about the potential for popular artifacts to yield the kinds of value and meanings that are inherent to the received masterworks. So that's one difficulty, skepticism about the humanistic value of popular culture. The other difficulty has to do with material culture itself, popular or otherwise.

Because the fact of the matter is that the overwhelming stock-in-trade of the humanities has been literary. Words, not material objects. The only humanities discipline that regularly deals with material culture is Art History, and until very recently, their subjects have been uncompromisingly elitist. The only other disciplines with a fairly long tradition of dealing with *popular* material culture are archeology and ethnography, both on the borderline between the humanities and social sciences. Times have changed and new bridging interdisciplines as well as renegade sub-disciplines have opened many doors for the examination of popular material culture: folk-life, cultural geography, historical archeology, industrial archeology, commercial archeology, agricultural history, history of technology, New Social History, American Studies and popular culture are a representative sampling of some of these interdisciplines and sub-disciplines. Most are in their first generation of scholarship and teaching; only a handful have achieved academic prestige as departmental units of colleges and universities. Many of their practitioners must endure ridicule, contempt and prejudicial discrimination for taking the popular material environment seriously.

The reasons for this state of affairs are easily given. The ultimate culprit is undoubtedly Plato, who most pointedly demonstrated that the farther one distances oneself from what the common herd thinks is the "real world," the closer one comes to the true reality of pure idea. As the centuries progressed, disdain for material things became fixed into the institutional hierarchy of the universities, and as the natural sciences (which *do* study material things) became increasingly distinct from letters, the humanities became exclusively verbal. Words about words about ideas. During the European Renaissance there were rumblings of discontent both with the academic and intellectual hierarchy and with the anti-materialistic methods of pursuing truth and beauty. Yet Leonardo da Vinci argued only in his unpublished notebooks, Rabelais' satire was too Rabelaisian for serious consideration, and Leon Battista Alberti's success in elevating the material crafts of painting and architecture to the dignity of professions was because he was humanist employing an arsenal of ethereal Neo-Platonic arguments from the ancient world.

There's also the matter of the company one keeps. American education is designed to graduate people from Show and Tell mentality. Those who can't hack a college prep verbal curriculum are siphoned into vocational training, an academic dead-end. Material things have generally been regarded as kid stuff, beneath the dignity of serious scholarship. And, if we adopt the Freudian idea that collecting things is an expression of the infantile anal instinct, we can label the research that *has* been done by antiquarian collectors of guns, dolls, stamps, bottles, campaign buttons, quilts, cars, spinning wheels, tractors, Toby jugs and Christmas plates, as "mere antiquarianism." Which in general it is, being limited to *identifying* and *pricing*, a long, long way intellectually from *interpreting* and *valuing*.

3. In 1989 the decorative arts museum that occupies a wing of the Louvre in Paris exhibited toys, including Mattel's Barbie dolls. Toys are objects of popular material culture that at once express and impress a society's human values.

To summarize briefly then, there are two major barriers to viewing popular material culture as legitimate subject-matters for the humanities, these being skepticism about the intrinsic value of any popular culture, and general neglect of material object as things that deserve equal footing with verbal documents. Both are matters of prestige, but both are also matters of inexperience. Popular culture studies and material culture studies are new kids on the block, and we all are a mite suspicious of new kids, until we've had some experience with how they think and act.

Turning to positive aspects of this wide-ranging, exciting new area of the humanities, popular material culture study has actually achieved prestige through the company it keeps. This company is not, of course, Dick Tracy, Fisher-Price toys or the *Antiques Price Guide*, and it certainly is not the American Historical Association, the American Philosophical Association or the Modern Language Association. The prestigious company has been museums, places like the Museum of Modern Art, the Field Museum of Natural History, Colonial Williamsburg, the Smithsonian Institution, the Henry Ford Museum and many other American museums of art, natural history and history as well as such foreign places as

Ottawa's National Museum, Britain's Victoria and Albert, Blist's Hill, and York; the Parisian Musée D'Orsay and the Louvre's Musée des Arts Décoratifs, and "open air" museums throughout Europe.

Why is it that museums—especially the large, famous ones—exude such a heady aroma of prestige? Historically, museums really have rather ignoble origins. Grave-robbery, smuggling, plunder of war, racist exploitation and the loony bequests of anal-compulsive collectors characterize the beginnings of many great museums, quite unlike the methods and motives of most libraries and colleges. Nevertheless, museums have served as pioneers in scholarship, as for example in the connoisseurship and authentication of art collections, in the botanic, zoological, geological and ethnological expeditions of natural history collections, and in the archival depth of state historical collections. Moreover, and most importantly, museums are privileged to touch the Real Things that are valued by humans. Let us see how the three predominant kinds of museums have legitimized popular material culture.

Although popular culture and mass-produced material objects have always been anathema to art critics and art historians, and their snobbery is still well entrenched, the decorative arts sucked museums into popular material culture. True, the original intention was to elevate the taste of *hoi polloi*, but the Victoria and Albert Museum in London began to collect manufactured popular objects in 1851, while the Musée des Arts Décoratifs did the same in 1870s. In Germany, the post-Great War Bauhaus was not a museum, but its purposes were to demystify the Artist, and to exploit mass-production methods to conjoin good design with utilitarian popular objects. Few items went into the intended mass-production that would bring Bauhaus taste into the reach of *volks* purses, but many went into museum collections. And they did spawn truly popular Woolworth, Montgomery Ward, Pier I, Crate and Barrel and Dansk versions. But the point is that art museums found themselves in the business of collecting mass-produced coffee pots, cutlery, chairs and luggage as well as elite Fabergé eggs and Christian Dior original gowns. A second inroad of popular material culture into the fine arts was in the discovery that primitive artifacts might be Art. The impetus came from artists' rejection of academic realism and Victorian ornamentation, but by the 1930s Picasso, Braque and Modigliani had sanctified African sculpture, and Mondrian, Mies and Wright had stamped the passports of Shaker furniture, Navajo rugs and Hopi pots. These objects were not machine-made popular culture, but they certainly were utilitarian material artifacts of the People. The distinction between what had been "primitive" art (now "folk" art) and cultivated "fine" arts had become blurred, particularly because the new aesthetic vocabulary of "abstraction," "mass," "form," "economy," "honest use of materials," etc. could be applied equally to a Brancusi sculpture, a Shaker stove, a Princess phone, or a San Il defonso Pueblo bowl. A third inroad in the fine arts museum came from direct challenges by Dadas and Futurists early in the century, and past mid-century, from the Pop art movement. Marcel Duchamp's 1917 urinal "Fountain" may not have been rushed into a permanent collection, (indeed it was lost, and the artist had to flush out a second version in 1951) but Jasper John's Ballantine Ale cans, Claes Oldenburg's oversized bag of french fries, Joseph Cornell's box assemblages and Duane Hanson's souvenir-and-camera-draped tourists made it into museums with breathtaking speed. The intent of artists

4. When an art museum such as the Netherlands' Kröller-Müller exhibits African sculpture next to cubist master-works, it validates ethnic popular culture as True Art.

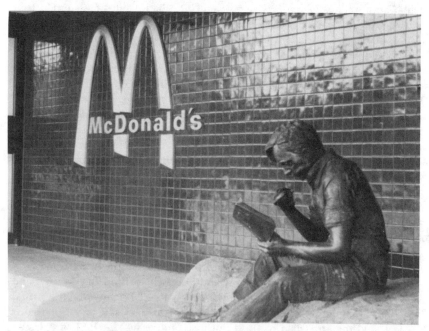

5. A perfect wedding of popular and fine arts material culture. Artists such as George Segal and Duane Hanson explored human psychology and sociology in realistic sculptures of ordinary people. When McDonald's joined Kansas City's genteel Plaza shopping district, they commissioned this sensitive "Out to Lunch" by Edward Johnson (1977).

3. **"B.K.F." Butterfly Chair** ❋
In 1938 three architects—Jorge Ferrari Hardoy,
Juan Kurchan, and Antonio Bonet—introduced
the butterfly chair. In 1943 it was selected for the
Museum Design Collection. Our faithful edition of
this now classic chair, with leather sling and trian-
gular iron frames that do not fold, is made in
Argentina for the Museum. 35H". $495.00.
members $445.50. **5472.** Brown. **5473.**
Black."

4. **Three-Wheel Trolley**
Elegant and easy to maneuver, this trolley was
designed by Enzo Mari in 1987. Features two
large glass serving surfaces for cocktails or tea.
Black coated aluminum with sturdy steel frame
and handle. Made in Italy by Alessi.
33½H×17⅞W×29¼L". **T5481.** $925.00.
members $832.50. Price includes shipping
within the contiguous U.S. Please allow 6 to 8
weeks for delivery."

❋ **MoMA exclusive.**

1—Sol LeWitt Rug **T5459**

6. The popular "butterfly chair" is available to anyone from such retailers as Sears Roebuck or Target. For a price—$495—though, you can be assured that it is an exclusive masterwork by buying from the Museum of Modern Art's catalog.

7. The tenets of Formal Criticism erased the line between technical products that are void of meaning and art that consciously expresses human values. MOMA's saw blade and ball bearings are lifted out of their intended environment of useful labor. Unlike consumer items such as cars and typewriters, where artistic design is intended, these are purely functional material objects that in use would be coated with pitch and grease.

such as these, and Andy Warhol and Roy Lichtenstein, as well as photographers of the commonplace was clear: there are meaningful arts and art forms all around us in the environment of commercial culture. Just as landscape paintings help us to see the beauty of the natural environment, so oversized soup cans, framed comic strips and welded autoparts can help us to see the world we live in, for better or for worse, but with the thoughtful, analytic humanistic attention that it deserves. The art exhibit that capped the movements to legitimize popular material culture, though, was the Museum of Modern Art's "High and Low" of 1990, tracing the contributions of mass culture to fine arts from the early Cubists' use of popular newspapers as source material. True enough, but a jaunt uptown to the Metropolitan Museum would show that such Dutch "little masters" as Jan Steen, Pieter deHooch and Adrien Brouwer were employing popular material objects as expressive of family values back in the seventeenth century.

Turning from art treasures to museums of natural history, anthropology is the key to popular culture. Visitors to the American Museum of Natural History may be primarily interested in animals, rocks, plants, planets and similar natural phenomena, but the scientific study of the physical and social evolution of humankind began to creep into the earliest museum collections before the mid-nineteenth century. The Wilkes Expedition in the 1840s set a pattern for careful observation of remote cultures, and primitive artifacts collections began to make their way into museums, which, by the end of the century, were themselves funding expeditions to collect examples of the total material culture of primitive societies. Once again, this is popular culture in the sense of culture of the people rather than mass-mediated culture. But for various reasons—not the least of which is that anthropologists were running out of isolated tribal groups to observe—museums began to expand "the story of mankind" into recent times and urban life. *Ergo*: commercial, mass-produced, popular material culture. Two examples may suffice. The Field Museum of Natural History's recent Polynesian exhibit begins with the geology of the islands and the introduction of flora and fauna. It then moves on to objects from their superb collection of century-old canoes, paddles, costumes, fishing gear, household goods and the like—but the exhibit ends with a town street whose shops are filled with tourist goods such as paper leis and camera supplies, household goods like canned foods, bolts of synthetic cloth and Hong Kong sandals. The Illinois State Museum in Springsfield is (rather strangely), a museum of natural history *and* of decorative arts. For years, its major anthropological dioramas have depicted Indian life. However, the last of these depicts the coming of French fur traders, bringing popular manufactured material culture in the forms of blankets, beads and axes. It is only natural that in developing a major new permanent exhibit, the evolution of Illinois community life (and the decorative arts of Illinois) will be expressed in such things as gas ranges, television sets, Barbie dolls, Tupperware and other objects, nearly all of which have functional cognates in the pre-Columbian dioramas. Let us now consider historical museums.

There are museums of history that lack popular material culture. Versailles, Blenheim Palace and Biltmore may fill the bill along with various other castles, villas and stately homes. But that's about it. Even Mount Vernon and Monticello are not exempt, because tableware, bedding, furniture are out of upper-crust popular molds, and both museums now interpret backstairs culture of slaves

8. Although the car is a mass-produced material object, a "Jesus-freak" invested it with deeper human values with such messages as "dedicate your work to God and your plans will be made." This was part of a brilliantly conceived major exhibit at the Tennessee State Museum on southern religious traditions. Is it art, history, or anthropology? It is unquestionably humanities.

and servants. Indeed, what is really interesting about Versailles, Blenheim and Biltmore is their places in the history of popular propaganda. Versailles, for example, was from the beginning open to the general populace. It was as unique and glitzy as Disney World; it was as calculated a political statement as Lenin's Tomb. It was and is, therefore, a kind of popular material culture, regardless of craftsmanship, cost and aristocracy, and don't you doubt it. A somewhat related kind of historic museum includes great medieval cathedrals and humble parish churches. Like such mansions as Chatsworth and the White House which are buildings that continue to serve as residences as well as being public museums, most of these, like Notre Dame, are functioning houses of worship as well as public museums of material objects. A guided tour of most of these churches will quickly persuade the tourist that carvings and stained-glass windows were used for popular education, their purposes not in the least elite or exclusive.

But generally when we think of historical museums it is not preserved living palaces and cathedrals that come to mind, but the museums of collected artifacts and formal exhibits like the Smithsonian's Museum of American History, the museums of the Colorado Historical Society, the Ottertail County Historical Society or the Atlanta Historical Society. Actually the range of kinds of history museums is astounding: historic homes like the Eisenhower home, museums attached to presidential libraries, state park museums such a Split Rock Lighthouse in Minnesota, reconstructed schoolhouses as on the Bowling Green

9. The city museum in York, England exhibits toilets as objects of local industrial history, as well as social history that has profoundly altered human behavior.

10. Shadowboxes flank the staircase to the exhibits of the Chicago Historical Society suggesting the range of popular material objects that are needed to document a community: chairs, musical instruments, clock, statuary, etc.

11. On a plane with the popularity of Dick Tracy is this Chicago Historical Society exhibit of T-shirts and sneakers. Is this worthy of the name Humanities? If it were an exhibit of coats-of-arms of European aristocracy, Florentine guilds, or an arm shaking a spear, we'd not question it. Typologically, the T-shirts serve the same function of expressing identity. Unlike coats-of-arms, though, these emblems are democratically inclusive rather than reserved for an elite few.

University campus, "living history" reconstructions like Colonial Williamsburg and Old World Wisconsin, industrial-technological museums such as the Henry Ford Museum, history exhibits in comprehensive museums such as Omaha's Joslyn Museum, archeological sites such as Mesa Verde, military sites like Fort Sumter, Halls of Fame, like Nashville's Country Music and Hayward, Wisconsin's National Freshwater Fishing Hall of Fame, specialized collections like Pensacolas's Naval Air Museum and the Baker Museum for Furniture Research in Holland, Michigan, or one-time exhibits like the Duluth Public Library's 1990 Centennial history...Had enough? There is more, but the point is abundantly clear. All of these are examples of understanding some aspect or aspects of human history by way of objects of popular, material culture. The closer the museum comes to employing social history as its interpretive focus, and the more the time emphasis is post-industrial revolution, the more the definition of *popular* becomes congruent with the usual conception of mass-mediated, mass-produced commercial culture, bringing us right back to Dick Tracy *et alia*.

But is it humanities? Are these things worthy of serious examination?

My answers are from the classics. But first, let me ask you to look around your present environment and see what material objects are not popular, mass-produced and mass-distributed? Second, if you are in your home or office, does this assemblage of things reflect your individuality and your values? Third, do you value your own being? We must go to the heart, because as one of the humanities' favorite texts says, "The unexamined life is not worth living." That's Socrates. Another favorite text is from one of Terence's comedies, which in Cicero became a guidepost for wide-ranging human curiosity and generous tolerance for humanity: "I am a human, and nothing that is human is alien to me." From Terence, we may adopt a stance of not prejudging the humble, abundant baggage of human lives. From Socrates, the lesson *is* to judge to examine all aspects of our lives and the lives of others', including the material baggage, and then to judge where the meanings are. The values of humanities are not intrinsic to a few rare objects. They are in the human meanings that we read into or out of things with thoughtful examination.

Suggested Reading

My *Outlaw Aesthetics* (Bowling Green UP, 1977) takes such popular material objects as lawn flamingoes and plastic Virgins and relates them to the humanities themes both historically and cross-culturally. Varnedoe and Gopnik's big exhibit catalog *High and Low: Modern Art and Popular Culture* (MOMA/Abrams, 1990) is as thorough a study of both popular materials and relevant modern artists and styles as could be hoped for. For manufactured utilitarian goods and their meanings for human values Siegfried Giedion's 1948 *Mechanization Takes Command* (Norton) continues to be a gift that keeps on giving. Methodologically and philosophically I think George Kubler's *The Shape of Time* (Yale, 1962) is particularly insightful about human valuing of material things. From a European view, Philippe Ariès and George Duby's collection of articles on *A History of Private Life* is now in English translation (Belknap/Harvard 1987-1989). The three volumes look at domestic life from pagan Rome through the Renaissance and utilize material objects as one of their tools to get into the sociology, psychology and spiritual lives of Europeans. Popular material artifacts are the very essence of outdoor museums, things and ideas interact in every day activities; Jay Anderson's *Time Machines: The World of Living History* (American Association for State and Local History, 1984) is the authority.

The foregoing books are all to some degree international in scope (though primarily in the Western European-North American hemisphere). For American popular material culture there is a wealth of sources available. The American Association for State and Local History, because of close connections with historical museums, has been a leader in publications that guide the interpretation of human values through material objects. Thomas Schlereth's *Artifacts and the American Past* (1980) and David E. Kyrig and Myron Marty's *Nearby History* (1982) are excellent introductions as well as being thoroughly authoritative. Collections other than the one in your hand edited by Ray Browne and Marshall Fishwick for Bowling Green University Press used major humanities themes as ways to examine popular culture (although the majority of the subjects are literary and media rather than material); these include *Icons of America* (1978); *Objects of Special Devotion: Fetishes and Fetishism in Popular Culture* (1981); *Forbidden Fruits: Taboos and Tabooism in Culture* (1984). The division of folklore study called "folklife" includes material culture. Simon J. Bronner is the editor of a series of books on American Material Culture and Folklife for UMI Research Press. The introductory volume (1985) bears the series title. Historical archeology, like all archeology, is based on material things. For brilliant humanistic interpretations of homely manufactured objects, James Deetz's *In Small Things Forgotten: The Archeology of Early and American Life* (Anchor Books, 1977) is already a classic, and William H. Adam's *Silcott, Washington: Ethnoarcheology of a Rural American Community* (Washington State University Department of Anthropology Report #54, 1977) is an interdisciplinary study of life styles as revealed through material culture that deserves more widespread attention.

Of Art and Entertainment

Jon Huer

The role of art—as distinguished from the arts—in the humanities may not be clear because often we tend not to tie the two together. Yet making pictures with the hands and paints is surely one of the oldest of human expressions. Sometimes these pictures have been used to educate, to entertain; sometimes they have been used to "inspire the human spirit." In all instances they have been used to communicate, to one degree or another, some emotion—identity, directions, promises, hopes, uplift. Consequently art has played a very important role in the statement and purposes of the humanities. In the following essay Jon Huer distinguishes between the two kinds of art—or several kinds of art— and points out some important conclusions.

Of all human expressions, Art, it is often said, is perhaps the most moving and affecting. If so, it is one of the profoundest of the humanities. Yet we often fail to recognize it as such, and often separate it into another role. There are, of course, "high" art and "low" art, or so we are told. It is worthwhile to examine the so-called distinction and see how both tie in and serve to rejuvenate the humanities.

All great works of art are said to give a "profoundly moving" experience to the art-public. Lesser works of art give a similar experience on a smaller scale. But why do we get this moving experience from art and not from entertainment? To be sure, we *do* become moved by some entertainment. We even cry at the movies. But, sooner or later, we feel intensely *ashamed* that we were moved to tears by the experience. Somehow we feel that we were fooled by some very clever entertainer. This feeling of shame almost never occurs when we are moved by art experience. The deeply moved audience at the performance of "Romeo and Juliet" or the "Fifth Symphony" is unlikely to wake up to shame.

Consumers of contemporary American culture have a tough time separating art and entertainment. Many cultural enterprises are presented as art, which should be more properly called entertainment. Many entertainers (Frank Sinatra, Michael Jackson, for example) are often called "artists." There is even a cable channel called A & E, for "Arts and Entertainment." Virtually everywhere art and entertainment are confused. Are they indeed two separate categories in human endeavors? Or, should they be *thought* of as two separate categories at all?

Below I will attempt to delineate art and entertainment as a way to answer the questions raised above. The task may be foolhardy and irrelevant. But our intellectual task may also bear fruit and help us think more clearly about art

48

and entertainment and the roles they play in advancing the humanities in our society.

Active vs. Passive Response

In art we involve ourselves actively and alertly. Art demands our active participation, and it is this very reason of active participation that we *go to* art in the first place. It is not to be played to lull us to sleep, hung to fill a space or read as an exercise in relaxation. With art the response and involvement must be total and absolute. There is no room for partially awake, or marginally conscious responses in art-experience. Art does not exist if it is not *experienced*. No art-experience is possible unless it is active and total.

In entertainment, on the other hand, no active involvement is necessary. Not only is it unnecessary, but it is also not in the best interest of entertainment if it requires active involvement. The first rule of entertainment is that it must require no strenuous or stressful involvement from the audience. It must be *entertaining*. It must be something we can participate in or disengage from *at will* with minimum thought required in the decision-making. We can take it or leave it. We do not go to entertainment; it comes *to us*. It seeks us out with extensive advertisement and with the promises of making our expense worthwhile. There is fierce competition among entertaining events to attract our attention. Entertainment pleases our senses with the minimal requirement for alertness and conscious response.

Public vs. Private Purpose

All art is a "public" endeavor, for no art can properly be called art if it remains a private event. By being public, an art work exists in the open, to be encountered and appraised as a public experience. Although created and experienced through individual processes, art acquires its public character as it is presented to its audience. Thus artistic creation is the most *public* of all human activities and utterances. No artist produces an artwork only to hide it from the public or to have it remain in private existence. All art experiences take place in public forums: in museums, in art galleries, in concert halls, and in printed media where everyone can see art and respond to it. Even when one listens to, reads, or views an artwork in private, one is still involved in the ongoing process of public judgement, experience, and appreciation. In that sense, the artist is more publicly open than he is often suspected because of the intensely private nature of creative processes.

Entertainment, on the other hand, pleases the private person. There is little or no dialogue, either historical or interpersonal, among those who are entertained. For, although they may be entertained at the same place, they do not form an audience to share the experience in a public dialogue. They may express their approval and disapproval, but such expressions cannot be carried any further than that. Individual fans have individually different reasons for their approval or disapproval. Entertainment is relevant only to the private purpose of the person in possession of the object. Its meaning and existence please and satisfy only that person alone. One buys and consumes it with no lasting significance attached to the article so bought and consumed. It is a matter of one's everyday life and one's private doings in it.

Internalized vs. Sensory Beauty

In art the sense of "beauty" we feel and reflect is not sensory at all. It is *felt internally*, rather than recognized externally through the senses. Within our inner imaginings and recreating, the feeling of beauty is rendered possible. When we hear Schubert's "Unfinished," we may call it a "beautiful symphony." But the beauty we refer to is "internalized beauty," that can be recreated only in our imagination, not through the senses. Art's beauty must be *artificially* created by the audience's active response and realization as the artist intended it. It is thus an intellectual, not sensory, process.

In entertainment, it is you-get-what-you-see, hear, smell, taste, or touch. There is nothing to internalize in entertainment. It is all on the surface, as all entertainment must be. There is no reflection necessary, no internalizing the experience, beyond the quick and superficial encounter. Judgement is also instantaneous. We approve or disapprove at the moment we see, hear, smell, taste or touch it. To be sure, we all enjoy entertaining things, but we do not enjoy the *same* entertaining things very long. Entertaining things must change at all times, and in quick succession in order to retain their attractiveness.

Ideas vs. Things

Every artwork is a metaphor for ideas. It is the very nature of art that it represents something other than itself. What are the ideas represented in "Hamlet," in the "Eroica," or in the Mona Lisa? What are their "messages"? Why did the artists create them? As metaphor, no artwork conveys its meaning directly. (Or else, all art would be science.) The meaning, or the idea, must materialize through the active internalization of the audience. An artwork whose ideas are instantaneously clear and direct to the mind, like a propaganda poster, is a failure. Art must *embody*, not *identify*, the ideas for its existence. On the other hand, an artwork whose ideas are never clear even over considerable time and space is also a failure; people simply lose interest. Neither artwork contains enough ideas to require an audience for its continuing appreciation.

Entertainment, on the other hand, cannot contain ideas that are not directly represented in itself. Propaganda posters, military marches, "social movies," political slogans, among others, have a clearly identifiable message that requires only the most cursory attention. All such messages are direct, concrete, and material. Ideas-as-ideas are difficult to be the subject of entertainment. The subject has to be something that the audience can identify and relate to immediately— money, sex, power, violence. A beautiful object in and of itself may be joy to own, enjoy, or cuddle, but not an idea to appreciate or reflect on. We may enjoy entertainment, but we rarely take its "philosophy" seriously. John Lennon may have had his ideas, but his music was entertainment first and last.

Revolutionary vs. Variational

Every true artist is a revolutionary and every true artwork a revolution. All great artworks are destructive to the status quo and contradictory to the established. They often emerge as a declaration for a new era, a new society, a new generation. Once such ideas are accepted as "inevitable," the artwork is a surprise that does not surprise, a deviation that becomes standard, a revolution whose existence is more justified than the order it defies. It is the power of art that what at first seems odd and impossible ultimately becomes inevitable and logical in the human mind. In the process, man may become freer and happier and more enlightened.

No entertainment ever overthrows the existing rules of pleasure and acceptance. It merely improves upon the already-existing. Black-and-white may become technicolor, low tech may become high tech, coarse pictures may become more lifelike. But all these are variations on the old theme. Nothing fundamental changes in entertainment because the fundamental human senses do not change. Even "original" novels, movies, games, what have you, must follow the rules of pleasure in human nature, although they may take a different approach. In television's fall lineup every "new" lineup is a variation of the "old" lineup. Every year it is a variation of the same theme, and the theme itself never varies. The consumer of entertainment does not allow himself to be displeased with his creature comfort, sensory pleasure or stimulation. While the entertainment product is never original, it is under obligation to vary its forms and presentation so that it *evolves*. Every year entertainment becomes more elaborate, more stimulating, more perfect—in short, more entertaining. The principle of entertainment, however, remains the same: even the caveman could enjoy our modern entertainment without much trouble, were he to walk into our high-tech world today.

Immortal vs. Transient

Every artwork is intended to be the definitive last word on the subject. A true artist says no more about the same subject, and moves on to another one. In this sense every artwork is intended to be immortal. But immortality, contrary to what it first appears to mean, is not a static state of being, a fossilized repose in a forgotten depository. Artistic immortality must be realized only through posterity, through the continuing judgment of living generations. Immortal art is permanent and unchanging because it is always self-generating and self-rejuvenating. Within all great works of art is contained this capacity for inexhaustible resources for self-renewal. Artistic immortality thus consists of this *capacity* to change to remain relevant for each new experience and each new generation. It is the same Shakespeare plays, the same Beethoven symphonies, the same Van Gogh paintings that enthrall each new audience. But they avoid obsolescence by being *ahead* of generations while being *in step* with history.

Every entertaining event, however overwhelming its effect at the time, is destined to be transient. It is here today and gone tomorrow. The entertainment that pleases is also the entertainment that bores. It must come and go at dizzying speed. By and large, every entertainment is a one-shot event, although some come back as reruns. Once seen, once read, once heard, entertainment value is spent from the experience and our entertainment desire demands something new. There may be "classics" in entertainment, which regularly find new audiences. But even they become old hats to be replaced by the new generation of transient spectacles that are bigger, better, and simply more entertaining. One bestseller writer must write another bestseller that is better-selling than the one before; a singer must sing a song that sells more records; one hit must be followed by another that is a bigger hit. It is an eternal race toward obsolescence.

Pain vs. Pleasure

Contrary to public perception, true art experience is painful as life itself is painful. Pain is the basic ingredient that makes up life, and the artist is perhaps more sensitive to life's suffering than anyone. Virtually all "great art"—in novels, plays, symphonies—is heavily loaded with human tragedy; virtually all "grand operas" have the hero or heroine die at the end. The artist gladly undertakes the painful process of creation for reasons known only to himself. He is not there to please the public, but to share his own vision of art for which he endures the great and private pain of creation. Art, like all other noble and sublime human endeavors, must struggle with painful self-doubts and reflections. It is not triumph over pain, but *in* and *through* it. When we hear the funeral march in Beethoven's "Eroica" the anguish and sorrow of its creator are overwhelming, yet his anguish and sorrow do not drown us in them. The painful experiences are Beethoven's to endure, and ours to appreciate. Every growing process is accompanied by pain. The audience grows too, achieving a new dimension of thought about man, society, and life not attained before.

Entertainment's total purpose of existence is to please its consumers. It is never intended to invoke or experience pain in its consumer. The very existence of entertainment means a pleased public. No entertainment is ever designed to impose its will and meaning upon an unwilling public. It is designed, planned, and processed to affirm the "pleasure principle," so to speak, that exists in human nature. It is a marketplace exercise in immediate gratification, whose effect of pleasure must be felt instantly and without reflection. It could be soft-and-easy music, pleasant landscape paintings, page-turner bestsellers, gorgeous nude bodies, exciting car chases on television, some of which may claim to be art. While art forces us to grow, entertainment *stunts* our growth. Permanently-entertained people are permanently juvenile. Entertainment caters to our smallest whims and caprice, and makes us less than wholly human.

Originality vs. Replication

Originality is possible only in human ideas, and true originality exists only in art and philosophy. Every artwork (and every philosophy) bears the signature of its creator, the artist (and the philosopher). With his sheer power of persuasion the artist forces his will upon us. He demands our submission to his *art*, but not our submission to *him*. Unlike entertainment which can be replicated by anyone, every artwork requires that there be an artist. Originality of artwork as conceived by the artist alone is one of the supreme contradictions of life. By all known logic, there should be no artistic originality, or no artist, but plenty of pleasing things around us. Logically, the wheel eventually leads to the computer. But there is no logic in the progression from Bach to Mozart to Beethoven to Brahms. Each artist is the creator of his own original ideas. One technology leads to its better model; but in art one artist is not necessarily an improvement over the other. Art cannot exist without originality, and originality makes an interconnection among them impossible.

In entertainment there is neither original creation nor the creator. Every entertainment can be manufactured by anyone with enough resources to do it. It can be mass-produced and -distributed in complete anonymity to its producer.

It is not the producer as a human being that produces entertainment, but his resources, including machines. Thus, every entertaining object looks and feels like every other entertaining object. It is a matter of which one does better, from one season to the next, from one bestseller to the next, from one gush of fad to the next. Every entertaining phenomenon has no memory of the other, and every phenomenon resembles exactly all the other phenomena before and after it. Unlike in art, consumers and producers in entertainment can remain totally anonymous. The consumer is neither interested in, nor cares about, who pleases his senses as long as his senses are pleased.

Craftsmanship, Means vs. Ends

Art requires craftsmanship as its first order of necessity. But it is subordinated to the larger requirement of art, that is, the creation of an idea. It is merely a means to that end. To the artist, his art-conception is the ultimate purpose, and his craftsmanship merely a tool, an instrument, a material resource to be employed. It is neither beauty nor ornament that the artist seeks in his art. It is an idea, a concept, a message that he is seeking to create. Because of this, the greater an artwork, the less evident is its craftsmanship. A great artist never tries to be clever or obvious with his craftsmanship. In great art craftsmanship is so totally immersed in the work that one cannot tell where one part ends and another begins. It is only in lesser artists that we see the evidence of craftsmanship in their artwork, thus distracting us from their art. In great artworks the audience merely *feels*, but cannot clearly identify, the fine seams of craftsmanship.

Every entertaining object, on the other hand, is a showcase, its craftsmanship evident at first glance. There is no second guessing. It must appeal to our immediate sight, hearing, and so on without hesitation or reflection. It must demonstrate its effect right there and then. The skill with which the entertainment is produced must be there for all to see. Subtlety of meaning and nuances are a deadly enemy of entertainment. All must be dazzling, eye-popping, attention-grabbing, side-splitting, stupendous, breathtaking, headline-worthy. It must stand or fall in the first minute of its existence. The audience will not give failed entertainment another chance. No second life is normally expected in entertainment.

Change vs. Conformity

Art is change. Every artwork represents a triumph over the reluctant heart, mastery over resistance, and change over inertia. Art reflects change while causing it by its own destructiveness. Static art dies out, for its relevance and meaning have been lost to the new generation, the new order, and the new world. The artworks that survive and achieve immortality are, ironically, those that never remain the same. The artworks change the times, yet change *with* the times as well. They remain permanent by never being the same to two generations, two social orders, or two worlds. In all this, the artist is the supreme agent of change. He is the logic and inevitability of change in one person. In him alone remain the mystery as well as reality of art.

Unlike art, entertainment cannot change itself, for there is no agent of change within itself. It must remain subservient to the demand of the consuming public. Its survival and prosperity are not insured by change, but by conformity to the established rules and the status quo. While unchanging in its fundamental makeup, its very existence depends on variations of the same theme and the reappearances of now-forgotten old themes. Entertainment is that part of human nature and society that has not changed much since humanity first demanded to be entertained. It still consits of tickling our fancy and funnybones. It cannot and does not change anyone's reluctant heart, for its very acceptance depends on *not* trying to change anyone's heart. Thus, entertainment remains the same in different packages, forever making its appeal to the human senses.

Art is a *specific* activity. A specific person (the artist) comes upon a specific urge to create. No one but the artist, perhaps not even himself, understands the mysterious ways in which this urge strikes the artist. Entertainment, on the other hand, is a *general* activity. Its production is tied to commerce and material resources, and the general desire in human nature to be pleased. Psychologists help the entertainment industry by figuring out what people want and what their natural inclination is. Entertainment is then produced to match the psychological profile of human nature and inclination. Once thus figured out, it is easy to mass-produce it.

But no one has figured out how art works or what drives the artist. Not that we haven't tried.

Pornography, Obscenity and the Humanities: Mapplethorpe, 2 Live Crew And the Elitist Definition of Art

William E. Brigman

The creative arts have always forced themselves into a special place in the affairs of human beings. Plato taught us that creators burn with a special fire bequeathed by God, and people who do not have—or have been denied the expression of—that fire have always been forced to content themselves with warming themselves with the heat generated. The creative arts have therefore always been the cutting edge of human expression. Sheltered from the criticism that has controlled most of the life of the majority of us, they have broadened and enriched our lives in many ways. But they have always been under suspicion and criticism by those persons who do not understand them. In the 1990s surely the arts are going to be tested and threatened in every way possible. Since they are so important to the development and continuance of the Humanities it is fundamental that we understand their role and how we must assist in that development. William Brigman outlines the problems and solutions below.

Definition of the humanities, their relationship to the arts and function in society take on dramatic significance in the context of pornography, obscenity and definition of art. The criminal prosecution of the Cincinnati Contemporary Arts Museum and its director, Dennis Barrie, for exhibiting the homoerotic works and nude children studies of photographer Robert Mapplethorpe sent a shudder through the arts establishment in America.[1] In large part because of the coincidence of timing, the criminal prosecution of the rap group, The 2 Live Crew,[2] for a live stage presentation in Florida and the conviction of a black Miami record store owner for selling one of their records, As Nasty as They Wanna Be, after a determination by a federal judge that the song was obscene, merged with the Mapplethorpe trial as evidence that the arts were under attack.

In the recent past the line between art, pornography and obscenity has been the focus of attention of a few scholars and numerous juries trying obscenity cases. In the mind of the arts establishment, however, the literary and artistic censorship battles were long over: it was unthinkable that "serious" art, artists, or museums could be prosecuted. The Mapplethorpe trial and the multiple 2 Live Crew trials abused, if they did not completely shatter, those illusions.

Nat Hentoff, while criticizing the art establishment for its naivete in thinking it was immune to censorship, expressed the horror typical of both the civil libertarian and the arts establishment at the new developments in an article entitled "We Are Entering A New Era of Repression," (*Penthouse*, September 1990, 153).[3] He begins:

> In Cincinnati on April 7—for the first time in American history—police entered a museum,...cleared the galleries of all visitors, and closed the doors....
>
> Until now, museums have been considered immune from the thought police. But that is no longer true. The Cincinnati precedent now holds museums to be in the same category as adult bookstores and movie theaters showing films....
>
> However the Cincinnati case comes out, we have entered a new era in pursuit of alleged obscenity and pornography in the United States. Not only X-rated films and various magazines are vulnerable. The arts establishment—including its prestigious museums and museum directors—is now subject to sudden visits by armed critics, writing down their shocked reviews of exhibits and handing out subpoenas.

There was a mass sigh of relief from the arts establishment when the Cincinnati jury, composed largely of individuals who had never been in an art museum before they were called for jury duty, found the museum director not guilty of pandering obscenity. This sigh of relief turned into euphoria when a Hollywood, Florida jury found 2 Live Crew not guilty of obscenity charges for its live stage performance: the forces of "art" (in different manifestations) had triumphed over the forces of ignorance.

For example, Richard Goldstein writing in the *Village Voice* was almost ecstatic:

> Why would a jury of ordinary Americans, who could always be counted on to see a threat to law and order in whatever turned them on, suddenly turn tail on history, giggling over what the Man calls dangerous? The answer has a lot to do with another honorable American tradition: contempt for authority. But there's a more subtle reason why many people have come to resent the policing of erotica. And that has more to do with marketing than with morality.
>
> It's been nearly 20 years since porn came out from under the counter. In that time, smut's gotten cheaper than a six-pack, and videotape has made filth a fixture of the home entertainment center for millions of Americans. Some of these folks, inevitably, end up on juries. (Even the good people of Cincinnati can cross the river into Kentucky to get their dose of dirt: no wonder they weren't particularly shocked by Mapplethorpe's tableaux.) A generation has grown up with access to erotica in the form of mass-circulation slicks like Hustler, as well as slasher films, music videos, and advertising that flashes sexual desire as an iconic strobe. A touch of lingerie, a glimpse of bondage, a quick crack of the whip: this is the hot sauce of American entertainment. And most of us have become accustomed (if not addicted) to a market economy that serves up an every more specialized menu of sexual fantasies, as fresh and hot as a delivery from Pizza Hut.
>
> ...What we've learned from the Mapplethorpe and 2 Live Crew cases is that right-wing repression is a paper tiger in America today. There may be 40 million of *them*, there are five times as many of *us*. And though true believers can wreak havoc with a business that stocks dirty records or videotapes, the market for such commodities is too diverse to be permanently suppressed....[4]

This "Doowutchyalike" analysis is premature, based on a set of incorrect assumptions, and the euphora is destined to be short lived. First, while it is true that the jury in Cincinnati acquitted the museum director in the Mapplethorpe case it is not true that they approved of the photography. One juror, James Jones, has stated, "[w]e had no idea that something like this existed." "As far as we were concerned," said another juror, Anthony Eckstein, "they were gross and lewd." Second, Goldstein's analysis concentrates on the trial of the members of 2 Live Crew for their live performance at the Club Futura in Hollywood, Florida, and ignores the judicial determination that some of their material is obscene and the conviction of a record store owner for selling it.

The acquittal of 2 Live Crew was not a manifestation of a new acceptance of erotica but rather the result of the extremely poor technical quality of the recordings of the live presentation made at the night club and the resultant inability of the prosecution to make a convincing case. If the prosecution had been able to present commercial records of the songs (which the judge properly prevented them from doing) or if they had been able to present a videotape of the live show, conviction would have been more likely. The acquittal is an aberration and it is inappropriate to build an argument on it. Prosecutions of 2 Live Crew records continue in several cities.

Treating the 2 Live Crew acquittal as an aberration and the convictions as the norm, this chapter examines why Mapplethorpe's homoerotic work which was personally objectionable to many members of the jury was judged non-obscene in Cincinnati, arguably the most erotically conservative city in the United States, and why the 2 Live Crew's dirty rap is unacceptable in Miami, Dallas, and other major cities.

Standing alone, and in view of the acquittal of the museum and its director, the Mapplethorpe case might not require a reassessment of the complex relationship of art and pornography in either the narrow legal context or the broader context of pornography and the humanities. However, when the Mapplethorpe acquittal is contrasted with the conviction in several of the 2 Live Crew cases, the reassessment is required. Moreover, the continuing F.B.I. investigation of "naturist" photographer Jock Sturges (some of whose works are presently being shown in a small Philadelphia art gallery) on "child pornography" charges indicates that the problem is not temporary for either the legal or artistic community.[5]

It cannot be seriously argued that Mapplethorpe's explicit homoerotic art is, per se, more acceptable to the mass society than is the explicit language of "the dirty boys of rap." Such an interpretation would also require the conclusion that the public is not concerned about the alleged "child pornography" in the Mapplethorpe case. It is also directly contrary to the statements of several of the Mapplethorpe jurors about their abhorrence of the materials. Rather, the acceptance of Mapplethorpe and the rejection of the 2 Live Crew is grounded in the elitist definitions of art, pornography and obscenity and the acceptance of the elitist definition by the public.

Throughout history, pornography has been defined in innumerable ways: it has been admired and scorned, praised and rejected, worshipped and denounced, exhibited with great fanfare and housed in secret. But, for all its controversial nature, one aspect has held constant: the level of acceptance on the part of the beholder has largely remained a function of that individual's social status. Pornography has been acceptable for the elite but not the masses.

Early in his book, *The Secret Museum*, Walter Kendrick discusses the problems that the explicit sexual relics of the newly discovered ruins of Pompeii presented to curators in the last century:

The matter was further complicated by the fact that mere preservation was not enough. Pompeiian artifacts were valuable because they formed a source of knowledge, and knowledge requires dissemination; somebody besides diggers and custodians had to view these things if their value was to be realized. While Pompeii was alive, anyone and everyone had had access to them, but from the first moment the first obscene artifact was unearthed, it was apparent that the ancient and modern worlds differed drastically in this regard. . . . What was required was a new taxonomy: if Pompeii's priceless obscenities were to be properly managed, they would have to be systematically named and placed. The name chosen for them was "pornography," and they were housed in the Secret Museum.[6]

Even more revealing is an introduction that M.L. Barre wrote to the 1877 catalog of the Secret Museum at the National Museum of Naples:

. . . we have taken all the prudential measures applicable to such a collection of engravings and text. We have endeavored to make its reading inaccessible, so to speak, to poorly educated persons, as well as to those whose sex and age forbid any exception to the laws of decency and modesty. With this in mind, we have done our best to regard each of the objects we have had to describe from an exclusively archaeological and scientific point of view. It has been our intention to remain calm and serious throughout. In the exercise of his holy office, the man of science must neither blush nor smile. We have looked upon our statues as an anatomist contemplates his cadavers.[7]

Implicit in the treatment of the Pompeiian artifacts is the intellectual, the elitist bias which has permeated art and especially erotic art and pornography throughout the modern era. For the elitist, art is an intellectual enterprise. It is perfectly acceptable to survey the works of great masters when displayed in a manner that is pleasing to intellectual members of society. A nude Goya, for example, hanging in a prestigious hotel in a major American city is visited and admired by many. The nude, lounging wistfully, arouses little dissent. Take the same concept of a nude female, sculpt, paint or photograph her straddling a Harley-Davidson motorcycle and place the piece in an establishment frequented by members of a lower class of society, and it is no longer art. The nude figurine perched atop a $200 an ounce bottle of perfume calls for greater social acceptance than one similarly adorning the mudflaps of a semi rig barrelling down the interstate.

Elizabeth Hess, writing about the F.B.I. investigation of Jock Sturges on "child pornography" charges, inadvertently makes the elitist distinction quite clear. In describing Sturges' work, which contains a series of 22 photographic prints of young girls on a "naturist" beach in France, she says:

Young girls pose, smack in the center of the frame: groups of children sleep lackadaisically on the beach; the family basks in the hot light of the sun. These folks truly look like they were born naked. They're totally relaxed with their own bodies and also relaxed in front of Sturges' camera. Almost too relaxed. There's not much going on in the work apart from the typical male gaze organizing each frame. The kids look somewhat bored. And *everybody* has a perfect, Coppertoned body. . . .

The odd thing is that Robert Mapplethorpe's work, which is much more extreme and dramatic, was easier to defend against his adversaries than these romantic, often paternalistic portraits would be. Mapplethorpe kept his models, especially when naked, at a theatrical distance, turning much of the work into critical commentary on his subject. Sturges brings us close to the surface, to the skin—and stops. Mapplethorpe's work demands debate over various notions of sexual progress; Sturges offers us uncritical images of traditional standards of "beauty." For Mapplethorpe, the bottom line in Court was whether or not his work is Art, and of this there could be no doubt; the photographer had already been welcomed into the canon.[8]

Only an artist or member of the critical elite would even try to argue that Mapplethorpe's seven photographs which show, among other things, a man urinating in another man's mouth, three photos of a man's anus penetrated by various objects, and a mans' finger inserted into a penis, is "easier to defend against his adversaries than [Sturges] romantic, often paternalistic portraits [of nude young children]." The writer is obviously referring to a defense based on the canons of art criticism, not mass attitudes.

This particular typical elitist concept of art has two elements: 1) Mapplethorpe's work has distance and Sturges' does not, and 2) Mapplethorpe had already been welcomed into the elite community of major artists. Compare Hess' elitist concept above with that of Susan Sontag in her essay, *The Pornographic Imagination*:

What makes a work of pornography part of the history of art rather than of trash is not distance, the superimposition of a consciousness more conformable to that of ordinary reality upon the "deranged consciousness" of the erotically obsessed. Rather, it is the originality, thoroughness, authenticity, and power of the deranged consciousness itself, as incarnated in a work.

While it is possible to disagree with Sontag's definition and to argue that it has its own elitist element (who is to judge the originality, authenticity, etc?), it does serve to highlight the traditional elitist concept of erotic art as opposed to pornography.[9]

For centuries, a painting or sculpture depicting nude bodies or suggesting sexual interaction has been acceptable if it met four basic criteria: 1) it has existed long enough to be considered classic—several decades or centuries; 2) it was created by well-known individuals; 3) it was housed in prestigious establishments or galleries; or, 4) it was owned by or viewed by members of the elite.

The Supreme Court gave its imprimatur to the elitist distinction between erotic art and pornography (or obscenity) in its second major obscenity case, Manual Enterprises, Inc. v. Day, 82 S. Ct. 1432 (1962), when it ruled that an item having redeeming social significance was by definition not obscene and explicitly said that "art" was not obscene.[10] (The concept had probably been included in Roth v. United States, 354 U.S. 476 (1957), but several commentators had suggested that the original formulation protecting "ideas" might not be broad enough to cover art which some would contend does not contain ideas in the usual sense of the term.) Subsequently, in Ginsburg v. United States, 383 U.S. 463 (1966) the Court reinforces, in an obverse sort of way, the elitist concept of art by holding that the manner in which an item was produced and sold was relevant to the determination of obscenity. Specifically, the Court held that a court could take notice of the fact that the publisher of *EROS*, Ralph Ginsburg, had attempted to get a third-class postal permit in towns like "Blue Balls" and "Intercourse."

However, the categorical approach to obscenity which indirectly embodied the elitist definition of art and literature was destined to be short lived. In 1973, Miller v. California, 413 U.S. 15 (1973), and its companion case, Paris Adult Theatre I v. Slaton, 413 U.S. 49 (1973), dramatically changed the ground rules. Whereas the rule from 1962 to 1973 was that an item with *any* ideational content or *any* redeeming social content could not be obscene, the new definition protected only material which contained *"serious* literary, artistic, political or scientific value." Since the decision was to be made by a local jury using local community standards, the decision was an open invitation for a local community to weigh the offensiveness of a presentation against its artistic value. Thus, the door was opened to prosecute artistic works which had been constitutionally protected prior to the Miller decision.

The seven homoerotic and nude children photographs contained in the much larger Mapplethorpe exhibit were precisely the type of situation for which the Miller rules were designed. In fact, they and the Sturges photographs are nearly perfect examples of the conservative obscenity paradigm developed by Chief Justice Burger in *Miller* and *Paris*: the pictures were clearly offensive to the standards of at least part of the Cincinnati community and it was up to a jury to determine if they had "serious" artistic value.[11]

The Mapplethorpe presentation, offensive though the homoerotic art may have been to certain members of the public, clearly fell within the elitist canons of art. After all, they were by a recognized photographer and had been displayed in several major museums. To the art establishment that was dispositive of the issue. However, for the conservatives of Cincinnati filth was filth regardless of its location. As Hess states regarding the Sturges photographs of nude children: "The feds don't care whether Sturges is an artist or not." Neither did the establishment of Cincinnati. For the courts, it was up to a jury to weigh the offensiveness of the material against its purported artistic value. The method of performing the calculus has never been stated. In theory, as stated in Miller v. California, the jury is the embodiment of contemporary community standards and its judgment is final. In fact, however, it is not certain that an appellate court would accept a jury determination that the offensiveness of an acknowledged literary or artistic masterpiece outweighed its value. In the very first case after Miller, the Supreme Court reversed a Georgia jury's determination that the movie "Carnal Knowledge" was obscene.[12]

To a very large extent any obscenity trial is an attempt to persuade the jury of the literary or artistic merits of the material on trial. In the Mapplethorpe case the prosecution took the position that the pictures spoke for themselves and there was no reason to show that they were not art. As a result, it presented only on art "expert." However, since the entire case of the defense rested on establishing that Mapplethorpe was a significant artist, that these particular photographs were an integral part of his work, and that when judged by the contemporary canons of art they possessed serious artistic value. Since none of the jurors had been to a museum in recent years, the task of the defense was to educate the "visually illiterate." Since most of the original jury venire and only two of the jurors had ever been to an art museum, and none had been in recent years, it was necessary to educate them in the canons of artistic values and criticism. In the 2 Live Crew trials the task was to educate the jury in the styles of contemporary rap music and to convince the jurors that rap and its message was legitimate.

The legal environment of the trial required that the education of the jury take place within the rules of evidence and the legal definition of obscenity. However, the thrust of the defense's case was the distinction between art and pornography (or obscenity). According to the local defense attorney, H. Louis Sirkin, the defense tried to show that "each image was put into the exhibition for one reason—serious artistic value. We thought that if we could convey that to a jury, we could win. No one else thought we could."[13] The legal battle began with the question of whether the seven photographs could be viewed in isolation or must be seen in the context of the entire show. Although the show's organizer testified that the seven pictures were "important for the retrospective" because they the only ones "that showed Mapplethorpe's ability to handle sequence," and that to omit them "would be to leave out a chapter in a novel or a segment of history," the judge ruled that they could be viewed in isolation.[14]

The first lesson in art appreciation had failed but the task continued with art experts carefully chosen not to offend Cincinnati sensibilities: no one presently residing in New York, and no wild-eyed radicals from Dayton or Cleveland. According to *The Art News* the defense witnesses were persuasive. According to one juror the art experts helped her to gain a new perspective on the bothersome images. "When the experts said this is why it's art, they were very convincing. One said that Mapplethorpe was depicting a lifestyle of the '70s that I never knew existed. [The Museum director who put the show together impressed me] with everything she said about Mapplethorpe personally, about putting together this exhibition. I didn't realize so much was involved—she said they went through thousands of pictures."[15] The jury also was disappointed that the prosecution put forward only one witness who's credibility was questioned.

The first defense witness, Janet Kardon, a museum director and the organizer of the show, set the stage for the education of the jury into the techniques of artistic criticism. She testified that Mapplethorpe was "one of the most important photographers of the 1980s working in the formalist mode." She also undertook to explain the highly controversial photograph of a man with a bullwhip in his anus in artistic terms:

The human figure is centered. The horizon line is two-thirds of the way up, almost the classical two-thirds to one-third proportion. The way the light is cast so there light all around the figure. It's very symmetrical, which is very characteristic of his flowers...."[16]

The education continued, both in direct defense testimony and in response to cross examination. Robert Sobieszek, senior curator of the George Eastman House International Museum of Photography, talked about content, composition and lighting in works of art. He contended that the photographs "reveal in a very strong, forceful way a major concern of a creative artist...a troubled portion of his life that he was trying to come to grips with. It's that search for meaning, not unlike van Gogh's"[17]

In the final analysis, the jury found the photographs lewd and objectionable but concluded they were serious works of art based on the testimony of the art experts called by the defense. Some of them suggested that the outcome might have been different if the prosecution had come up with credible witnesses to the contrary.[18]

The "art is protected and cannot be obscene" tactic is standard in obscenity cases and was used in the 2 Live Crew case as well. However, the task is even more difficult for non-traditional arts and non-traditional groups than it is for an established artist, even when that artist is very provocative.

John Leland, *Newsday* music correspondent, has testified for the 2 Live Crew three times since February 1990. Just as the museum curators and music critics attempted to place Mapplethorpe's work within the canons of traditional art, Leland's testimony is designed to place the 2 Live Crew within the context of black music. As the Village Voice relates, "he gives an entertaining annotated history of hiphop, which includes a stop in Miami for the birth of ghetto bass, as originated by Ghetto Style DJs, of which Luther Campbell is one of the founding fathers. Juror's eyes widen, no kidding."[19]

Professor Henry Louis Gates Jr., then Duke University and now Harvard University professor and literary critic, and one of the leading scholars of rap music, defended the artistic value of the 2 Live Crew's music to the jury by establishing it as part and parcel of a black oral and literary tradition extending over several centuries. Much like his counterparts in the Mapplethorpe trial he explained why works of art are rarely to be taken literally. The 2 Live Crew's music, he argued, "takes one of the worst stereotypes about black men—they're oversexed animals—and blows it up until it explodes.... When Gates compares 2 Live Crew to Archie Bunker, light bulbs go off in the jurors heads."[20]

In the Mapplethorpe and the 2 Live Crew trials, as in the standard obscenity trial, the prosecution tries to put literary and artistic criticism on trial. In the 2 Live Crew case, the prosecution asked Professor Gates,

'Does this work advance black culture?' Gates answers, 'Yes,' with a straight face. 'Are you saying that this is part of fighting for civil rights and fighting for equality? Are you equating 2 Live Crew to black leaders like Martin Luther King?' Gates hesitates, not even he can go that far. 'I never equated the two. There is difference between a civil rights march and exploding a stereotype.'[21]

What made the Mapplethorpe case different from the three 2 Live Crew trials held to this point, and what makes it different from the standard obscenity case was that a museum was on trial. As one lawyer in the case put it: "Six weeks [before the Mapplethorpe trial], museums and bona fide institutions were considered immune [from prosecution]. Suddenly, those presumptions have been stood on their heads."[22] The newspaper accounts indicate that the fact that the pictures were in a museum and considered to be art was a significant factor in the determination they were not obscene.

It is interesting to speculate if the outcome of the Mapplethorpe trial would have been the same if it had been a book of Mapplethorpe pictures that was the focus of the trial rather than a collection of photographs in an art museum. The outcome could easily have been different.

It would be easy to distinguish the Mapplethorpe acquittal from the conviction of the recorded 2 Live Crew album (not the prosecution for the stage prosecution) *solely* on the basis of the signification of artistic approval by being displayed in a museum. However, it would be incorrect to do so.

The 2 Live Crew record trials have two, perhaps interrelated, elements: race (or cultural relativism) and the war against rock and rap music. Charles Freeman, owner of E-C Records, who was convicted on obscenity charges for selling the 2 Live Crew recording, "As Nasty As They Wanna Be," which has previously been declared obscene by a federal judge, put the issue bluntly. "It's unfair," he shouted to reporters after the verdict was read. "The jury was all white. They don't know where my record shop is. They don't know anything about the goddam ghetto."[23]

Representativeness of the jury is almost always a concern in obscenity trials. The constitutional requirement is that the list from which the actual jury is chosen must be representative of the community as a whole, not that the particular jury trying the case be representative of the community or the minorities be represented on juries even when minorities are on trial. In *Miller v. California* (1973) the Supreme Court specified that local community standards should control the determination of obscenity and that the jury was the representative of the community for this purpose. The Court naively assumed that there was one community standard and that a jury of 6-12 people could represent or ascertain that standard. Both assumptions are incorrect. First, there are many different standards in a community. It is ridiculous to argue that the standards of the retirement community of Miami are the same as the Cuban areas of the city or that the Cubans and blacks share the same values.

One example of linguistic pluralism can make the point. The word "motherfucker" had its origin in the second most popular of all American pastimes, baseball. (Pitcher = Father; batter = Son; catcher = Mother; and plate umpire = motherfucker.) Although the word never became part of polite mainstream language and was used primarily by whites as an expletive, it was picked up by urban blacks and became a form of greeting for good friends and associates, especially those not recently encountered. To the typical white juror the word "motherfucker" can only imply incest and is an insult. To at least some urban blacks it is nothing more than a friendly greeting.

The defense in the trial of the live performance of 2 Live Crew unsuccessfully challenged six white jurors because they had no black friends. The defense attorney explained: "It's an unusual request, but it goes back to community standards. A large part of this community is African American, and as a result, these [white] jurors wouldn't be able to understand that part of our community." The prosecution countered to the press later in the afternoon that "[t]he basic premise behind this is that blacks can somehow relate to this music more, and therefore have lower moral standards. This music is obscene. It would be obscene if it was country western, reggae, or rock and roll."[24]

The District Attorney is wrong. The special audience to which a production is directed is a very real factor in determining its obscenity unless it can be assumed that there is only one possible audience. It is important for members of a jury to know minority word usage unless minorities are to be punished for nonconformity to white linguistic norms. Without sensitivity to different cultural norms obscenity trials can easily become weapons of cultural imperialism.

On the surface, racism does not appear to be an issue in the prosecution of 2 Live Crew records and prosecutors go out of their way to deny that it is a factor. Even the indictment in the live performance case belies such a conclusion:

...as live person before the audience, [they] did knowingly conduct, perform, or participate in, by words and/or conduct, a show or performance which was obscene...[which] included, but was not limited to, a rendition of 'C'mon Babe,' and an apparent version of 'Me S Horny,' said renditions consisted of verbal depictions of descriptions of sexual conduct, to-wit sexual intercourse, deviate sexual intercourse, as defined in Florida Statute Sec. 47.001, and actual physical contact with a person's unclothed buttocks, examples of which are: 'Let me stick my dick in you behind,' 'I'll be fucking you and you'll be sucking me, lick my ass up and down, lick it till your tongue turns doo-doo brown'...and in the course of said performance...did simulate an act of deviate sexual intercourse as defined in F.S. Sec. 47.001...examples of which are: placing the face of a woman into a very close proximity to the groin of one of the performers, Luther Campbell, and through the acts of another performer, Mark Ross, uncovering and exposing the breast of another female.[25]

However, the appearance of racial neutrality is deceptive because of the very nature of rap music and its relationship to the black experience in America. In an article in the New York Times entitled " 'Radical' Rap: Of Pride and Prejudice," Jon Parles traced the development of radical political rap as a "forum for urban debates." He points out that they are adamant and unanimous in their support of the teaching of the Nation of Islam, the Black Muslin group and that they "don't spout racist, anti-white rhetoric, although they do allude to Black Muslim genetic theories..."

Parles argues that "rap is replaying the schisms of civil-rights activism in the 1960s" and that for radical rappers, "black Americans are the victims of kidnapping (through slave trade), theft (of labor and culture), brainwashing (though education) and imminent genocide (through crack, AIDS and murder). The rappers urge re-education, discipline, unity and black self-reliance, while they are divided on how far to go in self-defense..." they have revived "questions of cultural nationalism, of violence versus nonviolence, of evolution versus revolution." He suggests that a difference is that the colloquy now takes place in recordings rather than the streets.[26]

It would be misleading to suggest that 2 Live Crew belongs to the "radical rapper" camp. As the Village Voice said, "[t]hese aren't 'righteous rappers'."[27] However, by the same token, the broader umbrella of cultural relativism does come into play. Nasty rap is an expression of ideas in a format unlikely to arouse the sympathy of a white jury. It is much easier to convince a middle class jury that it should give deference to an elitist concept of art as in the

Mapplethorpe case than it is to convince a white middle-class jury that what they consider to be lower class music and obscene words have value that should be protected.

In his classic study, *Art and Pornography*, Morse Peckham notes:

...if the artistic quality of pornography is generally judged to be of low caliber, such judgments emanate from the higher and cultural levels, the spiritual abode of people whose interest is both to make artistic judgments and to defend them, to maintain, as it were, the entrance requirement for matriculation in that area of behavior. As with all exclusive associations, an important ingredient is that membership in it should be exclusive and earned.... Hence in literary and other artistic criticism, an exceedingly important activity is the creation of the canon of what is to be accounted excellent, and its continual recreation, in response to the constantly changing cultural conditions and problems.[28]

Peckham's statement is valid but needs an amendment: in modern America where legal doctrine places the determination of obscenity in the hands of a jury chosen from the public at large it is necessary for the cultural establishment to persuade the masses which serve on juries to acquiesce in its elitist definition of art. Judging from the contradictory outcomes of the Mapplethorpe and 2 Live Crew trials, the establishment has succeeded.

Notes

[1]The best accounts of the trials are found in Robin Cembalest, "The Obscenity Trial: How They Voted to Acquit," *Art News* (November 1990) 136-141; Jayne Merkel, "Art on Trial," *Art In America* (December 1990) 41-51; Marcia Pally, "Cincinnati: City Under Seige," *Penthouse* (September 1990) 148-152, 156, 202, 211.

[2]The formal name of the group is "*The* 2 Live Crew." However, to avoid phrases such as "the The 2 Live Crew" the shorter form, "2 Live Crew" is used throughout the paper. The best article on the 2 Live Crew live stage trial is Lisa Jones, "The Signifying Monkees: 2 Live Crew's Nasty-Boy Rap on Trial in South Florida," *Village Voice* (November 8, 1990) 43-46, 171.

[3]Nat Hentoff, "We Are Entering A New Era of Repression," *Penthouse* (September 1990) 153.

[4]Richard Goldstein, "Doowutchyalike," *Village Voice* (November 6, 1990) 49.

[5]The Sturge case has received little attention outside of professional photographic circles and the San Francisco area. The case began in April, 1990, when the San Francisco police and the F.B.I. acting on the basis of a report from a processing lab raided the Sturges' office and took roughly an estimated 1 million negatives. Since that time the F.B.I. has assiduously searched for the families whose nude children appear in Sturges' photographs. It has questioned 46 families, primarily in France, about the circumstance under which the photographs were taken. The Paul Cava Gallery in Philadelphia has shown the photographs. See *The Village Voice* June 12, 1990 and January 29, 1991 for a fuller account.

[6]Walter Kendrick, *The Secret Museum* (New York: Viking Penguin, Inc., 1987) 11.

[7]Quoted in Kendrick 15.

[8]Elizabeth Hess, "The Accused: Jock Sturges, Harassed by the FBI, Shows His Work," *The Village Voice* (January 29, 1991) 49, 80.

[9]Susan Sontag, "The Pornographic Imagination," *Styles of Radical Will* (N.Y.: Farrar, Straus & Giroux, Inc., 1966) 47.

[10]The author is well aware of the legal distinction between "pornography" and "obscenity" or "hardcore pornography." However, in the public mind, and in this debate, the terms are usually used interchangeably. For those reasons, the term "pornography" in this paper is used to designate those creations which are not deemed to meet the canons of artistic presentation whether they meet the legal definition of obscenity or not.

[11]Apparently the attorneys and the judge involved in the Mapplethorpe case treated the two elements of the Miller obscenity test as separate. That is, a decision was first made as to the offensiveness to the community and a second decision as to whether the material had "serious" artistic value. Under this approach a finding that the material was serious art automatically protected it regardless of the level of its offensiveness.

An even better argument can be made that the Miller test requires the jury to treat two elements as one. That is, to determine if the artistic value outweighs the offensiveness of the material. Under such an approach a jury could decide that even a major artistic presentation is obscene.

[12]Jenkins v. Georgia, 418 U.S. 153 (1974)

[13]*Art News* (December 1990) 136

[14]*Art News* (December 1990) 137

[15]*Art News* (December 1990) 140

[16]Merkel 47.

[17]Merkel 47.

[18]Merkel 51

[19]Lisa Jones, "The Signifying Monkees: 2 Live Crew's Nasty-Boy Rap on Trial in South Florida," *Village Voice* (November 8, 1990) 171.

[20]Jones 171

[21]Jones 171

[22]Quoted by Alan M. Dershowitz, "Who Next?," *Penthouse* (September 1990) 156.

[23]Quoted in *National Law Journal* (October 14, 1990) 47.

[24]Jones 47

[25]Reprinted in *Village Voice* (November 8, 1990) 49.

[26]Jon Pareles, " 'Radical' Rap: Of Pride and Prejudice," *The New York Times* (December 16, 1990) Sec. 2, 1.

[27]Jones 47

[28]Morse Peckham, *Art and Pornography* (New York: Basic Books, 1969) 55-56.

Souls on Fire

Susan B. Laubach

For many, music, because it is the most natural and uninhibitable expressions of the human beings, is one of the most fundamental of the Humanities; it is the universal voice of the Humanities, color-, class-, ethnic-, nationality-, sex-blind. Even species-blind. If not the voice of the spheres, it is the universal voice of life on Earth. It is therefore the medium most directly the voice of "the heart" of people, and as such perhaps the most influential on and the most important to the true statement of the Humanities. Susan B. Laubach, in the following article, demonstrates the feeling, the outreach and importance of music in and to the Humanities.

The street-corner voices stopped completely as I climbed from my husband's car, and turned to get the crutches.

"See you at nine o'clock," I said nervously. Then I began to climb the steps leading to the entrance to the Ashbury AME church. Old and young men, slouching in doorways and watching in silence, looked at me and through me. I felt their stares. "White woman...What she doin' here?"

I was having my Humanities test in the place where Socrates and Plato thought it mattered most—out in the real world, in the market place, amidst *humanities.*

Jabbing the front door opening with one crutch, I hopped on my non-sprained ankle into the cool darkness of the church. Twelve sets of eyes swung to stare at the intrusion. Each held the same question. White woman. What she doin' here.

Balancing myself on the crutches, I began hobbling to the front of the church where members of the Souls on Fire Gospel Choir sat appraising me. The silence was broken by the director's voice. She said, "This must be the woman I was telling you about." My experience in liberation through the humanities had begun.

Why was I there? For anyone who has ever surreptitiously directed a symphony orchestra or played air guitar, the question is moot. At gospel choir concerts, I sang from my seat, annoying and embarrassing the people around me, no matter how quiet I tried to be. *My* secret desire had long been to be in a gospel choir. Not one of your pale white imitations...those music-readers and rule-followers whose renderings sound the same every time. No, I wanted to be in the foot-stamping, hand-clapping kind of choir that rhythm-walked down the aisle, calling us to "Come to my Father's House" with joy, with gusto. I wanted to be in a group that wasn't into blending. The only gospel sung that way that I knew of was sung by black people.

So, struck one day with that periodic stabbing thought "Life is too short" I decided to see if this was possible. I asked the Mayor in our town if he knew anyone in the local black Gospel choir *Souls on Fire*. "Sure," he said. "I know the Director. Why?"

"Could you ask her if she'd mind if I sat in on their rehearsals?"

He did that and I received permission to come to rehearsal on Tuesday night at 8 p.m., after the weekly business meeting. When the group began to sing from the choir loft, I joined in as usual from my seat in the audience. But this time it was go for broke. I sang it out loud. Oh, it wasn't gospelizing...I sang the melody like any other white person would, but I sang it with heart and with joy. They reacted with kindness. "Why, you know all our songs!" someone said at the end of the evening.

Now these people could easily have viewed my intrusion with resentment and alienation, adding to the already hostile atmosphere in a county known for its active Ku Klux Klan.

Instead, I was welcomed every week with shy hellos at first and then more familiar nods and smiles until that great moment when I asked Edith, our director, if I could sing with the group at the church service on Sunday. She looked stricken and murmured something about there not being a robe for me. But Reverend Joe spoke over her, "Sure, you can!"

And Mr. Scotty said, "She can wear Johnny's robe."

"He don't wear it 'cause he gets too hot," explained Miss Annie to me. Johnny was the piano accompanist whose music would make a lame man dance, who could set the most paralytic toe to tapping.

And so, in this realm of joy-singing black folks, each of whom had their solos to sing, I wore Johnny's robe and became a Soul on Fire. And eventually I, too, sang solos. Timid at first, weak and wobbly. But with the murmured voices around me urging me to "Sing it, honey!" "Let it out, girl!" "Oh, my, that's beautiful!" I became less afraid. I opened up my mouth and oh, I just...let it out.

For two years, my Soul was on Fire. Every Tuesday was a religious experience, every Sunday I was one with the Lord, singing and clapping in my Father's House, every "concert" trip became a journey of joy bumping over country roads in the rented yellow school bus driven wildly by a man named Duke.

Then my company transferred me back to the main office and my gospel-singing days were over. But what a time it was! There's been no joy just like that since. There is nothing similar to gospel singing in the ordinary life of a stockbroker. No opening of the soul, no liberating of the heart through song. Not to mention the fellowship and acceptance of a loving group of black people. That time was extraordinarily special.

And now, five years later, I reflect on those singing experiences and liken them to those of the ancients who, imbued with the Holy Spirit, began to speak in tongues. (Indeed, in the film "Say Amen, Somebody", a documentary about gospel music, a black minister is so overcome with emotion during a service that he cries out in an unintelligible language before falling to the floor.) Talk about liberating! It was more like soaring, like flying out of those little country churches into the sky with the birds than it was like choir singing.

My contribution to the group was minimal. I could be counted on to carry the melody. But gospelizing isn't something that one learns easily...you don't just pick it up and go, unless you're a lot more talented than I. No, I believe instead that real gospel singing is learned at someone else's knee, very young. It is something to be ingested. It grows in you, planted and tended through years of hearing voices circling melody, dipping and diving and soaring around it like kites on a windy day. The melody is respected harmonically but only occasionally followed...at the beginning of a song so that the listeners get the idea. There is no slavish devotion to it, just a touch with the toe every now and then.

Gospel's message in song is clearly this: everything's going to be all right.

My liberation was not limited to the singing. Membership in the Souls on Fire led me to join the Ashbury AME church. For the first time in several years, I looked forward to sermons on Sunday. It was easy to see why people went to services that lasted one and a half, sometimes two hours. It was the respite we needed, a mini-vacation from the world. But it was the singing of the songs that unchained my spirit....

Time and circumstances have altered my life to the extent that the Souls are no longer a part of it except in memory. My life is all white people now— white people, white bread, vanilla. Church music is from the hymnal, plodding and dull. When I sing out strong in a service, the children turn to stare. To tap the toe, to sway and snap is to invite smirks and significant looks between other parishioners. Odd, the looks say. That woman is odd.

Black people don't think that giving yourself to the music is odd. In fact, during my years with the Souls, it occurred to me that there was very little that one might do in the throes of the music that might be considered odd... *not* tapping the toe, for instance, would be odd at the Ashbury United Methodist Church or at any of the little country churches where we gave our Sunday afternoon "concerts." When parishioners rose in the congregation, clapping, snapping and stomping—sometimes climbing over the infirm and elderly to get to the aisle where movement was less restricted, it was not considered strange or unseemly. It was a welcome reaction which only encouraged us to sing louder and longer. Our songs had more or less informal endings: we could keep them going until Miss Edith gave us the signal to stop. And an enthusiastic, participative audience could prolong the service nearly indefinitely. It was always difficult to tell my husband exactly when I would be home.

Humanities, or in this context, music, was humanity in its fullest sense, transcending racial differences, transcending locked-up, rooted-to-the-ground senses of decorum. We, black and white, men and women, fat and thin, rich and poor, were connected in song and spirit. Would that it could go on that way forever.

Works Cited

Of the many books and articles about gospel music, Don Cusic's recent study is the most helpful; *The Sound of Light: A History of Gospel Music* (Bowling Green: Popular P, 1990). Cusic defines a music which leads to an understanding of our whole culture and our problems in the 90s.

From Genre to Medium:
Comics and Contemporary American Culture

Joseph Witek

One guiding elitist maxim has always been, "If you can't control it condemn it," and the reverse side of the maxim has always cautioned, "If everybody can understand and appreciate it, then it could easily get out of control."In other words if many people can engage in the expression and many people, children and adults—educated and uneducated—can understand and enjoy the work, then how can the elite continue to control? Such has been the fate of the comics in American society in the twentieth century, as Joseph Witek points out in the following essay. As he demonstrates, it is high time that all of us recognize the elements of the comics, the role they play, and the importance they will increasingly assert in society—with or without the conventional Humanists' approbation. Like the poor, the comics will always be with us. They do not want or need Social Security benefits, just an open and free market in which to work and express themselves. That seems to be asking very little.

For most of their history in this country, comics have been among our least respected forms of expression. To call violence in a movie "cartoony" or to speak of its "comic book" plot or to call anything "Mickey Mouse" has been to damn these things as superficial, hackneyed, trivial, and juvenile. Even in the egalitarian world of popular culture studies one of the foremost scholars of comics can still rightly say, "Among all forms of popular culture, we're at the bottom of the heap."[1]

Yet comics currently are one of the most dynamic cultural forms in the United States. In fact, so much is happening in comics today that an overview of American comics is difficult and a prediction of their future nearly impossible. What once was an exceptionally static field, with only superficial changes in mainstream comics since the institution of the Comics Code in 1954, presently is in the midst of what *Rolling Stone* calls "the sort of exciting creative explosion that film and pop music enjoyed in the '60s."[2] But the "explosion" metaphor misstates the nature of the process; those who follow the field know that American comics have been developing and diversifying for at least the last ten years and arguably since the underground comix of the late '60s and '70s.[3] As they have developed, comics have taken on an increasingly important role in the humanities.

It is true, however, that recent events have thrust comics forward in several ways. Big-budget movie and television productions have featured such comics characters as Batman, Dick Tracy, The Flash, and Swamp Thing. A series of high-visibility comics projects including Frank Miller's *The Dark Knight*, Alan Moore's *Watchmen*, and Art Spiegelman's *Maus: A Survivor's Tale* have garnered wide media attention.[4] Collections of comic strips such as Jim Davis's *Garfield* and Bill Watterson's *Calvin and Hobbes* routinely spend weeks atop the best-seller lists. Conservative media critics have even launched a new anti-comics crusade, and talk-show hosts cluck in dismay over sex and violence in today's comics, which until now haven't been much of a threat to anything at all since their heyday in the early Fifties.[5]

Behind this recent publicity lie far-reaching changes in comics and cultural attitudes about them. For decades comics publishing was dominated by a handful of comic-book publishers and newspaper syndicates, but today scores of artists and writers are producing comics independently in a wide variety of physical formats and distributional outlets. With the rise of the self-published and cheaply reproduced comics pamphlets called "minicomix," the visions and voices of women, the working class, and gays and lesbians, among other groups, are being seen and heard in our comics as they have never been before.[6] Today's gallery artists continue to use comics imagery in their work, as did such artists as Roy Lichtenstein and Andy Warhol before them, and the iconography of the comics has become familiar in the contemporary fine arts. Comics themselves now are produced in luxurious and expensive formats beyond the dreams of their pulp-paper forebears. And comics are no longer confined to the spinner display racks of the local convenience store. Most American cities of any size have at least one comics specialty shop, selling hundreds of different titles published every month along with several decades worth of back issues, and collectors' prices for comics are soaring. In academia, several full-length studies of comics have been produced and more are forthcoming.[7]

The many recent feature articles on contemporary comics in the popular press (often bearing headlines like "Bang! Zoom! Comics Aren't for Kids Anymore!") concentrate on issues of social status, suggesting rather nervously that comics have become more mature and respectable.[8] Some have, but that's only part of the story; comics are not simply moving up in cultural prestige but downwards and outwards as well. Comics formerly were found only in newspapers and on newsstands: now while museums and art galleries stage exhibitions of comic art, other comics creators hand out Xeroxed pamphlets of their work on street corners. Comics are considered for prestigious literary prizes; comics are prosecuted for obscenity. Comics explore such weighty matters as the psychological consequences of the Holocaust; comics pander (as they have always done) to the power fantasies of adolescent boys. While some cartoonists do aspire to social and commercial respectability, others turn to comics as a readymade tool for critiquing and subverting the values of mainstream America.

This proliferation of new styles and new approaches to the comics points to a fundamental shift in our ideas of what comics are and what they can do; we are beginning to reconceptualize the very nature of comics. Traditionally, comics in the United States have been defined by genre, according to their usually fantastic or humorous thematic content and rudimentary or exaggerated visual and verbal style. Hence, some people have become so accustomed to juvenility and naivete in American comics as to argue that adult themes are always inappropriate in comics, that stories with panels, pictures, and word balloons are by their very nature best suited for children. The phrase "the comics" itself conjures up for many people some timeless four-color Cartoonland where Snoopy, Batman, Little Orphan Annie, Flash Gordon, Pogo, Betty Boop, Mickey Mouse and Daffy Duck all live together in nostalgic harmony.

But increasingly today's comics creators and readers conceive of "the comics" not as a set of characters or of thematic concerns such as superheroes and talking animals, but as an expressive medium in itself, a method of depicting the world and human experience that blends words and pictures according to a well-developed set of narrative conventions. Americans have begun to see what Europeans and the Japanese long have accepted, that comics employ a medium of potentially unlimited range and sophistication.[9] Harvey Pekar, writer and publisher of *American Splendor,* a fiercely mundane and relentlessly autobiographical comic book, explains this growing view of comics:

People say, 'I like comics,' but that's like saying 'I like prose.' Well, OK, we all like prose. Comics is as wide an area as prose or film. It's a medium, and it can be used for any number of purposes, for fiction, for non-fiction. The fact that's its been used in such a limited way is crazy. Comics can be as versatile as any other medium. Comics is not an intrinsically limited form.[10]

The apparent error in grammatical number in Pekar's precise last sentence encapsulates the shift presently occurring. In the past, "comics" have been a plural "they," the sum total of all the newspaper strips and comic books that have ever been created, and the content of those strips and books has defined for our culture the central attributes of their narrative form. But increasingly for those who create, read, and think about them, "comics" is becoming a single thing, a medium of expression analogous to prose, and perhaps with even greater potential than its purely verbal counterpart. To liken a popular form such as comic art to such a fundamental medium of communication as prose once would have seemed monumentally pretentious or arrogantly trivializing. But a historical perspective reminds us that in the past both prose and film were scorned as vulgarities for the masses, just as comics have been. Whether comics will emerge as a major form of expression in our culture remains to be seen, but clearly many serious artists are now convinced that the comics medium can achieve effects otherwise impossible in even the most culturally respected forms of communication.

As ever, changes in cultural attitudes are accompanied by changes in language, and the ferment in the comics field has spawned a variety of new terms in the comics industry and among practitioners of the medium. The very phrase "the comics," with its connotations of broad humor and frivolity, has always been something of an embarrassment to those who try to expand the scope of the medium, since any attempt to be serious in comics clashes with the medium's very name. Various alternative terms such as "pictorial fiction" and "graphic narrative" have been put forward over the years to replace the phrase "the comics," but without lasting success. "Pictorial fiction" limits the genre of the medium unduly, since comics have dealt quite well with such nonfictional modes as biography, autobiography, history, and journalism.[11]

"Graphic narrative" is essentially misleading, since any exciting and vivid verbal account could just as well be called a "graphic narrative."

The basis of the comics medium is its combination of words and pictures in sequence, and any new term must avoid giving undue emphasis to either element of the equation. Any phrase with "illustrated" in it, *a la* "illustrated fantasy," fails when applied to comics. The essence of comics is that they are *not* illustrated texts, if we accept the traditional connotations of ornamentation and textual redundancy suggested by the word "illustrated"; in comics words and pictures form an inextricable narrative *gestalt*.

Art Spiegelman, comics creator and co-editor of the avant-garde graphics anthology *Raw*, recently has introduced the term "commix," as way of suggesting the crucial "co-mixing" of words and pictures that by anyone's definition distinguishes the comics from other types of visual narratives.[12] Spiegelman's neologism may perhaps become current, but it suffers because "commix" sounds exactly like the term it tries to replace, and is a variant spelling of "comix," the word used to distinguish underground comic books from their less controversial newsstand counterparts. But the very impulse to create it indicates how today's comics makers themselves are trying to redefine the medium in which they work.

Another master practitioner of the comics medium, Will Eisner, writer and artist of *The Spirit* comic book, has responded to this same problem of terminology by coining a phrase that enables the very distinction that I am making here between "the comics" on the one hand and their narrative medium on the other. In the first book to analyze the actual workings of comic art, *Comics & Sequential Art*, Eisner uses the latter term to distinguish between the narrative medium itself and its particular manifestations, newspaper comic strips and comic books.[13] Eisner's term has its own problems, not the least of which are its unwieldiness and its emphasis on the "art" element (not surprising in so talented, careful, and inventive a draftsman as Eisner). But "sequential art" at least does have the advantages of acknowledging the sequencing of pictures that distinguishes comic art from editorial and humorous cartoons, with their single captioned picture. Whatever the ultimate fate of Eisner's neologism, his book remains the best full-length treatment of the narrative grammar and syntax of the comics medium, and is required reading for students of visual narrative.

As our conceptual framework changes we also need more accurate terms for the people who make comics. When comics are regarded as purely commercial commodities, their makers are industrial producers, whether they are called "cartoonists" or "artists" or are simply ignored, as they have been for most of their history. But one of the major issues in the comics field today is the very definition of the people who type the words and put pens to drawing boards; as commercial and cultural relations in comics undergo extensive revision, comics artists, writers, and crafts people also are redefining themselves as something more than mere executors of corporate designs.

Production roles in the comics are becoming more complex as well. For example, although spectacular draftsmen traditionally have gotten the most attention in the comics, today writers as different as Alan Moore, Neil Gaiman, and Harvey Pekar have made their mark on contemporary comics without drawing pictures at all. Others have found new ways to work on comics, as when the outspoken proponent of self-publishing Dave Sim writes all the words and draws the figures and foreground elements of his *sui generis* animal comic *Cerebus*, while a collaborator draws the complex and detailed frames and backgrounds. Such diverse ways of making comics pose new questions of terminology that even the cumbersome formation "artist/writer" does not address. Is Alan Moore an "artist" because his scripts for comic books sometimes include detailed descriptions of each panel down to the patterns on the carpets and the graffiti on the walls? Is Harvey Pekar a "cartoonist" when he writes the most personal of stories to be drawn by an array of collaborators? Are those collaborators simply "illustrators" even though they determine much of the style, tone, and atmosphere of each story? As a result both of comics workers' attempts to control their creations as well as a fertile diversification of technical roles, the omnibus term "creator" is beginning to be used by both comics-makers and analysts alike as a substitute for the old roles of "cartoonist," "artist," and "comics writer."

This shift from "cartoonist" to "creator" is more than a semantic one; for comics makers, achieving the status of independent creative artists has serious economic as well as cultural consequences. American cultural attitudes towards comics and the development of the medium both have been profoundly affected by long-standing commercial considerations and by the formal attributes of comics as physical and cultural artifacts. To understand the cultural place of comics requires that we understand who owns them, who makes money from them, and how their commercial functions have affected comics as an art form.

Newspaper comic strips are usually copyrighted not by their creators, but by the distribution syndicates who market them. In the syndicate system, the narrative or aesthetic form of a comic strip is relatively unimportant. The essential characteristic of successful comics from the corporate point of view is the "property" or recognizable set of characters that can be licensed and merchandised. The most lucrative strips themselves are simply low-profit, low-overhead advertisements for the T-shirts, action figures, soft-drink glasses, and other products spawned by the popularity of the characters. The death of a strip's originator hinders the process not a whit; the "life" of a syndicated comic strip is perceived to flow from its characters, not from its creator.

Comic books too have been under similar corporate control. Until quite recently, nearly all comic books were produced under "work for hire" contracts, which conceived of artists and writers as free-lance technicians hired for the nonce to carry out the wishes of the comics publishers, with no more claim to their creations than a sign painter has to his billboard. The assembly-line production methods of the major comics publishers, with separate people to plot, script, layout, pencil, ink, letter, and color the stories, reinforces the conception of comics as mass-produced industrial commodities rather than as a form of artistic expression. Until quite recently, aspiring comics creators soon learned that they were expected to give up copyright, trademark, and most merchandising rights to anything they might create. The most famous (or notorious) example of how the comics industry regards its workers is that of Jerry Siegel and Joe Schuster, creators of Superman. Although Superman was the defining idea that made possible the entire comic book industry as we know it, established National Periodical Publications (later called DC Comics) as the premier comic-book publisher in America, and generated enormous marketing and licensing revenues, Siegel and Schuster were paid only standard industry rates until extensive litigation as well as the protests of comics fans convinced DC Comics to grant the men a modest stipend in their retirement. Cautionary tales like that of Siegel and Schuster steered ambitious artists away from the comic field for decades.

But as more comics creators produce work outside of the tightly controlled commercial mainstream, and as that mainstream itself opens up to new methods of producing and marketing comics to a wider audience, comic creators presently are asserting greater rights to their works.[14] Fifteen years ago individual ownership and control of comics creations was almost unheard of in the industry; even the original artwork was considered to be the property of publishers, not of creators. Today, comics such as Gilbert and Jaime Hernandez's *Love and Rockets*, Harvey Pekar's *American Splendor*, and Alan Moore and Bill Sienkiewicz's *Big Numbers*, as well as almost all of the minicomix, are controlled entirely by the people who make them. Creator ownership offers the possibility of a more equitable distribution of the money from comics; now creators at least have a chance to reap the rewards of creating a popular comic book or strip.

Yet the financial advantages of creator control of comics are far surpassed by the artistic and conceptual gains. Even the most successful comic books pay rather poorly by the standards of, say, best-seller publishing or movie screenwriting; the real money is in heavily merchandised properties like the wildly popular Teenage Mutant Ninja Turtles, not in the comics themselves. But the ability to retain artistic and editorial freedom is crucial to the social status of any artistic medium, and creator control thus becomes not only an economic benefit but a vital step in transforming the cultural concept of comics from a set of juvenile and commercial genres to a medium of communication and expression.

When comics are seen as a medium we also see that they can be used to say nearly anything at all, and that freedom can be disturbing or even threatening to those who are used to thinking of comics as essentially formulaic and juvenile. The current changes in American comics bid fair to transform the medium forever, and that transformation will forcibly evict comics from the cultural niche to which they have so long been accustomed. Comics in the past have been valued even by their greatest practitioners and their most enthusiastic admirers for knowing their place, for not taking themselves too seriously. Jules Feiffer, veteran cartoonist and one of the first commentators to write approvingly of American comic books, calls them "junk," and junk, he tells us, "is a second-class citizen of the arts."[15] Comics publisher Jeanette Kahn laments, "I'm sorry that comics are not the way they used to be when we were young. I hate to see the passing of the era when comics were part of the joy of being young."[16] In 1969, Charles Schulz, creator of *Peanuts* and the most influential of post-World War II comic strip artists, sensed the limitations imposed on comics and haltingly foresaw a time when comics would become more ambitious:

I am very proud of the comic strip medium and am never ashamed to admit that I draw a comic strip. I do not regard it as great art, but I have always felt it is certainly on the level with other entertainment mediums which are part of the so-called "popular arts." In many ways, I do not think we have realized the potential of the comic strip, but sometimes

I feel it is too late. With a little more tolerance and a little more dedication on the part of those who create the comics, perhaps we could do better.[17]

Schulz's equivocation is instructive; he knows that, given their history in this country so far, to call comics "great art" is at best pretentious. But Schulz also sees that the medium has the potential to be more than simply another form of mass entertainment. Schulz, the master of gentle humor, no doubt looks with little joy on contemporary comics with titles like *Hate* and *Raw* and *Anarchy*, yet they and dozens of other comics of all types suggest that comics creators are realizing that Schulz' assessment of the medium's potential is essentially correct.

Unlike most forms lumped together under the rubric of "popular culture," comics have no high-prestige analogue to lend them a cachet of respectability and to give perspective to their development as a medium. Popular literature, music, drama (including much television), and film all partake of long-established "High Art" traditions; their "popular" status stems from their style, content, and historical reception, not from their narrative form. Thus the various films of Woody Allen can run the gamut from the crudest slapstick to solemn Ingmar Bergman homages with no sense that the narrative form itself is somehow inappropriate to the subject matter. Even the comics' close relation, animation, has a tradition of avant-garde experimentation to establish its credentials as a "serious" art form.

But comics are presently developing their own levels of graphic and narrative sophistication. Part of that process does involve the creation of a comics *avant garde*, most easily accessible in *Raw* magazine. But another comics movement rejects "high art" pretensions and celebrates the heritage of unabashed vulgarity in comics, as in the recently defunct anthology *Weirdo*. Still others, such as Chester Brown's *Yummy Fur*, which combines bizarrely grotesque adventure stories with a relentless retelling of the New Testament, work in modes so idiosyncratic as to render problematic the very "high art/low art" distinction with which comics have been bludgeoned for so long.

A telling indicator of the potentially fruitful tensions in the field comes from the comics specialty shops, which are finding it ever more difficult to satisfy the demands of their increasingly disparate clienteles. The superhero comics which still dominate the comics business attract into the shops the younger readers whose high-volume business pays the monthly bills. Yet the superheroes hold minimal interest for many adult readers (including some of the shop owners themselves), who often prefer the lower-profit and erratically published independent comics and more expensive reprints of older comics. In addition, shop owners face legal troubles when adult-oriented comics are sold and displayed in the same place as works appealing to children and adolescents. As a result, some business people foresee the creation of different types of comic shops catering entirely to specific segments of the market.

If we view comics as a genre, such a development in retail distribution seems faintly ridiculous, as if hobby shops could no longer sell both HO and OO-gauge railroad trains in the same store. Yet the analogy of the comics medium with prose makes the fragmentation of the comics audience seem not only inevitable but long overdue. No bookstore or newsstand, no matter how complete, can pretend to sell everything published in prose in a given month. With the burgeoning of publishers, titles, formats, and creative approaches in today's comics, the ability of comic shops to make the same claim is fast coming to an end.

This stratification of the comics audience points to new cultural possibilities for the comics form. Whether the medium is called "commix," or "sequential art," or "the comics," or, as in France, *"Bande Dessinee,"* and whether those who make comics are called "cartoonists" or "creators," comics presently are stretching toward and eventually may attain the same conceptual status as prose or film. That is, comics embody an expressive medium with its own strengths and weaknesses. For some readers, when comics stray from their familiar (and socially enforced) stomping grounds of superhero adventure and talking animal humor, some essential innocence is lost. Yet more and more comics creators are willing to relinquish the paltry privileges which go with the status of "second-class citizens of the arts" in order to exploit the potentially limitless possibilities of the comics medium. As comics creators expand the scope of their work, comics and their creators will play an increasing role in the humanities.

Notes

[1]M. Thomas Inge, quoted in Ellen L. Coughlin, "Looking for Messages in Batman and Donald Duck: Researchers Turn to the Comics," *Chronicle of Higher Education* (September 5, 1990) sec. A, 4.

[2]Mikal Gilmore, "Daredevil Authors: Today's Real Superheroes," *Rolling Stone* (May 17, 1990) 57. For a short history of comic strips, see Maurice Horn, ed. *World Encyclopedia of Comics* (New York: Chelsea House, 1976) 37-46; for comic books see M. Thomas Inge, "A Chronology of the Development of the American Comic Book," in *The Official Overstreet Comic Book Price Guide* Ed. Robert M. Overstreet. (New York: House of Collectibles, 1990) 71.

[3]The influence of the underground comix on today's comics can hardly be overstated. For more on the underground comix, see Jay Kennedy, ed. *The Official Underground and Newave Comix Price Guide* (Cambridge: Boatner Norton, 1982); and Mark James Estren, *A History of Underground Comics* (Berkeley: Ronin Publishing, 1974).

[4]Frank Miller, Klaus Janson, and Lynn Varley, *Batman: The Dark Knight Returns* (New York: DC Comics, 1986); Alan Moore and Dave Gibbons, *Watchmen* (New York: DC Comics, 1986); Art Spiegelman, *Maus: A Survivor's Tale* (New York: Pantheon, 1986).

[5]For attacks on recent comics see Joe Queenan, "Drawing on the Dark Side," *New York Times Magazine* (April 30, 1989) 32; and "Thomas Radecki Interview," *Comics Journal* 133 (1989) 66-75.

[6]For more on minicomix see Kennedy, *Underground and Newave Comix Guide*; and Dale Luciano, "Newave Comics Survey," *Comics Journal* 96 (1985) 51-78.

[7]Recent developments in comics scholarship are summarized in Coughlin, "Looking for Messages in Batman."

[8]See, for example, Art Levine, "Comic Books Are Winning New Respect," *U.S. News & World Report* (September 21, 1987) 69; Peter S. Prescott with Ray Sawhill, "The Comic Book (Gulp!) Grows Up," *Newsweek* (January 18, 1988) 70-71; Jay Cocks, "The Passing of *Pow!* and *Blam!*," *Time* (January 25, 1988) 65-66.

[9]The Japanese *manga* tradition arguably is older than American comics themselves; while European comics are not demonstrably superior to American ones in the aggregate, Europeans generally have not considered comics to be essentially a juvenile medium. For further discussion see Frederick L. Schodt, *Manga! Manga!: The World of Japanese Comics* (Kodansha International, 1986) and Paul Gravett, "Euro-comics: A Dazzling Respectability," 42 *Print* 7 (1988) 74.

[10]Harvey Pekar, interview by author, tape recording, Cleveland, Ohio, 11 November 1988.

[11]For discussion of these modes in the comics, see Joseph Witek, *Comic Books as History: The Narrative Art of Jack Jackson, Art Spiegelman, and Harvey Pekar* (Jackson: UP of Mississippi, 1989).

[12]Art Spiegelman, "Commix: An Idiosyncratic Historical and Aesthetic Overview," 42 *Print* 7 (1988) 61.

[13]Will Eisner, *Comics & Sequential Art* (Tamarac, FL: Poorhouse P, 1985).

[14]For a fuller discussion of these and related issues, see "Special Section on Creators' Rights," *Comics Journal* 137 (1990) 65-106.

[15]Jules Feiffer, *The Great Comic Book Heroes* (New York: Bonanza, 1965) 186.

[16]Quoted in Queenan, "Drawing on the Dark Side," 86.

[17]Charles Schulz, "But a Comic Strip Has to Grow," *Saturday Review* (April 12, 1969) 74.

Animal Rights and the Humanities

Michael Pettengell

In an enlightened society, as we come more and more to recognize not only the complexity but also the opportunities afforded us, we must look more and more to humankind's place in the order of creatures on this earth. Among the traditional Humanists Darwin is a respected name in the social sciences, but he is often ignored in the implications of his observations about Humankind's place in the order of things. Less fear is evidenced about these implications among the physical scientists, who apparently have less to protect and are therefore willing to consider the ladder of creatures on their worth without knocking out any rungs. Pettengell's essay should cause us all to re-examine this ladder, humankind's rung on it and the full resonances of our call for the Humanities throughout our understanding and actions.

The deeper we look into nature, the more we realize that it is full of life, and the more profoundly we know that all life is a secret and that we are united with all life that is in nature. Man can no longer live for himself alone. We must realize that all life is valuable and that we are united to all life. From this knowledge comes our spiritual relationship to the universe.—Albert Schweitzer

The question is not, Can they reason? nor Can they talk? but, Can they suffer?—Jerry Bentham

The Humanities in the traditional use of the word refers to the study of artistic endeavors associated with human culture and civilization. As the disciplines within the university setting begin to broaden in scope and concept, students of the humanities tend not to concentrate solely on the great masterpieces of Western Culture. Increasingly, college textbooks are stretching the boundaries of the traditional canon to incorporate popular culture (including all types of written works and media), the women's and civil rights movement and, in short, to break down the burdensome hierarchy which has been so stringently in place for a hundred years.

And yet, in studying the humanities, what are students attempting to understand? The purpose of such study might be conceptualized by the statement, "We are trying to understand humankind, its quest for meaning, and its place in the world." In order to achieve this, one studies the popular and elite art (whether it be fine arts, architecture, music, or literature—politics philosophy, or events) and struggles to understand, deal with, and perhaps solve the complexities and questions concerning life on this planet. A program which precipitates this kind of intensive study would no doubt be heralded by such diverse critics as Allen Bloom and Ray B. Browne. And yet to truly understand our place in the world, the first hurdle to cross is the bias of the word itself...Humanities. This word contains as its root the human element and so creates an image which has become the center of most people's lives. The meaning of such a word is both narrow and blinding. It simply places as the center of all importance that solitary soul which was molded out of Christian theology; a creature whose duty it is to use, enjoy, and inevitably destroy all which it encounters. When we look within ourselves we see many dark and wonderful things, but if we dare look outside our human shell, we can experience in the mirror image emanating from the eyes of our fellow creatures the beginning of the answer for which we search.

Peter Singer, noted animal rights author and activist, states that the animal liberation movement "marks an expansion of our moral horizons beyond our own species and is thus a significant stage in the development of human ethics" (1). Although the argument between those who see humankind as part of the animal world and those who deem humans as superior to all other life has been simmering for many years, the boiling point has only recently been reached— the knowledge of atrocities committed against animals has led to rage and that rage has led to action. The oneness of humankind with the world is a concept prevalent in Hindu thought and other eastern philosophies and religions, but unfortunately much of this type of information is noticeably lacking within the academic curriculum, a victim of educational priority perhaps more than a blatant disregard for its ideas. In any humanities survey there is no doubt that the Ancient Greeks fill a substantial part of the make up of western thought. Slides, films, hand-outs and lectures will document to students the beauty of the human intellect, the importance of the ideal concept of art and life. And yet, it is Aristotle who may have first stressed that, in the words of Singer, "plants— exist for the sake of animals, and animals for the sake of man, to provide him with food and clothing" (2). This key concept is echoed in the book of Genesis in the Christian bible, and ever since has been gaining strength. The placing of humans above animals has not only become the center of western religious beliefs, it has spread throughout this culture's social values and acts as glue for one's own psychological well-being. This idea has been held in place by seemingly essential political and economical powers. Since the 1970s, a growing concern that this value system is unacceptable has brought on a kind of cultural revolution. At the core of the animal rights movement is a re-examination of humankind's place in the world and a general shunning of the speciesism which had become, up until that time, part of that ambiguous cloud of myths which Berger and Luckman, in their book *The Social Construction of Reality*, call "common sense." Of course, such a radical change in both the physical and psychological living patterns of daily life will, and always shall, meet with violent reaction.

Before the actual organized movement began there was evidence that, in the words of scientist Donald J. Barnes whose long battle with medical ethics led him away from further experimentation on laboratory animals, "change requires the reconceptualization of many, if not all, of our habits" (167). What attempts were made to familiarize the masses with the ideas of animal liberation were either blocked from public awareness, seen as misguided information from people outside of the moral center of "common sense" and therefore "crazy," or veiled and hidden in other forms. The later writings of Mark Twain are seen by even the most enthusiastic scholars of his work as the uniformed ramblings of a misanthrope. It is rarely, if ever, mentioned that the concepts of such works as *What is Man?* and *The Mysterious Stranger* are based on a new awareness of humankind's relationship with the animal world and not necessarily the heretical scratches of a man broken by sorrow and economic defeat. Typical of Twain's wit, such essays as "Was the World Made for Man?" poke fun at the so-called importance of humankind. In this piece Twain outlines the history of the earth while illustrating that each new species from the pteradactyl to the monkey was created for the use (whether it be for food or for the sheer pleasure of finding their fossils) of humans. He sums up his facetious argument:

Such is the history of it. Man has been here 32,000 years. That it took a hundred million years to prepare the world for him is proof that that is what it was done for. I suppose it is. I dunno. If the Eiffel tower were now representing the world's age, the skin of paint on the pinnacle-knob at its summit would represent man's share of that age; and anybody would perceive that that skin was what the tower was built for. (106)

Such a comparison, as ludicrous as it may sound, could be said to echo the more historic words of Thomas Jefferson, "...that all *Men* are created equal." Much of Twain's material which has bearing on the hidden intensity of the animal rights concept was either suppressed or published privately and anonymously. Only after Twain's death were these ideas linked to the great "funny man." Suddenly, his words are not so humorous. It is a tribute to the all encompassing "common sense" directive that the typical university student who may thoroughly debate the possibility of racism in *Huckleberry Finn* is rarely introduced to Twain's later works. In "Man's Place in the Animal World" Twain complains that there is one major defect in the notion that humans are equal to other animals in the world. And this defect, in the words of Robert Frost, "has made all the difference." Twain writes:

I find this Defect to be *The Moral Sense.* He is the only animal that has it. It is the secret of his degradation. It is the quality which enables him to do wrong. It has no other office...Without it, man could do no wrong. He would rise at once to the level of the Higher Animals. (86)

Unlike other outlets of pre-1970s animals rights attitudes, the writings of Mark Twain are blatant attacks of a system which gave no indication of permitting resistance, philosophical or otherwise, from outside forces. Not all such ideas have been so disconcerting.

Although they are more subtle, ideas pertaining to animal rights have occasionally showed up in popular films. Admittedly, the audience's observation and appreciation of the beauty of nature is usually coerced by filmmakers in the unmistakable abuse of animals on the screen. Disney films are adored by countless parents and children alike and pretend to establish the importance of animals to humanity while exploiting all manner of living creatures. Seemingly innocent, these films which delight and amaze all age groups are an excellent example of how western culture blithely witnesses (in this case for entertainment purposes) on a daily basis the wrongful treatment of animals. Since the study of films falls under the umbrella of humanities in many of the smaller universities, it is interesting to briefly take note of several popular films which at least hint at the issues manifested in the new animal liberation movement. It is not often that animal rights and the detective genre cross paths (although it might be admitted that each represents humankind's search for higher truth and meaning in a chaotic world) and yet *You Never Can Tell* (1951) starring William Powell, incorporating his tough guy persona on the heels of the noirish *Murder My Sweet*, is a story in which a German Shepherd inherits a large sum of money and is then poisoned. In animal heaven, where all benevolent creatures (excluding humans, interestingly) live in harmony, the canine is given a second chance and allotted a certain amount of time to find his murderer. In short, the shepherd comes back as William Powell, private eye. The humorous plot continues with Powell candidly crunching dog biscuits and growling at thugs. A most important theme in terms of animal rights in the film is worth mentioning. It is made clear that many humans were actually animals in earlier lives but were not noble enough to be accepted into animal heaven, which precipitates their purgatory-like existence as humans until they fulfill their obligation to the animal world. The intent of the film clearly establishes a link between humans and animals and even echoes, albeit in a lighthearted way, the radical ideas of Twain.

Not all popular films which deal with the animal rights issues are picturesque and humorous. *Planet of the Apes* (1968), for example, illustrates a much more brutal thesis. The plot of the film is familiar to most avid moviegoers and so does not need retelling here. The film places plainly before the audience, this time within the confines of the science fiction genre, the inhumane (this being yet another biased word which in the current trend is in need of re-examination) treatment of animals at the hands of humans by turning the tables on the audience. It is Charlton Heston, forever seen in the eyes of many as the devout biblical figure he once played, who is treated like an animal, and who is hard pressed to convince the ruling orangutans of human intelligence and worth. More recent films like *Harry and the Hendersons* and *E.T.* can be added to the small yet effective canon of films which illustrate a growing cultural concern with the treatment of animals.

The animal liberation movement is comparable to many movements in America (literary, artistic, and otherwise) which have attempted to clarify and understand humankind's place in the world. The movement is not clearly defined, nor is its boundaries shared by a typical group of people. The ideas and arguments presented by this dedicated, if not entirely regimented, group continue to flourish in all levels of social and economic classes. Tom Regan in "The Case for Animal Rights" states that the movement is committed to a number of goals including, "1) the total abolition of the use of animals in science; 2) the total dissolution of commercial animal agriculture; (and) 3) the total elimination of commercial and sport hunting and trapping" (13). Vegetarianism is a vital component of such an agenda, as is the shunning of leather goods and the use of only cruelty free products (including among other things cosmetics and household cleaning materials) where at all possible. Interestingly, as an example of the blindness and general unawareness of much of the populace which substantiates the concern of the activists, many people use products on a daily basis without knowing that these items have been cruelly tested on animals. Even more extraordinary is the fact that a number of these tests are reported to be worthless in light of human safety and effectiveness. Put plainly, and borrowing a slogan from an animal rights poster showing two chimps recently freed from the confines of laboratory torture, the movement proclaims that, "Animals are individuals who have a value independent of their usefulness to others." This fluctuating and developing manifesto operates within all types of popular culture despite aggressive opposition.

Like all movements of cultural importance the supporters of animal rights have surrounded themselves with components which seem to radiate symbolic meaning. Icons in the form of buttons, T-shirts, handbags, coffee mugs, posters, and pamphlets enable the various members to spread information to the uninitiated. By showing support in such a way, the group invites possible new members to join by offering attractive, new elements of fashion. Once this step is taken, the new members feel less vulnerable within the world whose values they had begun to re-examine and perhaps mistrust. The power-in-numbers theory is what has brought animal rights its popularity as well as the scorn from more traditionally minded outsiders. Large rallies have been held in recent years to promote animal rights activity, including a mass gathering in Washington, D.C. in 1988 and the highly promoted "Rock Against Fur" in New York City in 1989. These ritualistic celebrations strengthen the group and also recruit more members, especially from the segment of youth culture whose age signals the need for the re-examination of traditional American values. By combining rock-and-roll and animal rights, most notably illustrated by the popular singing group "The B-52s," the movement has used to its advantage an inherently rebellious popular art form to further its message.

As the movement has gained numbers and political power, certain figures have risen out of the swirling tide of supporters to lead the way. These heroes are figureheads whose actions and arguments are watched closely by other members. Consequently, these people are sometimes shunned by the majority of the population. Alex Pacheco, co-founder of the organization called PETA (People for the Ethical Treatment of Animals), is responsible for making the movement more visual through publications like *PETA News*. Other periodicals followed, such as *The Animals' Agenda*, and soon health food stores, co-ops, and selected book stores were incorporated into the movement's educational process. The writer who is noted as inspiring *PETA* and most of the other prominent organizations is Peter Singer, an Australian ethicist who published the influential *Animal Liberation* in 1975. As was evident in the civil rights movement in the 1960s, there is always a plethora of opinions concerning the use of violence versus the effectiveness of pacifist protest. Not all groups who believe in the animal rights credo are content to simply write letters to congressmen and join in peaceful demonstrations. Some sub-groups like ALF (the Animal Liberation Front) break socially accepted rules in order to free laboratory animals from what they see as inevitable torture and death at the hands of unfeeling human monsters, who perform their gruesome tests with government funds in the name of the deities of Progress and Science. Although the more moderate groups like *PETA* take no visible part in these activities, they lend support through reporting on the atrocities witnessed by infiltrators of laboratories and the often horrible conditions of animals freed by the militants. There are many cases of such abuse, including the continual bashing of the heads of monkeys; electrocuting the brains of quails and placing electrodes to the eyes of mice; starving bats to death; infecting the stomachs of kittens with deadly viruses; transplanting the brains of small dogs into the necks of large dogs while isolating other puppies in small boxes for up to nine months; trimming the whiskers of rats and dropping them into cylindrical tanks filled with water until they drown; crushing the legs of dogs; and injecting chemicals into the brains of cats (Ryder 46-55). Although it is difficult to justify such treatment under any circumstances, some might attempt to explain it by referring to the need in making medicines safe for human consumption. Unfortunately, this is not always the case. Thalidomide had no negative effects on laboratory animals and yet caused severe deformities in human infants. Another example of the uselessness of such testing occurred with penicillin, which did not have the desired effect on animals and yet was adopted for human use. It is doubtful that any feeling human witnessing these experiments would idly stand by unmoved. By condemning such activities through the medium of print, the movement as a whole remains in tact, a necessary defense against the powerful political forces which support the ideas and activities against which the animal rights movement fights.

At the heart of the animal rights movement is the concept that humans are not only one with other creatures, but are responsible for the suffering of animals even though they may not consciously be inflicting pain. It should already be clear that much of the population tacitly supports the use of animals by humankind even though they have not actively taken a political stand on the subject. Albert Schweitzer comments eloquently on the responsibility of human beings towards other creatures:

Whenever an animal is somehow forced into the service of men, every one of us must be concerned for any suffering it bears on that account. No one of us may permit any preventable pain to be inflicted, even though the responsibility for that pain is not ours. No one may appease his conscience by thinking that he would be interfering in something that does not concern him. No one may shut his eyes and think the pain, which is therefore not visible to him, is non-existent. (29)

Schweitzer illustrates that the drive for animal rights is more than improving the treatment of one's house pet. The message of this movement, it seems, attempts to further the argument which first became controversial with Galileo and Darwin. Humans, history relates, having at one time found themselves at the center of the universe, are reluctant to relinquish that position. Although figures like Darwin are always considered in the university curriculum, contemporary counterparts in attempting to substantiate the belief that humans are part of the animal world have only recently become visible within the liberal arts.

The first segment of higher education to be influenced in the development of the animal rights movement has been composition courses. With their emphasis on argument and the use of sources underlying collegiate writing, the composition courses have granted the animal rights debate more pages with each new collection of essays anthologized for student use. Two recent examples from St. Martin's Press can be found in *Elements of Argument: A Text and Reader* (1991) and *Our Times 2: Readings from Recent Periodicals* (1991). It will be interesting to note whether the movement receives any reinforcement from this new exposure, especially since this age group, as already stated, is particularly influenced by MTV and rock-and-roll and yet, especially in the more rural areas, may have rarely tested the sometimes thin ice of teenage rebellion. If, however, the current trend which has prompted the reinvestigation of all humanities classes is to be complete, animal rights will no doubt take a place in the conceptualizing process which attempts to define the importance of human work, thought, and its very existence.

Although emerging as a viable force within American culture only recently, the animal rights movement is forcing a new look from the eyes of students and professors alike. Of course, it is arguable that the university community is a somewhat pampered and isolated minority, and yet the ideas taught in the classroom do shape beliefs and actions of individuals even though the days of wanton destruction and protest on campuses are no longer a threat to the status quo. But it is a tribute to the animal liberators that their cause has pressed beyond the protective, cement walls of academia and that their actions are at last being presented to the masses, although many times without positive approval. However much the majority might find this new belief system a threat, animal rights groups have changed many people's lives in this country. Especially since at its core the movement deals with the clarifying and understanding of humankind's place even in an environment often devoid of natural forces, the so-called new animal liberation has become and will continue to be a new, interesting, and important force in American life and culture. As such it should constitute an ever-growing aspect of the Humanities, for the Humanities are the energies and guides which not only explain our culture but also direct us toward an enlightened expansion of it.

Works Cited

Atwan, Robert., ed. *Our Times 2: Readings from Recent Periodicals*. Boston: St. Martin's, 1991.

Barnes, Donald J. "A Matter of Change." Singer 157-67.

Elements of Argument: A Text and Reader. Ed. Annette T. Rottenberg. Boston: St. Martin's, 1991.

Our Times 2: Readings from Recent Periodicals. Ed. Robert Atwan. Boston: St. Martin's, 1991.

Regan, Tom. "The Case for Animal Rights." *In Defense of Animals*. Ed. Peter Singer. New York: Harper & Row, 1985. 13-26.

Rottenberg, Annette T. *Elements of Argument: A Text and Reader*. Boston: St. Martin's, 1991.

Ryder, Richard. "Experiments on Animals." *Animals, Men and Morals*. Eds. Stanley and Roslind Godlovitch and John Harris. New York: Taplinger, 1972. 41-82.

Singer, Peter., ed. *In Defense of Animals*. New York: Harper & Row, 1985.

–––––– "Prologue: Ethics and the New Animal Liberation Movement." Singer 1-10.

Schweitzer, Albert. *Animals, Nature & Albert Schweitzer.* Ed. Ann Cottrell. Washington, D.C.: Flying Fox, 1988.

Twain, Mark. *What is Man? And Other Philosophical Writings. The Works of Mark Twain.* Ed. Paul Baender. Berkeley: U California P, 1973. Vol. 19.

Additional Reading

Boas, Max and Steve Chain. *Big Mac: The Unauthorized Story of McDonald's.* New York: New American Library, 1976.

Clark, Stephen. *The Moral Status of Animals.* Oxford: Clarendon, 1977.

–––––– *The Nature of the Beast.* Oxford: Oxford UP, 1983.

Dawkins, Marian Stamp. *Animal Suffering: The Science of Animal Welfare.* London: Chapman & Hall, 1980.

Magel, Charles. *A Bibliography on Animal Rights and Related Matters.* Washington, DC.: UP Americ, 1981.

Midgley, Mary. *Animals and Why They Matter.* Harmondsworth: Penguin, 1984.

Regan, Tom and Peter Singer, eds. *Animal Rights and Human Obligations.* Englewood Cliffs, NJ: Prentice-Hall, 1976.

Rollin, Bernard. *Animal Rights and Human Morality.* Buffalo, NY: Prometheus, 1981.

Rowan, Andrew. *Of Mice, Models and Men: A Critical Evaluation of Animal Research.* Albany: SUNY P, 1984.

Salt, Henry. *Animal Rights.* 1892. New York: Avon, 1977.

Smyth, D.H. *Alternatives to Animal Experiments.* London: Scolar, 1978.

Collecting and the Humanities

A.D. Olmsted

The desire to search for, acquire and own—and often to display to others—objects is the drive that virtually makes collectors of us all. Gathering collectibles is one activity that removes many of the social and intellectual barriers between people. Doctors, lawyers, intellectuals, beggars and thieves—as well as housespouses and children—rub shoulders at auctions of antiques and newer materials and get into direct competition over acquiring ownership.

So the objects themselves become coins of commerce and the passing from one hand to another constitute an intermingling of humanity and thus the humanities. People who collect together, to speak tautologically, learn a great deal about themselves and thus stay together. Knowing about one another and staying together is the backbone of the humanities. Collecting, as A.D. Olmsted points out in the following essay, is an excellent classroom for teaching and learning those humanities.

Humanities: the branches of learning regarded as having primarily a cultural character and use including languages, literature, history, mathematics and philosophy. (Webster's Third New International Dictionary)

Popular culture is the practical-pragmatic Humanities. (Browne, 1987)

The world is divided into two classes. Not three or five or twenty. Just two. One is the great majority; the other is the leisure kind, not those of wealth or position or birth, but those who love ideas and the imagination. (deGrazia, 1971)

Introduction

As defined by Webster's, the Humanities are a small, elite world. It is comprised of academic teachers and researchers, who train professional curators, critics, artists and more teachers and researchers. These people educate and are supported by an elite, upper class which provides a milieu for high culture. Historically, the masses were exposed to this world through a public education system dealing with great art, music, literature and science. With the advent of the mass media, it was hoped that exposure to high culture via the broadcast and print media would educate and uplift the masses during their leisure hours. More people would love ideas and the imagination, as defined by the traditional purveyors of the humanities.

Instead, mass production and the mass media are seen to conspire in the decline of traditional humanities. With the exception of voices such as Browne (1987), popular culture is seen as antithetical to both high culture and the leisure kind who love ideas and the imagination (Rosenberg and White). It is accepted that

Popular culture is the television we watch, the movies we see, the fast food, or slow food we eat, the clothes we wear, the music we sing and hear, *the things we spend our money for,* our attitude toward life. It is the whole society we live in, that which may or may not be distributed by the mass media. (Browne 2) (emphasis added)

What is not accepted is the idea that education and leisure that loves ideas and imagination can be achieved by the practical-pragmatic Humanities.

Immersion in the world of public education has stereotypically lead to this result: "*Bouvard et Pecuchet* is the story of two men who acquire the income to do what they want but fall heir to it at too late an age for their adult studies to do them much good" (deGrazia). Recently, the example is a lottery winner who, after a consumer orgy, faces the same frustration. There is, however, an alternative, based not on purchasing power but on a leisure activity.

It is to buy what is scarce and rare; it is to collect. The virtue of pursuing collectibles rather than merely consumer goods is precisely that they have their own special scarcity. Collectibles are not available to anyone with means. Their availability is constrained by the fact that they are not the products of mass manufacture and can therefore claim to be unique (as in the case of art)...Collectibles, unique or very rare, must be hunted down, brought out of hiding, won away from other collectors. (McCracken)

After a brief overview of research on collecting and collectibles, the body of this paper will examine collecting and education (formal and informal) and collecting as an amateur leisure activity which merges the classic and practical-pragmatic definitions of the humanities in small integrated social worlds.

Collectors

Most children are collectors until about age twelve. At this age, the activity continues for some, but tends to drop off very sharply, particularly for girls. Most studies have reported many male collectors referred to as late-bloomers who have begun serious collecting in middle age (Dannefer). While early studies indicated overwhelming percentages of males among collectors, a more recent survey indicates that stamp collectors are now 49% female and coin collectors are 40% female (Crispell). Tomeh, Pearman and Schnabel note that while more women than men rate antique collecting as an interesting activity, more men then women carry out the activity of antique collecting. Although predominantly middle class, collectors include all elements of society, from unemployed and retired to upper class. Similarly, collectors are mostly young to middle aged adults, but children and the elderly are always well represented. Collecting has been observed in all national and political cultures.

Collectors share the motivations of a passionate interest in acquiring some class or classes of objects, a pleasure in organizing and completing sets of objects, and interacting with other collectors. Additional motivations include preserving culture through the objects, researching the objects, having fun, being independent of the work world, developing the self, and the potential of investing in the objects and making money.

Collecting

Collecting is the selective, active, and longitudinal acquisition, possession and disposition of an interrelated set of differentiated objects (material things, ideas, beings or experiences). *Accumulation* of possessions differs from collecting in that it lacks selectivity, may be simply a refusal to dispose of things and is no cause for pride. *Hoarding* is selective and active but focuses on utilitarian items that may be needed in the future. (Belk, R.W., Wallendorf, M., Sherry, J. and Holbrook, M.B., in press) (Italics added)

Ownership of a collection tends to be very individualistic, with shared collections definitely in the minority. Collectors, like other consumers, frequently refer to the pleasurable activity of hunting for a desired object. When this is done in the company of others, they are usually family members or friends, not other collectors. However, collecting is also intensely social, because it takes place in the social world of collectors.

Each social world of collectors is relatively small, and specialized on an object (Unruh; Olmsted). It is most easily observed at action scenes (Irwin), although much activity involves only the collector, the collection and often a wide range of reference literature. Similarly, collector to collector interaction is important, but seldom observed, except at action scenes.

For this reason, we have reports of collecting behavior; buying, selling, trading, hunting, and socializing at flea markets (Sherry; Maisel) garage sales (Herrmann and Soiffer) and auctions (Glancy; Smith). Dealers' shops, another important collecting scene, are not well researched.

While difficult to summarize, this literature suggests that collecting develops expertise about the object, skills for obtaining it, and a wide range of social contacts and interactions with other members of the collector's world. Because collectibles, discussed next, get their original meaning from the larger world, the collector also gains knowledge of, and contacts with, the culture that produced the collectible. Collectors frequently mention the possibility of either creating a museum, or donating their collection to a museum as a means of returning the collection and its information to the public. An increasing number of collectors are creating their own museums (Sobol and Sobol).

More frequently, the collector develops the collection and information about it, then shares it with other members of the collectors' world. This is usually first in conversation with other collectors—in verbal interpersonal exchange. A wider sharing involves letters to a collectors' publication, either asking or answering questions about new or unknown objects. Articles and books about collectibles are written by collectors. While relatively infrequent, these contributions are widely shared, as the journals and books are often placed in public libraries, as well as circulating in the collector's world. Such books may in turn become collectors' items themselves.

Very few collectors inherit their collections (Dannefer; Olmsted). When a collection is dispersed it returns to the collectors' world through the action scenes, to begin or extend other collections. Such items are frequently associated with the original collector, adding to the provenance of the object, and the information encoded in it.

Collectibles and the Collection

Collectibles, because of their diversity, are the least defined aspect of collecting. Danet and Katriel and Stewart have considered such aspects as size. Miniatures and gigantic objects are prime collectibles, particularly the miniature, due to its convenience. Age, rarity and association with famous people, places or times are collectible characteristics. But beauty is not only in the eye, but in the mind of the collector.

Underlying aesthetic behavior is the powerful human urge to classify the elements of the environment. This *taxophilic urge* manifests in...the human passion for collecting. (Morris 279)

Collectibles can be loosely defined (and separated from antiques and antiquities) as "...items mass produced during the Twentieth Century that cost less than $200 when they were made...People collect barb wire, hubcaps, lunch boxes and paperweights" (Crispell). And much more, of course, including things mass produced before the Twentieth Century, including guns, stamps, coins and so on.

Just as the organized collection separates sets of objects from accumulations and hoards, it also separates collectibles from necessities, souvenirs and mementos. Items are acquired for the collection, not to use, not to remind us of a personal visit, experience or memory. The collection is arranged not just to communicate the messages in the objects, but also to demonstrate the creativity of the collector, thus adding a meaning to the sum of the collectible parts.

The uniqueness of a collection is part of the creation of rarity among popular collectibles. The major part is, of course, wastage. Millions of miles of barb wire, millions of comic books, beer cans, stamps, and coins have been mass produced. They are used up, lost, damaged, recycled; in a word, consumed. Only those in collections or accumulations remain. Ferrel has discussed the degradation and rehabilitation of consumer goods from new through old, used and vintage. Rubbish theory also discusses this process (Thompson). Scholars studying circuses (Flint), working man's books (James), and train timetables (Schwantes) have thanked private collectors for preserving popular collectibles for their research needs.

Collecting and Formal Education

Psychologically, children's collecting is motivated by the rewards of acquiring and classifying (Durost 88). In conclusion this author suggests:

Because collecting activity seems to be an interest especially congenial to children, it may be that greater use of it could be made in enriching the curriculum for this group in the ordinary graded school system.

Because collecting seems to be midway between the two extremes of social and individual activities, the suggestion comes that it might be used with success in helping socially inadequate children make useful contacts with the social group. (Durost 94)

Morris points out that children who are bored in class by botany, geology and entomology can classify enormous amounts of information about their favorite football teams or popular music. Two literature reviews on collecting (Olmsted, Formanek) indicate that Durost's work signalled an abrupt end to such research (its revival is discussed below). The suggestions made for the educational use of children's collecting have been largely ignored beyond the "show and tell" level. Because children's collections are of everyday, mass produced items, this oversight obviated collecting as one avenue by which popular culture could be formally used as "medicine for illiteracy and associated educational ills" (Browne). Current research and a possibly unique elementary school curriculum are more encouraging.

Danet and Katriel are studying children's collecting in Israel. Furby has done the same in the US and Israel. Formanek has just begun a study of collecting among elementary and high school students in New York (Personal communication). Closer to the educational front lines, Vandergrift discusses how her personal collection of children's books enhances her lectures and her relationship to her students. "It is often the only way they will see some of the items they are yearning to touch and examine" (93). In addition, "collecting Nancy Drew or Judy Blume or Little Golden Books may be a solid contribution to future scholarship" (94). History, lifestyles and the anti-war and feminist movements are singled out as topics which could integrate book collections and the classroom.

Intrigued by this article, Paley examined collecting being done by his nine and ten-year-old students. He was "struck by the intelligence, rigor and commitment which marked their activities" (31). He concludes:

Encouraging children to share personal interests and accomplishments in school study programs emphasizes the critical idea that all knowledge is socially constructed, that the curriculum is created by people whose personal interests are the fundamental basis for the dynamics of scholarly inquiry and subject development. While this view is hardly a revolutionary concept (indeed for John Dewey consistently argued the same point nearly one hundred years ago), it bears repeating since so much conventional educational practice continues to encourage student recall repetition, and memorization of an abstract, impersonal body of material has little connection to their daily lives. (Paley 33)

In what may be the only example of its kind in North America (Formanek, personal communication) the Department of Education in Alberta, Canada has utilized this idea as part of language learning. Using a basic resource book called Zoom Shots (McInnes, Garry, Hearn and Hughes, n.d.) collecting may be used to achieve goals as follows:

Children are born collectors. Like all human beings, they collect experiences, "things," ideas, feelings, attitudes and related languages every day.

Children usually collect "things" with some intent—hockey cards, rocks, Scout badges and so on. Their collections are as different and unique as themselves. The act of collecting, however, and the common interest that surrounds it, offers an opportunity to share and learn from one another. (Instructor's manual, Zoom Shoots, n.d.)

Operationally, children are encouraged to read poems, stories, books and newspaper articles about collecting. (Many of these demonstrate different meanings of the world collecting.) They may present, display, discuss and classify their own collections.

Junior high schools encourage collecting as a form of cultural enrichment, and teachers often sponsor collecting clubs among students (Shutiak). Similar clubs exist at universities, although the only course known to be offered is one in art collecting, offered by New York University, Continuing Education. For this reason, the education of adult collectors is more individual, and informal. However, as interest in collecting, and adult education continues to rise, perhaps collecting will form a larger part of formal education, by definition including the new humanities.

Collecting and Informal Education

For many of us, public participation in the humanities is represented by the great "learned amateurs." These men (and occasionally women) have usually been incorporated over time into the traditional humanities, and often came of sufficient wealth and position to support the leisure (non-work) researches which made them famous. The major theme of this paper is that the collectors of popular collectibles are also of the "leisure kind," only they explore, collect specimens and report from the world of popular culture, and over time, are helping to create the practical, pragmatic humanities.

Collectors are amateurs who participate in leisure on a scale from casual to serious (Stebbins). Serious collectors are noted for their interest in history, both of the period during which their chosen object was produced and used, and the history of the objects themselves (Tomeh et. al., Serven). Learning this history is done during leisure time, not according to a formal curriculum. The classrooms are the action scenes described earlier, the teachers are initially other collectors, dealers and auctioneers who are members of the collectors' worlds.

Collectors' worlds eventually produce their own literature.

When John Goins first published his book *Pocket Knives, Markings, Manufacturers and Dealers* it filled a void in the information available to knife collectors. It very quickly became a standard reference for me and for many others who collect and research knives. (Goins 3)

Such collectors' texts are frequently mentioned in every collector's world, as are auction catalogues, retail catalogues, price guides and how to do it books for collectors. This example is used because it also gives us an account of how and why the book was produced.

The collecting of pocket knives and other articles of cutlery is a hobby that I have found very rewarding. Collecting information on old defunct firms is, for me, also part of that hobby. The information contained in this book is the result of almost thirteen years of research...By far the greatest amount of information was obtained from the Office of Patents and Trademarks...In a few instances dates were derived from markings on knife handles and pictures from old catalogs which picture knives with readable markings. City directories were also used, and these dates were generally very accurate.... I have found that some town histories conflict with each other. (Goins 5)

Collectors' words also create their own languages, and the ability to speak the language is, as usual, a sign of membership. Like the more classic languages, they are learned both by participation and from books. An illustrated glossary of the blade styles includes some which can be interpreted by the uncultured; pen, screwdriver, spatula, and my favorite, the melon tester. However, recognizing a Wharncliff, sheepfoot, muskrat or spay blade, and the origin of the name, requires a deeper education (Parker and Voyles).

Not only does this brief account of one popular collectible demonstrate a leisure education in history and language, it also demonstrates the natural philosophic study and classification of objects, and, like most other collectors' worlds, attempts a moral philosophy. A section on knife collecting etiquette includes general politeness, rules of deportment at shows and honest representation and pricing. It concludes:

Many of the old-time court-house traders operated under the premise "Do to me first 'cause I'm gonna do it to you if I get the chance." That premise is the best way to destroy a hobby.... (Parker and Voyles 27)

To this point, this section could have been titled "Formal Education in Collectors' Worlds," as it has dealt with research methods, reference books and is, except for the leisure motivation and lack of classrooms, a parallel to formal education. However, the collector's classrooms are the places where he buys things; flea markets, garage sales, auctions, dealers' shops and shows. The teachers are the vendors and other collectors, often one person combining both roles. Rather than cite other people's anecdotes, I will try to illustrate this with my own. The social interactions involved also illustrate the social nature of collecting discussed below.

Twelve years ago, as a late-bloomer, I resumed my interrupted career as a collector of revolvers and pistols manufactured by the English firm of Webley and Scott. One revolver I bought was easily identified, as the book (Dowell) had already been published, and my collectible was clearly pictured and discussed. However, inletted into the grip is a small shield-shaped plaque indicating (on the reverse side) that the revolver was a prize won in a target rifle match at the famous Bisley competitions in 1894. On the facing side is a fairly elaborate crest.

Letters to Webley and Scott and the Bisley organization informed me that their records had respectively been destroyed in a WWII bombing raid and were unavailable or lost. I began taking the plaque with me to auctions, shows and museums. Over the years, I have found that the object is eight carat gold, backed with sterling silver, not copper and tin, as I had thought. The hallmark on the silver establishes that it was made in Birmingham at the appropriate date. This information came from a dealer who also deals in jewelry.

A collector of military medals assured me that the crest was not European military. He referred me to another collector who was knowledgeable in heraldry. This expert showed me that, due to certain markings, it is a town or city crest. As towns and cities sponsored target matches during the period, this datum seems reasonable. However, the definitive answer still escapes me. While the research is incomplete, the social interaction has been rewarding. Ownership of an object which puzzles all members of my collectors' world carries a modicum of status (see Shoop, below).

In another case, I spotted a piece of porcelain of a type that my wife and I collect at a mall collectible show. However, I did not know what the item was. Neither did the dealer, so I bought it at a much reduced price, on the understanding that if I found out what it was, I would tell the dealer. A member of the family identified its use; I went back and told the dealer and we all had a good laugh. Ironically, a year later, "the book" on this porcelain was published, showing and identifying the piece. It would have reduced the fun, and raised the price.

In this section, I have demonstrated the effort and resources associated with learning about popular collectibles. In the next, I will discuss the personal and social rewards.

Sociability and Collecting

It has long been an accusation that both the material and symbolic worlds of mass society produce isolated, atomistic individuals who independently enact identical mass responses.

In the world of symbols, such as political campaigns, social primary groups were rediscovered (Katz and Lazarsfeld). Consumers of material culture are still seen as subject to buying available objects in a highly impersonal manner. The price is fixed (no bargaining), the vendor is a bureaucrat, paid a salary to run a cash register, is often ignorant of the product, and has no personal interest in the object. The worker(s) who produced the object is/are unknown and alienated. Brand names are simply identification, linking the product financially to a giant multinational corporation. Acquiring such objects, in such a manner, is definitely an unsocial interaction.

Collecting involves quite different levels of social involvement, as does buying used, pre-owned or secondhand goods. Ferrell provides an excellent discussion of how used popular culture objects are degraded from *new* to *old* or *used*, and then rehabilitated to *vintage* or collectible in our terms. This partly due to the physical condition of the object, but it is also a social construction. In the case of collecting, the categories created by collectors (Alsop) the act of classifying the objects (Morris) and the consequent exchange of objects (Smith; Maisel; Olmsted) are all creative and stimulating social activities. Well established collectibles are categorized, priced and sold in a manner approaching that of new items (Ferrell). Even at this level, however, both the vendor (dealer or auctioneer) and the collector must be personally knowledgeable about the object's classification and value. When objects are moving from old to collectible, and such knowledge is lacking, value is adjusted, as in the porcelain example above.

One very creative collection is based specifically on lack of knowledge. It is a collection of *insolts* (I never saw one like that) (Shoop). Collecting kitsch, considered the ultimate in bad taste (Dorfles) can become a humorous and playful activity (Henry). Generally, kitsch and insolts are low in economic value, but discovered at an action scene will soon produce a buzzing knot of social exchanges, often resulting in a constructed identification. At the more serious level, collectors often are consulted by dealers and auctioneers, given special status for their specialized knowledge.

At flea markets:

One can accumulate a wealth of knowledge by eavesdropping on the informal lectures some consumers deliver in the course of their search. The sheer joy of evaluation—of intellectual showing off with no adverse consequences—seems to be a powerful mechanism of engagement with the market. (Sherry 26)

Collectors, among other hobbyists, are well known for these lectures (Stebbins 1982).

Still at the flea market, Maisel reports rewards in the form of the *killing*: for a collector this would be an unexpected find which would not take place at a collectibles store. The *Edenic vision of sociability* is replete with "nice" people, good vibes, finding nice things and sharing one's own pleasures. *Character tales* include the dealer who buys a piece of silver for five dollars and then hands over fifty more because the silver is antique and worth over two hundred (501-02).

Many collectors find the auction the most exciting scene of all. While disagreeing on its economic merits (many think the prices and commissions too high), auctions have long been known as places to see and be seen (Towner). Furthermore, auctions are seldom made up of random collections of individuals. Whether art, guns or general collectibles, attenders form a sense of community, based on their shared view of the worth and value of the goods they pursue (Smith). Auctions are staged so that:

Whatever else an auction might be, it is generally a good show: the intense emotionality, the expressive gestures, the plots and counterplots, the dreams, the despair...(Smith 108)

Each lot is a separate drama, with all but a few of those present members of an audience. If the audience is pleased with the performance they applaud at the end of the bid. A new high price for an item, the contest among bidders, and a skilled auctioneer are all roles in the drama (Smith 128-29).

Encompassing all collectors' transactions, from the impersonal catalogue order to the event of the auction is the shared view of the worth of an object. While Smith's use of the term "auction community" is a good one, it implies a shared physical presence from auction to auction. Based on research in second hand clothing stores, Wiseman developed the term *quasi-primary interaction* associated with interactions she observed. Generalized to the flea market and garage sale scenes discussed here, she suggests that the sociability and conviviality occurs at the scene but ends at the store entrance (43). With the exception discussed below, this term describes the collector who both actually and metaphorically steps from the everyday mass society dominated world into a leisure world of sociability focused on objects which once were mass commodities and are now the center of one of the many collectors' worlds.

According to McCracken (1988) the evocative power of objects allows them to form bridges between the real world and an ideal cultural world through the process of *displaced meaning*: "cultural meaning that has deliberately been removed from the daily life of a community and relocated in a distant cultural domain" (104). For individuals, this is most often the discovery of "a personal golden age in which life conformed to their fondest expectations or noblest ideals..." (McCracken 108).

Between the individual and the entire culture is the group of collectors who share an image, thereby creating the quasi-primary group discussed above. Popular culture has a positive power in this area: the golden ages of radio, television, movies and music all create relatively distant cultural domains, and the artifacts to evoke them. In the world of gun collectors, this creates several levels of identity. For example, the Eastern frontier, Davy Crockett, and Fess Parker are all symbolized by the Kentucky or Pennsylvania long rifles. The American West, the cowboy and John Wayne are represented by Colt Peacemakers and Winchester rifles. An additional level of identity occurred recently when Mel Torme used a local radio interview to notify fellow Colt collectors in the area that he would like to hear from them. Such identifications with an era, an icon, an actor or actress and famous fellow collectors are quite common. The recent record purchase of a rare baseball card by Wayne Gretzky gives the same pleasure to card collectors.

Real world advertising promises similar rewards for purchasing new consumer products. According to McCracken, such "bridge" goods work when their purchase is anticipated, but must be replaced by others when the goods are acquired, for their promise is not fulfilled.

The appropriate substitute strategy here is collecting. The uniqueness or great scarcity of collectibles allows them to serve as objects beyond one's reach and bridges to the displaced meaning. (McCracken 115)

Ironically, many collectors define advertising material as collectible, truly finding the message in the medium.

In this section, we have suggested that collectible popular culture objects also provide bridges of sociability to other people, in a leisure world based on the new humanities.

Summary

It has been said that the method of studying popular culture is:

...to take the commonplace, the anonymous, the trivial, the everyday, and apply to them the same degree of serious attention that has been given to masterworks, to leaders and to great events. (Schroeder 320)

This accepts the premise that the practical-pragmatic humanities are commonplace, and what we buy is trivial, compared to the great events and masterworks of the traditional humanities. Here we have suggested that baseball cards and bisquit tins are comparable to artworks and antiquities.

Similarly, we have suggested that collecting popular culture is a leisure activity which involves competence in specialized language, literature, history, the mathematics of classification and exchange, plus at least a rudimentary philosophy and research component. However it is at the level of creating people that are educated, in a leisure activity (de Grazias "leisure kind") that collecting and the two humanities most positively interact.

"Because it is fun" is the quick response to the question "Why do you collect?" This fun also includes work: finding, identifying, researching and acquiring the right object. It also includes creating the categories for the collection, identifying and acquiring the appropriate objects and in so doing becoming a learned amateur in the area, an "expert." This results in either sharing this expertise interpersonally or in writing, thus enjoying scholarly expertise.

All this is done in a sociable social world, based on a common interest in certain objects. Social interaction is with the object(s), with fellow searchers at action scenes, and the literature of the field. Collectors can learn about, and identify with famous people, who either owned or collected the treasure object, and displace themselves to other times and places, often considered golden ages.

There are at least a few hints that the knowledge created in the leisure worlds of collectors can be integrated back into the formal education system, and perhaps also integrate the two humanities.

Classification, logic and statistics are inherent in baseball cards. Basic communication and art are equally present in comic books. Popular music contains at least the basic do ra me of musical structure. Some, if not all, school children would be less bored if their trivial, everyday passions were included in the otherwise icy hand of the standard curriculum.

Middle-aged, middle-class people are often superbly trained vocationally, but fear leisure time and retirement. Those who become collectors report the creative and humanistic pleasures of their leisure time. Similarly, the constant pressure of the consumer society can be bridged by collecting as a leisure activity.

A recent article by Highsmith (in press) suggests how collector-produced material such as a comic book collectors' guide can aid the creation of a focused university library collection of comic books. Many museums now have curated collections of everyday objects. Such validations of popular collectors can be a strong force in integrating the two humanities. It is to be hoped that it will not make collecting boring, and it will not devalue the humanities.

Works Cited

Alsop, J. *The Rare Art Traditions*. New York: Harper & Row, 1982.

Belk, R.W., Wallendorf, M., Sherry, J., and Holbrook, M.B., (in press). "Collecting in a Consumer Culture." *Highways and Buyways: Naturalistic Research From the Consumer Odyssey*. Eds. R.W. Belk and M. Wallendorf. Provo: Association for Consumer Research.

Browne, R.B. "Popular Culture: Medicine for Illiteracy and Assorted Ills." *Journal of Popular Culture* 21 (1987): 1-16.

Crispell, D. "Collecting Memories." *American Demographics.* November (1988): 38-41.

Dannefer, D. "Neither Socialization nor Recruitment: The Avocational Careers of Old Car Enthusiasts." *Social Forces* 60 (1981): 395-412.

Danet, B., and Katriel, T. "Thing magic: closure and paradox in collecting." Working paper no. 2. Jerusalem: Hebrew University Departments of Communications and Sociology.

de Grazia, S. "Transforming Free Time." *Mass Culture Revisited.* Eds. B. Rosenberg and D.M. White. New York: Van Nostrand Reinhold, 1971. 25-60.

Dorfles, G. ed. *The World of Bad Taste.* New York: Bell Publishing Co., 1968.

Dornell, W.C. *The Webley story.* Leeds: The Skyrac Press, 1962.

Ferrel, J. "Degradation and Rehabilitation in Popular Culture." *Journal of Popular Culture* 24 (1990): 89-100.

Formanek, R. "Why they collect: Collectors reveal their motivations." *Journal of Social Behavior and Personality* 6 (1991): 275-286.

Flint, Richard W. "A Selected Guide to Source Material on the American Circus." *Journal of Popular Culture* 6 (1973): 615-19.

Furby, L. "Possession in Humans: Exploratory Study of its Meaning and Motivation." *Social Behavior and Personality* 6 (1978): 49-65.

Glancy, M. "The Play World Setting of the Auction." *Journal of Leisure Research* 20 (1988): 135-53.

Goins, J.E. *Pocket Knives: Markings of Manufacturers and Dealers* 2nd. ed. Knoxville: Knife World Publications, 1988.

Henry, L.D. Jr. "Fetched by Beauty: Confessions of a Kitsch Addict." *Journal of Popular Culture* 13:2 (1979): 197-208.

Hermann, G. and Soiffer, S.M. "For Fun and Profit: An Analysis of the Urban Garage Sale." *Urban Life* 12 (1984): 397-491.

Highsmith, D. (in press). "Developing a 'Focused' Comic Book Collection in an Academic Library." *Acquisitions Librarian.*

Irwin, J. *Scenes.* Beverly Hills: Sage, 1977.

James, L. *Fiction for the Working Man, 1830-1850.* London: Oxford UP, 1963.

Katz, E. and Lazarsfeld, P.F. *Personal Influence.* Glencoe, IL.: Free P, (1955).

Maisel, R. "The Flea Market as an Action Scene." *Urban Life and Culture* 2 (1974): 488-505.

McCracken, G. *Culture and Consumption.* Bloomington: Indiana UP, (1988).

McInnes, J., Gary, M., Hearn, E., and Hughes, M. (N.D.). *Zoom Shots* Toronto: Nelson.

Morris, D. *Manwatching: A Field Guide to Human Behavior.* London: Jonathan Cape, 1977.

Olmsted, A.D. "Morally Controversial Leisure: the Social World of Gun Collectors." *Symbolic Interaction* 11 (1988): 277-87.

———— "Collecting: Leisure, investment or obsession?" *Journal of Social Behavior and Personality* 6 (1991): 287-306.

Paley, N. "The Collection Connection: The Educational Value of Childrens Collections." *School Library Journal* May (1990): 31-33.

Parker, J.F. and Voyles, J.B. *Price Guide to Collector Knives.* Orlando: The House of Collectibles, 1983.

Rosenberg, B., & White, D.M. (Eds.) *Mass culture reunited*. New York: Van Nostrand Reinhold, 1971.

Schroeder, F.E.H. "Popular Culture Methodologies: A Bibliographic Afterward." *5000 Years of Popular Culture: Popular Culture Before Printing*. Ed. F.E.H. Schroeder. Bowling Green, OH: Bowling Green U Popular P, (1980).

Schwantes, C.A. "The Joy of Timetables." *Journal of Popular Culture* 9 (1975): 604-617.

Serven, J.E. ed. *The Collecting of Guns*. Harrisburg, PA: The Stackpole Company, 1964.

Sherry, J.F. Jr. "A Sociocultural Analysis of a Midwestern American Fleamarket." *Journal of Consumer Research* 17 (1990): 13-30.

Shoop, S. "The Insolt Collection." *Collecting: The Passionate Pastime* Eds. S. Johnston and T. Beddow. London: Viking, 1986.

Shutiak, L. "Collections a Favorite Subject Among Students." *Calgary Herald* 16 March 1986, E8.

Smith, C.W. *Auctions*. New York: The Free P, 1989.

Sobol, K. and Sobol, J.M. "Homegrown Museums." *Canadian Geographic* April/May (1991): 74-82.

Stebbins, R.A. "Serious Leisure: A Conceptual Statement." *Pacific Sociological Review* 25 (1982): 251-72.

Stewart, S. *On Longing: Narratives of the Miniature, the Gigantic, the Souvenir, the Collection*. Baltimore: Johns Hopkins P, (1984).

Thompson, M. *Rubbish Theory: The Creation and Destruction of Value*. New York: Oxford UP, (1979).

Tomeh, A.K., Pearman, W., and Schnabel, J. "A Profile of Antique Collections." *Journal of Popular Culture* 17 (1983): 75-83.

Towner, W. *The Elegant Auctioneers*. New York: Hill & Wang, 1970.

Unruh, D.R. "The Nature of Social Worlds." *Pacific Sociological Review* 23 (1980): 271-96.

Vandergrift, K.E. "Collecting With a Purpose." *School Library Journal* Oct. (1986): 91-95.

Wiseman, J.P. "Close Encounters of the Quasi-primary Kind." *Urban Life* 8 (1979): 23-51.

The Humanities and Cultural Criticism:
The Example of Ralph Ellison

James Seaton

To have been of the past, even to think of and respect the past, is not ipso
facto *to have been wrong or now irrelevant. As James Seaton points out in
the following essay, the time line of ideas is just as continuous as art critics
insist it is in the history of art. And as Seaton correctly cautions it might well
be a serious mistake to unplug the life-sustaining ideas of tradition before we
have new machines to provide present-day sustenance. Seaton's ideas are certainly
relevant and pertinent.*

Literature, history and philosophy continue to be taught at American
universities, but the humanistic tradition which once informed the disciplines
making up the liberal arts seems obsolete, needing not so much rejuvenation
as resuscitation. A new super-discipline has arisen, most often referred to as
cultural studies, which promises to replace the humanistic tradition as the
unifying rubric under which all aspects of human activity are to be studied.
The conception of human activities as symbolic texts provides the charter which
allows literary critics, presumably skilled in rhetorical analysis, to claim the
ability to survey all of human life. This charter, however, requires that this
rhetoric be conceived as entirely non-referential, since any suggestion of a reality
beyond the text would impugn the authority of the cultural critic. If the study
of the humanities once seemed to offer insights into oneself and into human
life in general, cultural studies is premised instead on the rejection of such
possibilities. As Stanley Fish points out, there is no insight to be obtained, since
the "rhetoric" of both texts and human activities is simply "another word for
force" (517). Just as the analyst of wars goes beyond the bounds of social science
in considering which of the combatants is "right" and which "wrong," the
cultural critic oversteps his or her professional expertise in inquiring about the
truth or beauty of the texts subjected to rhetorical analysis. The humanities,
however, depend on a view of human life which allows questions of truth, beauty
and goodness to arise. If the humanities themselves are ever to be rejuvenated,
a revival of a tradition of cultural criticism unavailable to the proponents of
cultural studies is in order.

According to Jacques Barzun, the phrase "cultural criticism" first appeared
in print in Lionel Trilling's essay on "The Sense of the Past," published in
Partisan Review in 1942 and included in Trilling's most influential work, *The
Liberal Imagination.* Barzun says the phrase "arose spontaneously" as he and

Trilling sought to explain what sort of work would be required of the students who enrolled in the seminar the two taught for twenty-five years at Columbia. For Barzun, the connotations of the phrase are almost exactly the opposite of those conveyed by the same phrase today. The cultural criticism taught by Barzun and Trilling is a "non-method" which "presupposes the factitiousness of theory and the unsuitability of system" in attempting to account for works of art and literature (84). The "spirit of cultural criticism" is a kind of higher common sense informed by historical understanding—Trilling's "sense of the past" (83). Their cultural criticism is not a separate discipline, since it possesses no specific methodology or theory of its own; its tools are rather judgment and tact, qualities that can be encouraged and conveyed but not systematized.

In "The Sense of the Past," Lionel Trilling finds a "charter to engage in cultural history and cultural criticism" in a passage from David Hume (185). Hume, one of the greatest philosophical skeptics, seems an unlikely source for an affirmation of the studies generally considered much more problematic than the natural sciences whose pretensions to knowledge of reality were rendered suspect by the *Treatise of Human Nature*. But it appears that Trilling goes to Hume precisely because he is seeking something other than a charter to explain art away by reference to circumstances—instead he is seeking what he calls "a charter to deal with a mystery" (185). Hume does indeed provide Trilling's "charter" when he points out that creative artists do not live in isolation; if it is impossible to penetrate the mind of the individual artist or writer, it is possible to learn something about what Trilling calls the "gross, institutional facts" (193) of the larger society, and thereby make some reasonable inferences about the work of art itself, according to Hume:

The question, therefore, is not altogether concerning the state, genius, and spirit of a few, but concerning those of a whole people; and may, therefore, by accounted for, in some measure, by general causes and principles. (185)

Trilling seeks no more, since he is interested in cultivating the historical sense, the sense of the past, rather than in devising a methodology for the operation of which personal sensibility would be unnecessary.

Whether or not Jacques Barzun is right is claiming that the phrase "cultural criticism" first occurs in "The Sense of the Past," it is clear that the essays which make up *The Liberal Imagination, The Opposing Self* and *Beyond Culture* are part of a tradition which began long before the joint seminars at Columbia. Trilling's own model was undoubtedly Matthew Arnold, who initiated the self-conscious use of literary criticism as a basis for a criticism of society. Just because Arnold recognized that the social function of a literary study no longer seemed self-evident, he felt compelled to explore the ways in which the study of literature could contribute to clarifying the dilemmas of the larger society. Today, of course, Arnold is remembered most often as an advocate for the study of "the best that is known and thought," a defender of a canon based on "high seriousness," a traditionalist and a liberal humanist.

Arnold was indeed all these things. That is enough, for some people, to end the discussion. Terry Eagleton is generous enough to point out that his critique should not be taken to imply "that Matthew Arnold supported nuclear weapons" but he finds Arnold guilty of the moral equivalent: Arnold, like most critics, "...strengthened rather than challenged the assumptions of the power-system" (195). If this charge means that Arnold preferred reforming liberal democratic society to taking his chances, as Eagleton himself would prefer, on the success of "the socialist transformation of society," Arnold is probably guilty as charged (211). In this debate, Eagleton of course enjoys the advantage over Arnold of having been able to consider a number of attempts at "the socialist transformation of society." Whether he has profited from this advantage may be left to the reader to decide.

What is important is that Arnold recognized that the study of literature was no longer self-justifying, even for the elite for whom university educations were available. But Arnold was not concerned with the elite alone. In his essay on "The Function of Criticism at the Present Time" Arnold calls for a criticism whose governing attitude should be *"disinterestedness"* (270), which refuses to "lend itself" to "ulterior, political practical considerations about ideas" and instead makes it its business

simply to know the best that is known and thought in the world, and by in its turn making this known, to create a current of true and fresh ideas. (270)

Terry Eagleton argues that Arnold emphasized that "literature should convey *timeless* truths" as a means of "distracting the masses from their immediate commitments...and so ensuring the survival of private property" (26). In one sense Eagleton's criticism does not go far enough. Arnold not merely argued that literature was not primarily concerned with immediate political issues, he insisted, much more scandalously for Eagleton, that even criticism should aim at disinterestedness rather than engagement. Having said all this, however, it would still be a mistake to categorize and then dismiss Arnold's critical practice as just another example of "middle-class ideology" (26).

Arnold himself urges critical "disinterestedness" not merely for its own sake but also because he believes that criticism can thereby achieve its fullest social impact. The example he offers in "The Function of Criticism at the Present Time" refutes any perception that Arnold's creed entailed an avoidance of unpleasant social realities through immersion in the Great Books. Arnold quotes a politician expatiating on the glories and the virtues of "...the old Anglo-Saxon race...the best breed in the whole world..." (272) and another on the greatness of England:

I look around me and ask what is the state of England? Is not property safe? Is not every man able to say what he likes? Can you not walk from one end of England to the other in perfect security: I ask you whether, the world over or in past history, there is anything like it? Nothing. I pray that our unrivaled happiness may last. (272)

One of the effects of such complacency is to make political change almost impossible, but Arnold argues that complacency will not be penetrated by mere political advocacy. Nor does Arnold attempt to answer by referring to a work of "high seriousness." Arnold instead quotes a story "on which I had stumbled in a newspaper." He argues that it is one of the tasks of criticism to make connections such as he is making between apparently disparate events—in this case, the speeches he quotes and the facts reported in the newspaper story. The critic, at least the cultural critic, must take account of such stories as Arnold finds in the newspaper:

A shocking child murder has just been committed at Nottingham. A girl named Wragg left the work-house there on Saturday morning with her young illegitimate child. The child was soon afterwards found dead on Mapperly Hills, having been strangled. Wragg is in custody. (273)

By itself the story would be terrible but without wider implication. Arnold uses his critical skills to drive home how the newspaper story refutes the speech-makers:

And "our unrivaled happiness";—what an element of grimness, bareness, and hideousness mixes with it and blurs it; the workhouse, the dismal Mapperly Hills,—how dismal those who have seen them will remember;—the gloom, the smoke, the cold, the strangled illegitimate child! "I ask you whether, the world over in past history, there is anything like it?"...and the final touch,—short, bleak, and inhuman: *Wragg is in custody.* The sex lost in the confusion of our unrivaled happiness; or (shall I say?) the superfluous Christian name lopped off by the straight-forward vigour of our old Anglo-Saxon breed! (273-74)

It is true that Arnold does not follow up with a call for "socialist transformation" or even any proposals for welfare reform. The critic, he argues, will persuade "the practical man" who makes speeches like those quoted—and who forms the audience for such speeches—only by the exercise of a disinterestedness which will finally overcome the suspicion that such criticism has an ulterior motive, is interested in something other than the truth. Whether Arnold's strategy is wise may be argued; Jean-Paul Sartre and others have argued eloquently on behalf of a criticism of engagement. After reading such passages, however, it seems difficult to accept Eagleton's characterization of Arnold's criticism as merely a technique for "sweetening" "the pill of middle-class ideology" with "the sugar of literature" (26). A criticism which can take account of the fate of a Wragg at the same time that it attempts "to learn and propagate the best that is known and thought in the world" seems worth salvaging.

Anyone who reads Matthew Arnold's criticism with some of the "disinterestedness" he admired will find evidence that Arnold was concerned about society as a whole. If he argued that criticism should call attention to "the best that is known and thought in the world," it was because he thought that the dissemination of this "best" in society at large would have an invigorating and finally ameliorating effect on social problems, even those problems of crime, poverty and disease which seemed most remote from the realm of high literature.

Except for such notable passages as the one quoted on newspaper prose, however, Arnold spent little time examining works of popular or mass culture. The critics who have continued Arnold's tradition, however, have demonstrated that it is quite possible to pay serious attention to works outside of any particular "canon" without losing sight of the standards implicit in their own sense of "the best that is known and thought in the world." A critic demonstrates respect for works of popular culture in taking them not merely as documents to be examined but as expressions of human feeling and thought, to be confronted with one's whole self as one encounters the great works. In doing so, the critic enriches and even rejuvenates the humanities and the humanistic tradition, remaining true to Terence's saying that "nothing human is alien to me."

There are many examples of such criticism that could be cited, even—or especially—from critics usually dismissed as elitists. One thinks of T.S. Eliot on Marie Lloyd, the dance-hall singer, Edmund Wilson on The Ziegfeld Follies or on a best-seller like *The Robe*, Lewis Mumford on cities, Robert Warshow on *Shane*, or Lionel Trilling on "The Kinsey Report." Except for Trilling himself, none of these authors saw themselves as disciples of Matthew Arnold, and T.S. Eliot defined his own views in some measure by his opposition to Arnold. All these critics, however, shared a willingness to examine the common life with the same seriousness they brought to their study of the monuments of high culture. Their limitations are not the limitations of a method but rather of individual sensibility. Each judged the products of popular or mass culture with the standard they acquired by studying "the best that is known and thought." None patronized the so-called masses by supposing that what they personally despised was still good enough for other people. None avoided personal involvement by adopting the social scientist's pose of objectivity.

The essays of Ralph Ellison, however, go further than those of any of the critics mentioned in working out a rationale for treating works of popular culture according to the highest standards available. More than the rest, as well, he has explored the political implications of his cultural criticism. His essays, finally, demonstrate the power of sensibility and imagination as opposed to methodology. "The Little Man at Chehaw Station," an essay in Ellison's latest collection, *Going to the Territory*, will serve as a representative example.

Ellison tells us that he first heard about the "little man behind the stove" at Chehaw Station as a student at Tuskegee Institute during the mid-1930s. His informant was Hazel Harrison, "a highly respected concert pianist and teacher" (3) whose talents had been recognized in Europe by composers such as Sergei Prokofiev but whose race had prevented such recognition in the United States. She tells the incredulous Ellison that, while it is always important to always play one's best, "in this country, there's something more involved" (4). Here, she says,

"...you must *always* play your best, even if it's only in the waiting room at Chehaw Station, because in this country there'll always be a little man hidden behind the stove...
There'll always be the little man whom you don't expect, and he'll know the *music*, and the *tradition*, and the standards of *musicianship* required for whatever you set out to perform!" (4)

Chehaw Station itself "was a lonely whistle-stop" (4) which, the young Ellison pondered, "was the last place in the area where I would expect to encounter a connoisseur lying in wait to pounce upon some rash, unsuspecting musician" (5).

As the narrator of *Invisible Man* broods over his grandfather's injunction to "overcome 'em with yeses..." (16), so Ellison ponders the meaning of Hazel Harrison's "little man at Chehaw Station." The figure comes to have several meanings for him. He associates the little man "with the metamorphic character of the general American audience...that unknown quality which renders the American audience far more than a receptive instrument that may be dominated..." (6-7). The little man has strong likes and dislikes: "Being quintessentially American, he enjoys the joke, the confounding of hierarchical expectations..." (11). On the other hand, "...he is repelled by works of art that would strip human experience—especially American experience—of its wonder and stubborn complexity" (13).

A description of the taste of the "little man" leaves one wondering about the sources of that taste. Ellison suggests that "the man behind Chehaw's stove" might serve

as a metaphor for those individuals we sometimes meet whose refinement of sensibility is inadequately explained by family background, formal education, or social status. (8)

Perhaps no human being can finally be explained entirely on the basis of environment or circumstances or heredity, but Ellison suggests that "America's social mobility, its universal education, and its relative freedom of cultural information" (8) brings such unpredictability to the fore. Given such uncertainty, "...the chances are that any American audience will conceal at least *one* individual whose knowledge and taste will complement, or surpass" (9) the artist's own. The cultural effect of democracy, thus, is not to depress taste to the same low level but to prevent the simple correspondence of social class or status to cultural tastes or knowledge.

Ellison makes his case by recourse to experience rather than statistics. He presents for the reader's inspection scenes representative, Ellison asserts, of a culture peculiarly American. On a "sunny Sunday afternoon on New York's Riverside Drive" Ellison runs across

a light-skinned, blue-eyed, Afro-American-featured individual...[who]...disrupted the visual peace of the promenading throng by racing up in a shiny new blue Volkswagen Beetle decked out with a gleaming Rolls-Royce radiator...

Clad in handsome black riding boots and fawn-colored riding breeches of English tailoring, he took the curb wielding—with an ultra-pukka-sahib haughtiness—a leather riding crop. A dashy dashiki...flowed from his broad shoulders down to the arrogant, military flare of his breeches-tops, while six feet six inches or so above his heels, a black Homburg hat, titled at a jaunty angle, floated majestically on the crest of his huge Afro-coiffed head. (22)

Who was this individual? The very difficulty of classifying him according to some "rigid ethno-cultural perspective" (23) suggests to Ellison that he is quintessentially American:

Whatever his politics, sources of income, hierarchical status, and such, he revealed his essential "Americanness" in his freewheeling assault upon traditional forms of the Western aesthetic. Whatever the identity he presumed to project, he was exercising an American freedom and was a product of the melting pot and the conscious or unconscious comedy it brews. Culturally, he was an American Joker. (24)

Whatever the artistic or literary tastes of this "American joker" might be, they could be as little predicted by his social class or income as his personal appearance.

Ellison tells another story that makes his point even more emphatically. In the late thirties he found himself in the basement of a tenement in Harlem where he heard

male Afro-American voices, raised in violent argument. The language was profane, the style of speech a Southern idiomatic vernacular such as was spoken by formally uneducated Afro-American working men. (33)

As the young Ellison listened to the voices and gradually became aware of what the argument was about, he began to feel that "a bizarre practical joke had been staged" (33), since

the subject of their contention confounded all my assumptions regarding the correlation between educational levels, class, race, and the possession of conscious culture. Impossible as it seemed, these foul-mouthed black workingmen were locked in verbal combat over which of two celebrated Metropolitan Opera divas was the superior soprano! (34)

When Ellison discovers that the four have been appearing in operas at the Metropolitan as "the finest damn bunch of Egyptians you ever seen" he begins to laugh "in appreciation of the hilarious American joke that centered on the incongruities of race, economic status, and culture" (37).

Perhaps this is the "American joke" to which Henry James referred when, in a famous passage of his study of Hawthorne, he lists all the ways in which the United States differed from the older, hierarchical societies of Europe and thereby made things so difficult for the novelist, concluding that "The American knows that a good deal remains; what it is that remains—that is his secret, his joke, as one may say" (352). In any case, Ellison's understanding of that joke enables him to move from considerations of the tall-tale as folk art to tributes to Charlie Christian and Duke Ellington to appreciations of more canonical figures like Hemingway and Faulkner without the crutch of categorization but with a readiness to be surprised by the unexpected in both art and life. It is one of the greatest defects of contemporary cultural studies, on the one hand, that the rigors of methodology assure that there will be no surprises, that any investigation will only turn up a confirmation of the assumptions with which the study begins.

Ralph Ellison clearly knows a good deal more about the figures described in his essays than Matthew Arnold knew about "Wragg." If "poor Wragg" appears only as a victim, the personalities who crowd Ellison's essays are always granted a full humanity. Yet I do not think it is a mistake to connect Ralph Ellison's essays with a tradition of cultural criticism which may be conveniently dated to Matthew Arnold's essays. Like Arnold, and like Eliot, Trilling, Wilson, Warshow, and Mumford, Ellison brings the insights derived from a study of literature to a consideration of the political, social and cultural dilemmas facing society at large. Ellison, however, probably surpasses all the critics mentioned in his ability to recognize the artistic possibilities of genres outside so-called "high culture." In doing so he enlarges, enriches, one might even say rejuvenates, a tradition of cultural criticism whose revival would go far to hasten the rejuvenation of the humanities as well.

Works Cited

Arnold, Matthew. "The Function of Criticism at the Present Time." *Lectures and Essays in Criticism.* Ed. R.H. Super. *The Complete Prose Works of Matthew Arnold.* Vol. III. Ann Arbor, MI: U of Michigan P, 1962. 258-85.

Barzun, Jacques. "Reckoning with Time and Place." *The Culture We Deserve.* Ed. Arthur Krystal. Middletown, CT: Wesleyan UP, 1989. 75-86.

Eagleton, Terry. *Literary Theory: An Introduction.* Minneapolis: U of Minnesota P, 1983.

Ellison, Ralph. *Invisible Man.* 1952. New York: Vintage, 1972.

———. "The Little Man at Chehaw Station." *Going to the Territory.* 1986. New York: Vintage, 1987. 3-38.

Fish, Stanley. "Force." *Doing What Comes Naturally: Change, Rhetoric, and the Practice of Theory in Literary and Legal Studies.* Durham: Duke UP, 1989. 503-24.

James, Henry. *Hawthorne.* 1872. *Literary Criticism: Essays on Literature, American Writers, English Writers.* New York: Library of America, 1984. 315-474.

Trilling, Lionel. "The Sense of the Past." *The Liberal Imagination: Essays on Literature and Society.* 1950. New York: Doubleday, 1953.

Black Studies and The Humanities:
An Alliance Forged Through Fire

Joyce Pettis

Scholars and scholarship often respond only to pressure, even to threat and demonstration. Such has been the belated awareness among most scholars of the need for study of the lives and life-styles of at least one-tenth of our population, the Blacks in America—and throughout the world. Finally, they are becoming visible, and scholarship, as Joyce Pettis points out in her insightful essay, is finally coming to grips with the opportunities afforded by that scholarship. The essay has all kinds of ramifications for rejuvenating the humanities.

Significant changes in the humanities curricula that moved it from parochialism toward inclusiveness should and can be traced to the onset of Black Studies. Initially, neither group embraced their alliance favorably. Black Studies advocates insisted on autonomy and separatism from conventional university structures while administrators and professors resisted Black Studies programs, preferring instead the Eurocentric education firmly in place in American colleges and universities and resenting the political imperatives of Black Studies advocates. However antagonistic each group was to the ideology of the other, the interdisciplinary nature of Black Studies logically dictated its inclusion under the humanities umbrella. Indeed, its addition offered an opportunity for the humanities to eliminate elitism and to live up to its philosophical objectives. A group commissioned to study the humanities affirmed the philosophy and definition: "Through the humanities we reflect on the fundamental question what does it mean to be human?" Through continual inquiry the humanities reveal

how individuals or societies define the moral life and try to attain it, attempt to reconcile freedom and the responsibilities of citizenship, and express themselves artistically. The humanities do not necessarily mean humaneness...but *by awakening a sense of what it might be like to be someone else or to live in another time or culture, they tell us about ourselves, stretch our imagination, and enrich our experience. They increase our distinctively human potential*...The essence of the humanities is a spirit or attitude toward humanity. They show how the individual is autonomous and at the same time bound, in the ligatures of language and history, to human kind across time and throughout the world. The humanities are an important measure of the values and aspirations of any society. (emphasis added, Commission 1-3)

I have quoted extensively here because the mission of the humanities contained within the statement encompasses and necessitates the inclusion of marginalized and underrepresented cultural/racial/ethnic groups in the objective of learning about others and consequently gaining self-knowledge. Before the late sixties the humanities violated the very ideology that had defined its mission. To become inclusive meant drastic changes in the active practices of university humanities divisions.

"The humanities (excluding history) were always the most Eurocentric of American scholarly fields. English, literature, philosophy, art history, and music were, in the sixties, the fields least touched by subject matter having to do with black Americans," Nathan Huggins writes to the Ford Foundation in a commissioned report (39). Certainly these were the very areas, including history, where African American experiences were plentiful and shaped an accurate and meaningful representation of the American experience. They called attention not only to the global nature of the black experience but also to the presence of other ethnic groups and their interaction with and influence on the dominant culture. In their insistence on Black Studies programs, advocates explicitly urged the demise of the warped view of human experience that advocated the intellectual tradition of only one group of people and proffered that view as universal. Black Studies therefore pointed the way toward multicultural studies and the heterogeneous characteristics of so-called American culture. Walter Enloe and Rancy Morris, writing from the Hiroshima International School, Japan, reinforce in the eighties the argument made by Black Studies scholars and students in the sixties:

[The disciplines of] traditional humanities education...focus primarily on the western cultural tradition. If we are able to be true to the ideal of a global world view, this is obviously an incomplete approach to what it means to be human. The enforced dichotomy between western and non-western traditions is, by its very nomenclature, an arrogant and ethnocentric expression of what is important and what is not. Such a dichotomy encourages the study of human differences rather than stressing features common to the family of mankind. (78)

The rise of Black Studies curricula in the nation's universities is connected to the success of the Civil Rights Movement, desegregation, and substantial enrollment of African American students at predominantly Anglo American universities. Instituting the programs was far from an easy accomplishment, however. The experience of students in different parts of the country—at Earlham College, Richmond, Indiana, and at Cornell University, Ithaca, New York— for example, reflects the turmoil that surrounded Black Studies. In 1968 in their demand for a curriculum inclusive of Black history and culture, students at Earlham demonstrated and took over a small retreat cabin where part of the college faculty was meeting (Hatchett 14). At Cornell in January 1968, black students protested the "covert racism" of a white professor and subsequently armed themselves and occupied the student union building. According to Nathan Huggins, the adversity in establishing a black studies program was occurring simultaneously, and agreement was reached September 1968. The administration resisted requests that the program be established as "an autonomous all-black

college" initially, but made some concessions by mid-May 1969 "in the wake
of the most potentially explosive racial conflicts ever on a northern campus."
Neither autonomous nor all-black, the program was "one of the most separatist
and most political in the country" (24). Like other efforts to legitimize the African
American experience, resistance and accusations of standards being lowered
pursued efforts to offer Black Studies programs.

In the days of their inception in the late sixties and early seventies, the
validity of Black studies programs was questioned by many academicians. Some
of them offered the argument that these programs fostered a separatist perspective
for African American students which countered the objective of an "American"
education. The "nihilist, irrational, or anarchistic tendencies" of separatist
doctrines were pointed out by other opponents (Cruse 5). That Black Studies
programs had their origins in politically charged climates rather than in an
academically sanctioned "search for truth" made them automatically suspect.
Whether a viable intellectual tradition could support a study of the Black
experience was another question. Donald Henderson lists other objections to
the inclusion of Black Studies programs, including the charges that they offered
circumvention of rigorous academic performance in conventional programs; and
that they trained black revolutionaries (10-11). Others charged that there would
be no jobs for graduates trained in Black Culture and History. In addition to
its academic base, the liaison services of Black studies programs such as counseling
and retention, black graduate student recruitment, affirmative action in staff
and faculty hiring and promotions, and community programs were targets of
attack. Such services were said to offer preferential treatment and to coddle
students.

Although organizers and advocates of the programs often dissented about
their structures—whether they should be programs or studies or departments
or institutes or centers—and disagreed about whether the name most appropriately
might be Black, Afro-American or Africana studies, they agreed on the necessity
of instituting Black Studies on university campuses. Black Studies has become
the accepted designation, according to Nick Aaron Ford, "for all studies primarily
concerned with the experience of people of African origin residing in any part
of the world." It includes the experiences of "Africans, Afro-Americans, Afro-
Asians, Afro-Europeans, and African descendants of the Caribbean and other
island territories" (3). Although there was less disagreement about the essential
content of the programs, their function in the university, their grounding in
black intellectual tradition, and their role in shaping an Afrocentric perspective
in students, diversity among the programs established was the rule rather than
the exception.

Courses in art, history, literature, intellectual thought, music, language and/
or linguistics in Black Studies programs that were born amidst tense conditions
non-conducive for their growth and survival have flourished in most instances.
They have immeasurably enriched the humanities curricula in the universities
of the nation and in doing so have wounded (and rightly so) the concept of
Eurocentric studies, although advocates of Western tradition have entrenched
themselves for a battle. Revitalizing the humanities has most noticeably occurred
through the inclusion of studies that call attention to the specific history and
culture of different groups within the American culture mosiac and through

ongoing scholarly research in these fields. The artistry of African American women, whether expressed in their flower gardens or from their sewing baskets, has become a part of scholarly inquiry, as has, for example, the mental and physical survival of Harriet Jacobs, an enslaved 19th century women living in North Carolina; and the 1890s rhetoric of articulate feminist Anna Cooper, calling for an end to the second class citizenship of African American women. The inclusion of these women as well as myriad subjects in the African American experience has not only enlarged knowledge in the humanities but has formed a context for reversing the calculated subordination and distortion that had previously attended scholarly studies of Black life in academic disciplines.

Intellectual inquiry about the African diaspora as well as about interaction and influence between African Americans and the dominant culture in the United States has never been more active. The research of a new generation of African American scholars, many of whom began as undergraduates in Black Studies curricula in the late sixties and seventies, as well as scholars not of African ancestry has stimulated intellectual inquiry in the black experience. Much of this research encourages the development of cross cultural and interdisciplinary courses, particularly in history, literature, and the social sciences. Moreover, since many Black Studies programs emphasize community empowerment, their outreach efforts deserve recognition for helping to alter the racist image of predominantly white universities in black communities. Assisting the black community in acknowledging a changing university responsive to its total community also has the potential of creating interaction between humanists and marginalized members of the community and of extending the inquiry of the humanist beyond university walls.

Black Studies curricula, according to a report commissioned by the Ford Foundation, has become useful in recruiting Black students. Recruitment personnel point out the courses to substantiate the commitment of the university to addressing the culture and history of its ethnic and minority student population. Support services such as tutoring programs and counselors trained in Africentric psychology that are connected to Black Studies programs guarantee that special needs of students have been anticipated and provided for. Programs that two decades ago were disparaged have now become critical to university recruitment and retention of African American students.

Just as the Civil Rights Movement created the impetus for the Women's Rights Movement and became a model for its organization and protest tactics, (Loiacono 26), Black Studies models have provided the impetus and organizational model for several other minority and ethnic/racial-specific programs, among them women's, Hispanic/Latino, Asian American, Jewish, and Native American studies. These programs, too, have functioned in the best interests of the humanities in fulfilling its mission to investigate what it means to be human. Both the courses in Black Studies and other ethnic/racial studies programs have forced the humanities to incorporate the Other as a vital part of human experience.

The impetus of Black Studies in the humanities and the presence of other ethnic/racial studies programs have provided the thrust for multicultural studies underway at many universities and in high school curricula. Administrators at the University of Texas, to cite one example, believe multicultural education will be crucial to education in the 1990s. Multiculturalism in reference to university curriculum "means ensuring that courses in each college and school reflect an appreciation of the contributions that all cultures have made to civilization," according to Texas Vice Provost George C. Wright (4). When contributions of ethnic or racial groups purport equity with traditional courses, however, resistance ensues. Predictably, the response to multiculturalism, both on campus and in the community, recalls memories of the response that Black Studies initially received, but with slightly altered debate. This time around, opponents say that "some courses are a subterfuge for professors wishing to push narrow political agendas" (Wright 4). Fear that tradition is being sacrificed or eroded for inclusiveness and diversity seems the element most common to arguments against change. Concern that education is being underserved and diminished somehow when the culture and experiences of other groups become part of academic inquiry is merely thinly disguised racist bunk by those who wish to maintain the dominance of Eurocentrism. In northern Wisconsin, with the purpose of fighting racism, a curriculum in public education that includes the history and culture of the Chippewa Tribe has been mandated because the experience of Native Americans is misrepresented and distorted. One vocal opponent objected to the proposed curriculum because it does not teach equality, saying, ironically, "We're all the same" (9 April 1991, PBS-WUNC). No one argued for equity, of course, when the experiences of the Chippewa were omitted in the schools.

As happened with the birth of Black Studies, much of the debate and battle about multiculturalism will occur in the humanities. Even the terminology of change—accusations that a revolution is underway—remains the same. In the sixties, humanities divisions resisted the concept of Black Studies but more than two decades later have apparently accepted them and bask in the glory that many Black Studies scholars reflect on the university. The debate surrounding multicultural education offers yet another chance for the humanities to take the positive lead in asserting that multicultural education, as Black Studies curricula have illustrated, neither impairs nor denigrates the university education. The humanities by virtue of its mission and ideology has the opportunity to participate responsibly in the process of reconfiguring what we mean by "American culture" and what society values; has the opportunity to participate in the opening of minds too long closed and to insure that the minds of a new generation remain open. Moreover, if implementation of multicultural education is undertaken with positive expectations, humanities scholars will have created an opportunity to interact with and influence a public that often misunderstands or devalues what the humanities accomplish in the effort to understand human experience in society. Black Studies programs should become the model for how the humanities must respond to the fire surrounding multicultural education.

The best reward for promoting and incorporating a multicultural perspective in the university, as two decades have proven is true of Black Studies, will accrue to the students, the future humanists and population of tomorrow's world. It is they who will interact among the diverse population predicted by the U.S. Department of Labor to make up 29 percent of the additions to the work force between 1985 and 2000 (*Black Issues* 4).

When the legitimacy of Black Studies programs was under debate, perhaps the most eloquent arguments in their behalf belonged to those advocates who postulated that the curriculum would immeasurably enhance not only the sense of presence in the world community for Black students but also build self esteem and racial pride in the knowledge gained from the courses. Courses in the history, art, music, literature, or philosophy of African Americans as well as other ethnic and racial groups also perform a vital function in the education of all students who avail themselves of the information. The mission of the university committed to comprehensive education for all its students is obligated to create and maintain an atmosphere of openness. It can not be suspected of supporting the view that certain courses of study exist only for certain ethnic or racial groups. With the weight of the university behind them, both Black Studies and ethnic studies curricula in alliance with humanities divisions might reasonably achieve the comprehensive education that they strive to offer.

An argument for an expanded curriculum in the humanities that is reflective of the changing world population is also an argument for expanding students' course requirements in the humanities. Certainly it is an appeal that all students in the university be required to enroll in a course whose focus addresses the multicultural composition of the nation. This proposal seems minimal at best, but can continue the process of inclusiveness that began in the midst of anger, resistance, and fire in the 1960s. Attitudes in the humanities have changed since that charged period. No other alliances need be forged through fire; they should be made because through the spirit of openmindedness and commitment to understanding, the humanities continues its inquiry into understanding about all people and enriching the experience of being human.

Works Cited

Commission on the Humanities. *The Humanities in American Life*. California: U of California P, 1980.

Cruse, Harold. "The Integrationist Ethic as a Basis for Scholarly Endeavors." *Black Studies in the University*. Ed. Armstead Robinson, Craig C. Foster, and Donald H. Ogilvie. New York: Yale UP, 1969. 4-12.

Enloe, Walter and Randy Morris. "A Global Perspective for the Humanities." *The Crises in the Humanities: Interdisciplinary Responses*. Ed. Sara Putzell-Dorab and Robert Detweiler. Spain: Jose Porrua Turanzas, S.A., 1983. 75-90.

Ford, Nick Aaron. *Black Studies: Threat-or-Challenge*. New York: Kennikat P, 1973.

Hatchett, David. *Crisis* Feb. (1988): 14-21.

Henderson, Donald. "What Direction Black Studies?" *Topics in Afro-American Studies*. Ed. Henry J. Richards. New York: Black Academy P, 1971. 9-26.

Huggins, Nathan. *Afro-American Studies*. New York: Ford Foundation, Office of Reports, 1985.

Loiacono, Stephanie. "Blacks and the Women's Movement." *Crisis* 96:9 (1989): 45-46.

"Texas Grapples With Multicultural Curriculum Issue." *Black Issues in Higher Education* 7:22 (1991): 4.

Rejuvenating the Humanities—Learning Communities

Jack Estes

The cauldron of ideas in American education supposedly boils constantly and throws redhot ideas that set us all ablaze. Unfortunately generally the cauldron is merely a hot-mud pot that marks us not as clean advocates of new and useful ideas but as thinkers who are too slow to get out of the way of the dust of the past. In other words, often the upsurge of ideas is not a growth of new ideas so much as regrowth of old timbers. But not always. Occasionally new ideas do get mixed in, sometimes with consequential results. Such, as discussed below by Jack Estes, has been the experiment of the TESC. This is a cauldron into which experiment was thrown and out of which bubbled some bright and useful ideas, not for education alone but for the growth and expansion of the Humanities.

Higher education in the state of Washington nearly lost its balance twenty years ago with the establishment of a new four-year college. Known as The Evergreen State College (TESC), the school soon developed a reputation as the "hippie school," the students soon acquired the labels "greeners," and conservative legislators soon developed some concerns about the way they had voted.

Because of the pressures of the sixties, this new college broke with traditional colleges and universities by offering courses with no grades, by admitting students based partially upon their non-academic qualifications (so as to add to the multicultural makeup of the campus), by hiring faculty with no chance of tenure or rank, by providing no separate and discreet classes, and by removing from the faculty any requirement to publish.

TESC created two main credit-gathering methods: "contracts" and "programs." With contracts, students create their own individually adapted courses in which they can work one-on-one with a faculty member; one student, for example, wrote a novel as her quarter's work, studying with a faculty member who was both a critic and a novelist herself. With programs, students work in larger group courses which are results of coordinated efforts involving two to four faculty members and which last from one quarter to three quarters.

Now, after controversy and challenge, after three presidents (including former Sen. Dan Evans), and after nearly twenty graduations, TESC has emerged as one of the top small liberal arts colleges in the entire country. When other colleges are having trouble filling their spaces, TESC has a long waiting list. And when other colleges are busy analyzing and scrutinizing their curriculums, TESC has become a model.

One outgrowth of this system has been a state-supported association called The Center for the Improvement of Undergraduate Education, better known as "The Center." This association has been challenging educators to look at their curriculums and at the multi-cultural makeup of their student body, encouraging colleges and universities in the area to experiment with educational processes and various forms of assessment, and—perhaps most emphatically— to work with various forms of "learning communities."

I've been spending the past several months studying these learning communities, hoping to find out just what all the enthusiasm has been about. I've been visiting colleges and universities around the Puget Sound region to find out who's doing what, and why and how it's working (or even *if* it's working). Mainly, I want to know why these faculty counterparts of mine at other colleges seem to be so excited about teaching when I have been feeling so burned out and so anticipatory of retirement.

Learning communities is a term which refers to any classroom system in which groups of students and groups of professors combine their work. This system could consist of a coordination of syllabuses between an American literature professor and an American history professor, for example, to encourage students signed up for both classes to find the connections between the subjects. Or it could go so far as to become what The Center refers to as "coordinated studies programs," the jewel of the learning community approach.

The coordinated studies programs are known to turn around a faculty member's dragging career and a student's dark future.

What have I found out about these programs? This much is true: they are only limited by three factors: administrative support, colleague cooperation, and imagination. A typical course might include professors from three diverse disciplines—humanities, social sciences, and natural sciences, for example— working together under a single general theme—The Global Village, to suggest one that has been done. Such a course enables students to recognize connections among such disciplines that they would only coincidentally run into on their own, if they do at all. It also enables faculty to work with colleagues whom they respect but with whom they may have only a passing-in-the-mailroom acquaintance. It nearly always results in a renewed appreciation for one's colleague's discipline.

In Washington, these courses may have started at The Evergreen State College, but they have since been adopted by several other schools, particularly—and with a vengeance—by the community colleges. Washington's extensive two-year college system has discovered coordinated studies (thanks to the Center) and has found out how to adapt it to their programs. Among the methods of adapting these courses, the two-year schools offer these programs as types of gathering places for more standard courses. In other words, students don't receive credit for taking a coordinated studies course (which probably would not be recognized by transfer institutions); instead they receive credit in the traditional courses that are included within the overall coordinated studies theme.

In order to illustrate what all this means, I'll use the example of The Televised Mind, one of the most popular of the coordinated studies courses. This course began in 1986 at Bellevue Community College and has since been re-presented at three other colleges. In this course, three or four professors (the number varies somewhat from institution to institution) team up during one quarter to explore with their students the effects of television on American values. The students earn fifteen to eighteen quarter credits for their work. This, as you might guess, is the only course each student will take for that term; likewise this is the only course each of the professors will teach during that term.

My first response to a description such as the one above was great envy. It sounded too good to be true. What was the catch? I've since learned—and those who have done it emphasize—that the faculty members involved have never worked harder than with these courses. The classes are large, needing sixty or seventy students in order to justify the number of faculty. In addition, the classes need to meet at least as many hours each week as they are granting in credit. Thirdly, regarding the faculty work involved: these courses need to be carefully— scrupulously, in fact—planned prior to their being offered and during the quarter. A professor can't very well wait until the last minute and put together what he or she will be doing that day; instead each class day is developed "by committee." We all know how long that takes.

The Televised Mind course could, as an illustration, meet from Tuesday through Thursday from 8:30 to 2:30 with an hour off for lunch (although the lunches are frequently taken as a group). During the days, the faculty schedule discussions, writing workshops, group projects, films, guest speakers, student presentations, and seminars. Amount of lecturing varies from faculty member to faculty member, but generally the traditional lecturing is discouraged. One way the large class is handled (since the lecturing is minimalized) is through "seminar groups," referred to by the experienced professors as the key to a successful coordinated studies course. The seminar groups meet once or twice a week for ninety minutes to discuss the readings or other assignments among themselves, faculty members serving only as facilitators. Faculty also hold a seminar, sometimes known as the "fishbowl," in which they get together to discuss the book or article of the week and to which the students may come to observe. Remember that these students are frequently freshman or sophomores, students who haven't had much experience with the seminar mode of learning. The fishbowl gives them an opportunity to observe what a seminar can be, how through the give-and-take of a freely discussed topic some interesting ideas can emerge. They then, theoretically, will model their own seminar performance after these observations.

With The Televised Mind course, students receive credit for a choice of courses from the fields of anthropology, English, history, and sociology—eighteen credits maximum in all. Each faculty chooses which credits to offer. On the student's transcripts, only the courses which the student finally decides upon will appear. Here is where these courses vary from those multi-disciplinary courses which colleges have frequently offered. Even TESC, after which the entire system modeled these courses, gives credit for the coordinated studies course rather than for the separate courses which might make up the course.

Another change is that the community colleges offer traditional grades for the students in these courses, unlike TESC which offers no grades. On the other hand, this subject of grades is still being experimented with. Much more self-assessment seems to be in vogue rather than the normal teacher-to-student one-way assessment. Faculty also cooperate with their colleagues to give the single grade for their entire program rather than try to break the grade down according to the various courses. For example, in The Televised Mind, a student might receive an A- for all eighteen credits rather than have each instructor grade according to his or her discipline (e.g., a B in English 101, An A in Sociology 110, and a B+ in History 120).

Students are generally fascinated with coordinated studies courses and frequently sign up for other courses taught in the same manner. When they do go back into a more conventional classroom, they often find themselves frustrated by their distance from the instructor and their alienation from their classmates. In their coordinated studies programs, they had come to know their classmates in ways that they never get to know them in other classes. Coordinated studies classes encourage group work and cooperative education rather than individual endeavors. Students frequently eat lunches together; they go on field trips together; they work on papers and videos and slide presentations together. Several programs require student work within the community in which the students find social services to perform that somehow relate to the course they're studying: tutoring, counseling, political organizing, helping the homeless, coaching, reading to the elderly. Work such as that not only makes a difference in the students' lives but also draws the students together in unique and special ways.

The Televised Mind, as I explained, focuses on the ways in which the media, particularly television, affect each one of us. As part of the study of this topic, students need to develop a media literacy beyond which they possess at the beginning of the course. One important component of media literacy is an understanding of the tools; therefore, each student is required to create a video (ten to thirty minutes long) in which some aspect of their community is examined. The idea is not only to help the students learn about scripting, shooting, and editing but also to help them learn about point of view, about how they can manipulate truth through what they choose to show and how they choose to show it.

This aspect of the course relies upon some access to the tools, and faculty have become rather creative in this area as well. In some cases, the students make use of community access opportunities from the local cable companies; in others, they make use of their own or their parents' cameras. Rough editing can be taught with the use of two VCRs, although most colleges in the Puget Sound area now have straight-cut editing units for the use of students.

Coordinated studies courses are centered on themes, and the themes vary from faculty team to faculty team. Basically the single ingredient that shows up on most themes is a heavy emphasis on writing. Consequently, nearly every coordinated studies course includes an English composition component. It seems to be the way in which these colleges have responded to the call for Writing-Across-The-Curriculum. But usually the English composition instructor isn't the only professor who grades the writing assignments. This is shared just as all the other aspects of the course are shared.

Here are a few other themes which have been used in area colleges in their coordinated studies courses:

a. English and Business classes taught in a course called "Rethinking the Future: The Workworld of the 21st Century" (a course which uses the *Wall Street Journal* as one of its primary texts);

b. English and Philosophy classes in a course called "Autonomy and Community: The Dialectic of Liberty";

c. English and Literature in a course called "In Search of Meaning: A Study in Drama";

d. English and Speech in "Turning Points: Crises and Choices";

e. English and Philosophy in "Self-Discovery";

f. English, Philosophy, and Anthropology in "Religion and Culture: the Sacred in a Disenchanted World";

g. English and Math in "The Joy of Math and English";

h. English, History, and Literature in "The American Character";

i. English and International Studies in "Cultural Pluralism: Language, Life and Labor";

j. English and History in "Our Heritage: A Search for a Common Past";

k. English, Philosophy, and Psychology in "The Self: Looking Inward";

l. English, Biology, and Sociology in "People and the Earth: In Search of Harmony";

m. English, Philosophy, and Anthropology in "The Self and Society";

n. English, Biology, and Psychology in "Of Body and Mind";

o. English and Sociology in "Our ways of Knowing: The Black Experience and Social Change";

p. English, Sociology, and History in "Life, Liberty, and the Pursuit of Happiness."

As I said, the imagination is really the main limiting factor in finding themes. In theory, the more diverse the disciplines the more intriguing the course. A popular culture study, for example, could easily include professors from science as well as the humanities. As a means of adding a new look to the humanities, such a course could explain the ways in which technology has contributed to the growth and impact of popular culture (the printing press, film, television, computers, fax machines, etc.).

Besides the need for writing as a way of expressing the ideas about any of the courses studied, the use of English composition classes has another effect: it helps fill these courses. Since composition is a required class—and a challenging class—at most undergraduate institutions, students look for opportunities to get that course over with. The coordinated studies courses provide such opportunities. In fact, frequently these courses allow students to sign up for two or three different composition courses, depending on which ones they might need.

There are problems with these courses, however. For one, as already mentioned, faculty work harder than they do in their traditional courses. A faculty member needs to work with his or her colleagues in thinking out a course and in planning each step. No longer can that individual make all the decisions by him- or herself. Furthermore, a professor is required to work with these colleagues all quarter long. Arguments sometimes arise, as you might expect, and the professors need to work things out or face a long and uncomfortable term. Ideally, of course, the loads of work are fairly equally shared. One administrator I interviewed somewhat sadly mentioned that he did have one course which split during the fifth or sixth week. It caused all sorts of problems, but the faculty simply couldn't get along any further, and one walked out. (That was the only instance I heard of, however, in which such a problem occurred.)

Another problem for some faculty is that the time commitment means very little time for one's own research and writing. This isn't much of a problem in community colleges where such work is usually downplayed, but in four-year colleges this could certainly be a concern. On the other hand, coordinated studies courses offer opportunities for students to do their own presentations at regional conferences. As program chair for the Northern Pacific Popular Culture Association, I have had the joy of including several students from such courses on the regional programs. They have frequently stolen the show, and their presence has certainly been a shot in the arm for the conference as a whole.

Coordinated studies courses require administrative cooperation. Such courses need to be promoted, particularly at first and often in special press releases or posters. And the administration must assure that the course will be taught even if only half the allotted students sign up. Too much work goes into the development of the course ahead of time for the faculty to have the course dropped if it is under-enrolled. Occasionally, in fact, a faculty team is given a reduced load or a stipend to develop the course. (Actually, in Washington, The Center provides some "seed money" to get such courses started.)

Small schools with one-person departments provide particular problems. This is another area in which administrative support is required. If we have only one person teaching all the history classes at the school, for example, then that teacher may not be able to put all his or her efforts into a single course for the entire quarter. The administrator must be willing to hire a part-timer for that quarter, or perhaps must be willing to forego the offering of one or two courses ordinarily offered.

Another way this difficulty is handled is by creating a ten-credit coordinated studies course rather than a fifteen- or eighteen credit course. This way the history professor might be able to offer the courses ordinarily offered and still participate in the coordinated studies.

Another problem with the coordinated studies programs is that students don't have the same freedoms of withdrawing that they often do in traditional courses. If this is the only course the student is taking for the term, and if it is worth fifteen or eighteen credits, then that student may not be able to drop out after the fifth week or so. A consequence of this, however, is that the completion rate of students in coordinated studies courses is usually well over ninety percent.

For both the students' and the faculties' sakes, The Washington Center strongly recommends that a contract (known as a "covenant") be drawn up and signed by all participants in the program. This spells out as clearly as possible the expectations of students and the expectations of faculty. Some programs have actually assigned the development of the covenant as the first project for the students.

The coordinated studies programs, of course, have several variations. One popular variation is referred to as "linked courses." In this type of course, two or three courses are connected through a seminar. In this way, three professors could teach their discreet classes, but these classes would be coordinated around a central theme. Students would be encouraged to sign up for all three, but they wouldn't be required to do so. A separate seminar would enable these students to meet together and discuss the topics that they had in common. Such a seminar is often facilitated by what's termed a "master learner," an upper-division student or even a retired faculty member who sits in on all the classes involved and then attends the seminar to work with the students. Mainly the professors involved don't care too much for this approach since it defeats much of the significance of "learning communities," particularly that element of interaction among the faculty. On the other hand, it does give the students the opportunity to make those important connections among their classes, those connections which are so often glossed over or even missed entirely without some sort of guidance.

Learning communities have given Washington education and Washington educators a powerful jolt. Faculty who were ready to retire are finding new reasons to teach. They're finding themselves filled with opportunities to experiment with their courses, to include those elements of their disciplines which might have excited them to begin with. They're able to include non-traditional elements of education in their courses: popular film, rock and roll music, dinner parties. And they're finding students who are no longer merely going through the paces in order to earn grades but who are going beyond the assignments time after time, who are willing to work harder than usual since the courses are so frequently connected to what they see in the "real world." This is a system in which teachers actually teach and students actually learn.

Did someone say something about "rejuvenating the humanities"?

Architecture and the Humanities

Rodney Douglas Parker

Even the most casual observer among us realizes the impact that our built environment has upon us. If we are what we eat, wear, read, see, we are also the physical environment we have built to live in. That environment, driven by democracy, is becoming ever-increasingly an everyday, vernacular environment. Architect Louis Sullivan once observed that architecture is something designed to raise the eyelids. Such an idealistic philosophy is, for better or worse, giving way to a more realistic point of view. People are no longer exactly content to have architects who apparently never lived in a high-rise or worked in a hundred-story office building design a skyscraper a mile high. But such architects must take into consideration the human element, which might refuse to work in such an artificial separation from mother earth. People fear that they might discover that such an office building is like the high-rise housing for the poor which has now been declared unacceptable, and designed by architects who knew nothing about the poor. Architecture, as Parker points out, is sibling to the humanities, and as such should not forget its origins.

Architecture is often thought of as the technical discipline of building structures for human occupation. In this conception, architecture becomes chiefly a specialized branch of engineering, with architects being more or less technologists who only design specific-use constructions such as shopping centers, schools, or hospitals. Ironically, this notion of architecture as the science of building construction has led to an additional concept of the opposite extreme, namely, architecture as expressing the personal taste of avant-garde geniuses. With these two polar views we find perhaps the routine understanding of architecture: either as idiosyncratic expressionism or the mere result of construction science.

Apart from these extreme conceptions lies yet another—one that is probably more accurate and more profound. This more substantive conception emerges when we view architecture in light of the humanities. Following Browne and Marsden ("Non-Work Time and the Humanities") we may define the humanities as "those elements in culture which respond to the basic human needs in all of us...the ties that bind us together as *homo sapiens*." Given this definition, it can be argued that architecture is more profitably understood and more accurately construed as an art that responds to some of our most vital needs—physical, mental, spiritual and cultural—as human beings. Further, it can be stated that out of human needs grow basic values. Thus, rather than being solely the science of building construction or mere solipsistic expression, architecture can be shown to be more profoundly the humanistic discipline which in effect recognizes, shapes and preserves fundamental human values. As such we can say that architecture, like the humanities, helps tell us who we are and what we have been. To go a step further, we may provisionally consider the relation between architecture and the humanities a reciprocal one. Inasmuch as the examination of human thought, values, and institutions is the chief subject of the humanistic disciplines, these disciplines both support and are supported by the art and interpretation of architecture. We shall examine both sides of this reciprocal relationship. To fully understand the character of architecture, however, we will concentrate primarily on architecture's contribution to humane studies.

To be effective, the practice of architecture, like the practice of its sister visual arts, requires an either open or implicit contact with humanistic studies. The great Renaissance architect Leon Battista Alberti offered some sage advice for painters that applies as well for architects. In his treatise *On Painting*, Alberti counseled the artist to become as "learned as possible in all the liberal arts."[1] Particularly in order to identify subject matter of substantive content, the artist, Alberti advised, should associate regularly with poets and orators. *Invention*, the choice of subject matter, was the real key to a successful artwork:

Therefore I advise that each painter should make himself familiar with poets, rhetoricians, and others equally well learned in letters. They will give new inventions or at least aid in beautifully composing the [dramatic content] through which the painter will surely acquire much praise and renown in his painting.[2]

More recently, architect David Clarke has made a point quite similar to Alberti's. Clarke observes recent "high" architecture's failure to make contact with the general public; he warns that as a consequence, the future of the profession may be in jeopardy. To halt the increasing erosion of public support, Clarke recommends the re-integration of architectural education with the needs of society. A crucial first step in this process should be "that future architects be taught liberal arts in the college of liberal arts."[3] Through this direct contact with the humanistic disciplines architectural students would better "learn about the culture and society they are supposed to design for," from people much like their future clients. This grounding in the humanities is essential, says Clarke, but not just as a source for clever ideas. More importantly it prepares for the development of astute critical judgment, "the sort of judgment that supports sound decision-making and allocation of resources."[4]

Currently, if the architect is to stay tuned to his or her client society, much more than the study of standard canonical works of literature and history is required. Society now develops at a rapid pace in ways never imagined before. The kind of humanistic study necessary now must broadly embrace the vehicles of both popular and formal culture, culture that includes advertising, the electronic media, film, popular music and print journalism. The clients and users of this and future generations of architecture evidence their needs in a growing variety of ways. They are as likely to show their values through patronage of commercial television, movies, and weekly magazines as through the latest literary theory or the ascendant style in classical music. The mind of the contemporary public does not restrict itself to well-worn paths as it seeks expression and entertainment. To fully understand contemporary culture, the architect now needs to constantly monitor any activity, at all levels, where human effort and thought have left expressive marks.

The humanities, thus more comprehensively taken, aid the architect in understanding the essential conditions of his or her work. Put differently, they foster a refined awareness of the people, issues and ideas to which the architectural design must respond. But to the extent we can see architecture resting on a foundation of humane thought and values, we can also see architecture as both embodying and helping promulgate those same values and convictions.

Several thinkers have advanced our understanding of the substantial connection between architectural form and human values. G.W.F. Hegel's seminal discussion of the philosophy of art formed the critical groundwork of twentieth-century architectural theory. Lecturing in the 1820s, Hegel asserted that man has an essential need to externalize his consciousness, to make his thoughts visible in the objective, material world. "[M]an draws out of himself and puts *before himself* whatever he is and whatever else is," says Hegel; moreover man "as spirit *duplicates* himself...and only on the strength of this active placing himself before himself is he spirit."[5] In this need lies the origin of the work of art, and consequently the work of architecture. Human beings artistically use built form as one means of placing before themselves an objective correlate of their subjective reality. Man in this manner consciously alters the exterior world of nature to manifest his own being, thus managing "to strip the external world of its inflexible foreignness and to enjoy in the shape of things only an external realization of himself."[6] In this attempt to strip the world of its uncanniness, humans strive to make themselves feel *at home*. And it is with this sense of at-homeness, familiarity, and self-recognition that architecture establishes *places* for human preservation and habitation.

This removal of nature's strangeness was best reflected for Hegel in "romantic" or Gothic architecture, for him the highest form of the medium. In the Gothic church the sense of enclosure was dominant, says Hegel. Its sanctuary strictly avoided the fully open colonnades typical in Greek temples. Rather, this romantic "Germanic" architecture aspired to release the worshipping assembly from the external world of nature. Combined with soaring shafts, pillars and pointed arches, the fully enclosed interior physically concretized the needs of a freely aspiring assembly of worshippers preoccupied with inward contemplation.[7] "The spatial enclosure corresponds to the concentration of the mind within, and results from it," states Hegel. The Christian assembly concentrates itself on its inner life while simultaneously seeking an "elevation above the finite," the everyday world of nature.[8] Romantic form not only manifests this value, for the medieval faithful it served to preserve and encourage it as well.

German art theory, of course, was immediately influenced by Hegel's thinking. The art historian Franz Kugler followed Hegel and offered one of the more insightful characterizations of the role of monumental art and architecture. Human thought, in addition to needing outward projection, requires being grounded to a definite place or *locus* where it can remain openly accessible.

The source of art lies in the need of mankind to bind his thought to a stable location, and then to provide a form for this localization of thought, for this monument which would be the expression of that thought....[9]

Echoing Hegel, Kugler affirms man's need to bestow the material world with signs of the spirit. Moreover, with this investment man strives "to impart perpetuity to the transient and invest in the objects of the world a sense of the eternal." Framed more specifically, the work of architecture can be viewed as a concretized *locus* of human values and thought, the non-verbal "expression of that thought." As such a locus, the architectural work establishes and erects a *place*, a place which serves as a permanent, stable point to which we can always refer ourselves. This stable locus both orients us within a community and reminds us, as members of a culture, of what we have found important. In this capacity architecture, the built locus, shows our selves back to ourselves.

In this century, the correspondence between human thought and architectural form has been affirmed by the art theorist Rudolf Arnheim. For him this correspondence is not the result of a simple translation process; immaterial thought is not somehow "converted" into the totally alien medium of solid architecture. Quite the contrary, human thought from the beginning is already "architectural." More precisely, Arnheim insists that any ordered thought, whether it be the analysis of a process or the logical development of an argument, needs to be laid out spatially. "When the human mind organizes a body of thought, it does so almost inevitably in terms of spatial imagery."[10] This tendency of the mind accounts not only for the notion of "architectonics" as the abstract systemization of knowledge, but also for the noted frequency of architectural metaphors in our everyday language.[11] Thus human thought has an inherent visuo-spatial component, and further, argues Arnheim, "any organization of thought assumes the form of an architectural structure."[12] Conversely, this spatial character of thought clearly implies that knowingly or unknowingly, architecture "presents embodiments of thought when it invents and builds shapes."[13]

The argument that architecture embodies and conditions human thought and values is further reinforced by architectural historian Norris Kelly Smith. What Smith finds particularly important is architecture's power to image human organizations: guilds, governments, corporations—virtually any social institution. This ability became crucial when civilizations developed to a point where individuals, having acquired enough self-conscious freedom, began to see their private interests as potentially disconnected from those of the larger society and the state.[14] Threatened by the divisiveness of private self-interest, the greater social order thus needed a convincing image of social stability to project to its citizenry. Monumental architecture came in at this point, effectuating a persuasive counter to latent forces of social and political disruption.

In such a role, argues Smith, architecture essentially became the art of established institutions. An institution constitutes a stable, reliable framework which structures a pattern of human relatedness and group membership. The individual needs institutional membership, for the institution embodies premises for "making decisions, passing judgments, determining goals." Such premises are valuable to the private citizen, as they serve as criteria used for personal evaluations and decision-making. To go further, as social life becomes more complex and more unpredictable, this basic individual need for an accessible set of guiding values correspondingly increases. Architectural form thus presents a model or paradigm of communal membership and attendant systematized value, a model that in effect both communicates and fortifies the existing social order.

Like a building, the institution claims for itself a size and a power to endure which greatly exceed those of the ephemeral human being. By virtue of its size, its stability, and its permanence, it is able to shelter and protect its members, not simply from the elements but from that destructive individualization...with which every urban society is in some measure threatened. A building may be said to be a work of architectural art, then, insofar as it serves as a visual metaphor, declaring in its own form something...about the size, permanence, strength, protectiveness, and organizational structure of the institution it stands for (but does not necessarily house).[15]

This relation between institution and building Smith sees in the architecture of Frank Lloyd Wright. The primary institution which Wright's designs advocated and proselytized for was the American family and its values. Domestic architecture, naturally, became the specialty in which he was unsurpassed, and the Robie House in Chicago often is considered his consummate masterpiece.

Yet Wright's work can be seen as championing another social group's constellation of values, one which before his efforts had received only meager expression in residential building. These were the values of Midwestern Americans, reflected perhaps first in the Prairie Style and later in Wright's Usonian houses. Wright's designs stressed horizontal extension, a feature, for him, that affirmed the freedom of the western plains and the American highway.[16] The rise of this new domestic expression recognized and validated the increasing western movement of America's population; older Eastern seaboard vernaculars—such as the colonial house—no longer provided sufficient acknowledgement for a migration pattern that was well underway and needed to be encouraged. The importance of the western American experience now has fixed expression in our domestic architectural culture, namely in the form of the ubiquitous ranch house, a vernacular strongly influenced by Wright's Usonian designs.[17] Found nowhere outside of North America, the ranch house tacitly reminds us of what we value and why we are distinct as Americans.

Both Arnheim and Smith observe the power of architecture to communicate the nature of human organization and institutions. In this capacity architectural form corporealizes a non-verbal record of human society, a function not unlike that of the more generally verbal disciplines of the humanities. Architecture not only constitutes an element that responds to basic human values, but it also helps configure and record those values visually and concretely. In observing this ability, Hegel and Kugler stressed "high art" and monumental architecture; nonetheless, as we see in the ranch house, architecture hardly has to be grand or "official" to perform this role.

In this regard, art historian Alan Gowans maintains that virtually all historic artifacts and artworks, whether "official" or popular, were designed to serve an essentially social purpose, chiefly one of persuasion and affirming conviction to the culture's unstated values. In Gowans' analysis, art of earlier epochs served four basic functions for society: 1) substitute imagery—replicating the appearance of a person or thing so that it could serve as a stand-in for the original; 2) illustration—serving as a visual narrative and record of events and experiences; 3) beautification—embellishing and ornamenting objects to communicate their function and mark them as products of human activity; 4) conviction and persuasion—making "tangible symbols and visual metaphors" of attitudes, assumptions, and beliefs that a society already held as a community, or that the society supposedly ought to hold.[18] However, the notion of "taste" associated with this art was not the chief controller of artistic creativity; rather the tacit, operant ideology of the culture formed the real foundation of artistic production. This production in turn created and shaped what was interpreted as "taste." This operant ideology comprised "the unstated and largely irrational presuppositions on which conscious and formulated ideologies are always based."[19]

Gowans repeatedly stresses that regardless which particular ideology may rule, art has always served the two functions of persuasion and conviction. These two concepts deserve further elaboration. Persuasion may have several alternate intentions, two of which are a) perpetuating the convictions of the preceding era, especially when (or because) those convictions are losing their hold; and b) propagandizing the new paradigm or "Model," either by theme (new appealing images offered by the paradigm), or by style (new expressive detailing and associations for the paradigm). In this connection, we might well remember the observation of Smith and Arnheim, i.e., architecture's power to metaphorically portray new social organizations.

The process of securing conviction involves visually illustrating, symbolizing or embodying the established Goal. This is done first for those already personally converted, to shore up and enhance their newly-acquired beliefs. Secondly, producing conviction requires spreading awareness of the Goal throughout the wider society, as the new ideology begins to command larger resources.[20] As a tool for convincing the general public, architecture excels. "Architecture is the pre-eminent Art of Conviction," asserts Gowans. By publicly displaying its ideas in the form of bold visual metaphors, architectural form epidictally serves to anchor the established operant ideology. Put differently, "whenever one of these movements realized its goals to the extent of getting power, architecture has provided large, permanent, three-dimensional images of the new Establishment's ideals." Phrased even more simply, architectural works function as the 3-D billboards of establishment views, whether that establishment has cared to identify itself openly or not.[21]

Returning to the four functions of art, Gowans explains that one can view these all as subsumable under the broad function of conviction and persuasion. What a culture decides to illustrate or make substitute images of, and what it considers tasteful or beautiful—all these are conditioned by the operant system of ideological conviction. Given this, historic artworks are not to be understood as the purely passive reflections of a culture, the manifestation of the "spirit of the age," or the result of personal tastes. Rather just the opposite: historic artworks, especially architecture, in fact generated a particular notion of "taste" or *Zeitgeist* and persuaded people to accept it. Artworks "were the tools by which successive civilizations were shaped." What artifacts, artworks, and architecture actually record are the successive tacit ideologies held by various societies throughout history.[22]

Using Gowans' insights, we can begin to see that architecture functions much like a non-verbal mode of rhetoric, the classical art of persuasion. In classical Roman rhetoric, an argument's major premise was called the *locus*, or place. A persuasive argument started from a *locus* or place which recognized the existing values held by the audience. Such a *locus* was essentially also a definite element of the existing social, cultural and political "topography." As this "topography," the underlying unquestioned mental attitudes of a civilization constitute the most inertial, refractory and unchangeable element of its culture. This taken-for-granted substrate—what may be called the operant ideology—appears to the members of the society as self-evident; it also thereby determines what other "truths" will be judged as similarly self-evident. Consequently, ideas and new attitudes can "only develop in minds already accepting their presuppositions; and these presuppositions cannot be forced in, nor picked up by chance observation." And by implication, if any new attitude, trend, concept, or idea is to be adopted by a populace, its chief premise must already be contained within that locus of presuppositions in relation to which the culture evaluates everything.[23]

In grounding itself on those unstated presuppositions, architecture carries out its rhetorical function. It creates potent images of conviction—visual metaphors that proclaim, "This is what we should be convinced of!" With an example Gowans illustrates this point. During the feudal age, as in other times, architecture endeavored to make "great three-dimensional symbolic allusion to those truths" which were held to be self-evident. For feudalism, the unquestioned truth was Heaven beyond earth; it was constantly offered as the paradigm to be used for all worldly organization.[24] The Gothic cathedral aspired to the image of the Heavenly city; as such, it in itself became a *locus*, a place to which medieval citizens could always refer as a mediating standard for all their temporal, worldly endeavors.

Following Norris Kelly Smith, Gowans concurs that the prime function of architecture is to enhance the belief in society's institutions. Architectural styles did not simply spring from some pervasive spirit of the times. On the contrary, evidence indicates that the purpose of architecture was to *create* the spirit of the times, "to set out in large, permanent symbolic forms the convictions of leaders or rulers of society at any given time as to what official ideals should be." Hence, any new architectural taste was the result rather than the cause of reigning architectural styles. People came to approve of new stylistic form because they could relate it back to ideological convictions and operant presuppositions they in fact already held.[25]

Yet, the power of society's major institutions was never (and is never) monolithic. In any period there could be minority tastes associated with deviant architectural styles (Prairie School architecture and the work of Louis Sullivan are in fact two such examples). But simply put, "such dissenting taste grows out of convictions different from those which dictated the dominant tide of taste at any given moment." Whether dominant or marginal, styles are determined by "shifts in social, political, or religious presuppositions." As these new constellations of belief win acceptance, they make new visual forms seem attractive and older forms less so, "first to individual precocious 'leaders of taste,' then to broad masses of people generally." By implication, then, any major change in well-publicized architectural taste reflects an already established shift in society's unstated ideology, its underlying mental "topography."[26] Likewise, any marginal, minority or "grassroots" trends in architecture indicate the existence of dissenting ideologies and potential counter-cultures.

Gowans' discussion suggests we must look at all varieties and modes of architecture if we desire to know explicitly what kinds of belief systems are asking for continued support. Measured by sheer proliferation, the International Style and its descendants still dominate our commercial landscape. Our domestic architecture, on the other hand, still does not fully accept this "new Modernism" of the twentieth century. Our homes are still mostly "colonials" and ranch houses, though short-lived alternatives like the California Bungalow quite likely bespeak the existence of suppressed counter-ideologies. The abstract crystalline thinness of our glass office towers, the horizontal emphasis and selective historical associations of our housing stock—all these point to an operant but latent constellation of cultural premises and values. The exact nature of these unstated values and their correlate institutions is beyond the scope of this paper. That notwithstanding, what we should grasp at this point is the role architecture performs as a material recorder and advocate of the systemized thought and value.

Pulling together the observations of Hegel, Kugler, Smith, Arnheim and Gowans, we may perhaps elaborate the following view of architecture's role in society and its relation to the humanities. To sustain ourselves, our identity, and our community, we need to constantly find outward correspondences to ourselves—especially our subjective life. We look for these correspondences, these *alter egos*, in other persons and in objects and artifacts of the material world. These alter egos are the objectified, externalized image of ourselves and our social organizations; with them we must have regular contact, whether directly or indirectly. As our material alter egos, architecture and the humanities perform this function. Architecture models our transient subjective life in stable built form; the humanities record that life chiefly in verbal works and timeworks. Given their common purpose, the distinction between built and verbal records appears insubstantial. The humanities and architecture are essentially one.

We can also see architecture as engaged in the function of persuading and convincing. Succinctly, it can be said that architecture functions as a non-verbal mode of general rhetoric, the classical humanistic discipline of persuasion. Architecture necessarily rests on a base of collective, unstated, pre-reflective premises and beliefs. Those premises correspond to uncontested human needs and values serving as the sedimented ground of a culture. Yet, our internal images of ourselves and our institutions are not completely stable; we frequently experience doubt and uncertainty about our role as individuals and our relation to the established social order. Using the uncontested values and premises of society, architecture wordlessly convinces us of the social order's protective permanence; furthermore, it silently persuades us that the official ideology of the establishment deserves our support. Thus, directly or indirectly visible in architecture are the institutions, values, and beliefs that form the subject matter of the humanities. And to repeat, as a persuasive art, architecture is in essence a mode of rhetoric, one of the traditional humanistic disciplines. Here again, the distinction between architecture and humanism blurs to become virtually insignificant.

In sum, we use architecture as a humanistic discipline to build *places*, the stable visible images of our thoughts and our values. We require these images to feel at home in the world, to shelter our individual and civic identities in the face of biological transience and political uncertainty. We thus need architecture, along with all the humanities, to help remind us who we are, what we have been, and even where, possibly, we may yet be going.

Notes

[1] Leon Battista Alberti, *On Painting*, trans. John R. Spencer (New Haven: Yale UP, 1966) 90.

[2] Battista 91.

[3] David Clarke, "How Architects Became Irrelevant," *Connoisseur*, Apr. 1989: 139.

[4] Loc. cit.

[5] Georg W.F. Hegel, *Aesthetics: Lectures on Fine Art*, trans. T.M. Knox (Oxford: Clarendon P, 1975) 30-31.

[6] Hegel 31.

[7] Hegel 686, 688.

[8] Hegel 685.

[9] Franz Kugler, *Handbuch der Kunstgeschichte*, 2nd ed. (Stuttgart, 1848) 3; quote trans. Michael Podro in *The Critical Historians of Art* (New Haven: Yale UP, 1982) note 19, 221.

[10] Rudolf Arnheim, *The Dynamics of Architectural Form* (Berkeley: University of California, 1977) 271, 272.

[11] For example, "a *well-buttressed* argument," "her theory's *foundation*," "you've backed yourself *into a corner*." For more see Lakoff and Johnson, *Metaphors We Live By* (Chicago: University of Chicago, 1980).

[12] Arnheim 272.

[13] Arnheim 274.

[14] Norris Kelly Smith, *Frank Lloyd Wright: A Study in Architectural Content* (Englewood Cliffs, NJ: Prentice-Hall, 1966) 8.

[15] Smith 9-10.

[16] See Frank Lloyd Wright, *The Natural House* (New York: Bramhall House, 1954) 67.

[17] According to Wright, *Usonia* was Samuel Butler's term for the United States.

[18] Alan Gowans, *On Parallels in Universal History* (Watkins Glen: Institute for the Study of Universal History, 1974) 11.

[19] Gowans 13.

[20] Gowans 101-102.

[21] Loc. cit.

[22] Gowans 16-17.

[23] Gowans 24.

[24] Gowans 67.

[25] Gowans 100

[26] Gowans 100-101.

Go and Catch a Falling Star:
The Humanities in a Post-Modern World

Marshall W. Fishwick

The "isms" and labels are upon us. It is easier to mark a tree as we wander through a thicket, to number a post along the highway than to remember its characteristics, to label a motion or movement than to understand it. So on the time line of human existence we have progressed somewhere toward, through or past modernity. The label really makes no difference, as Marshall Fishwick points out in his essay below; it is really the state that matters, the conditions of existence. The conditions of the Humanities in our contemporary world— no matter how we label it—are fragile but promising. Fragility does not necessarily mean danger of being destroyed. But it does mean that time for thought is upon us. There are stars in the constellation of possibilities. It is time we went along the rainbow of promises and brought back some hard-nosed realities in the Humanities.

"Go and catch a falling star"—an intriguing idea. Perhaps we are all star-stuff; planet earth evolved when the heavens erupted, and we still gaze up at the star-lit dome. Sometimes falling stars light up the heaven, streaking through space, fading away. Behold the cosmic mystery.

One of my first nursery rhymes was "Twinkle twinkle little star," and it twinkles still in my imagination. Stars are always twinkling and falling—on earth as in heaven. Pop stars, sports stars, movie stars, super stars...we scream, stare, shrug as they fade quickly into that long good night.

Wise men followed the star to Bethlehem; Stars Fell on Alabama; Romeo and Juliet were star-crossed lovers. Caesar was constant as the Northern Star, and Milton greeted "The bright morning star, day's harbinger." The story of the humanities is the story of stardom—of shining understanding.

I do not intend to use heavenly stars merely as an analogy with those on earth. The meteor is the metaphor—my "star" is the humanities themselves. I want to examine the concept and theory, not merely the exemplars. My basic discipline for the star-search will not be astronomy but anthropology.

Our goal is to do as Emerson suggests: "Hitch your wagon to a star." We shall heed Emerson's sage advice as to how to find the best material for understanding the world in which we live: study "the meal in the firkin; the milk in the pan; the ballad in the street; the news of the boat; the glance of the eye; the form and gait of the body." Walt Whitman insisted that a mouse is miracle enough to stagger sextillions of infidels. His nineteenth-century contemporary, Soren Kierkegaard, couched the same thoughts in more philosophic language. The study of the humanities, as well as existentialism, would do well to ponder Kierkegaard's words: "Most systematizers stand in the same relation to their systems as the man who builds a great castle and lives in the adjoining barn."

Each of these three quotations is close to the earth; they deal with firkins, mice, and barns. Much of twentieth century scholarship, produced in seminars and library stacks, is far removed from the earth which is the womb and hub of our existence. It is the earth alone, as A.C. Spectorsky reminds us in *The Book of the Earth*, that we may touch, probe, pat, smell, work with—and on which we live, toil, and dream. Culture and land surface are interwoven, and interact in countless directions. Basically, the United States is a two billion acre farm.

On the land are names with which a poet could fall in love—Dry Bones, Nantucket, Machopongo, Bubbleup, Roanoke, Lake June in Winter, Okloacoochee Slough, and Lost Mule Flat. This land, Scott Fitzgerald noted, drew forth one of the greatest of all human dreams. "For a transitory enchanted moment man must have held his breath in the presence of this continent, compelled into an aesthetic contemplation he neither understood nor desired, face to face for the last time in history with something commensurate to his capacity for wonder."

We live not on one but two soils. The first is physical, and from it springs the crops which sustain our bodies. The second is spiritual and feeds another part of us. From the second soil springs the tradition which cements us together. An enduring civilization must plant seeds in both soils. It must draw not only from the land, but from what love and poetic feeling can make of those who work it. Here is the sinew of the soul, without which human meaning evaporates.

Two soils, two strengths. One strength is of the earth, the other of the human spirit. To study them separately and understand them jointly may be one way to catch a falling star.

The Greeks had no specific word for "culture," but the Romans not only used it ("cultus" means to break the soil) but exported it through laws, buildings, and spectacles. In a sense, they invented the "entertainment industry"; their Colosseum in Rome is still overwhelming. Our capital in Washington is an updated Rome. We are the latterday Rome.

Popular arts involve the duplication and multiplication of sights and sounds. They are designed for the millions, reflecting values widely dispersed in, and approved by, society. They depend on, and resemble, electricity—invisible, indefinable, powerful.

Hence the paradox: we think we "know everything" about popular culture, yet we seem to know next to nothing. Who can predict a trend, a fad, a best seller? Why do the most unlikely people (Elvis and Bruce Springsteen, for example) become the King and the Boss? How does a book rejected by dozens of publishers (*Jaws*) become a best seller? Why do people suddenly start twisting, eating goldfish, wearing worker's clothes, saying WOW?

Who knows? Aren't relativity and tolerance required in cultural as well as in moral or political judgments? Isn't it better that different cultural segments try to understand instead of condemning one another?

Endless bickering about mob taste, mass audience, and elitism, Benjamin DeMott notes, ranks as the most wasteful activity on the contemporary intellectual scene. Why not approach various aspects of our complex culture in terms that focus, not on the gap between them, but on likenesses among the human activities that make folk, popular and elite humanities possible and more extension of the same whole?

What is most remarkable is not multiple differences, but the way in which things congeal and make a totality—a "way of life." Elements of folk culture, coming from the least educated and sophisticated, are fundamental and inexhaustible. Absolute lines between various cultural forms and levels are artificial. Jazz is labeled "the great popular art form" of the last half century; but are not musicians like Benny Goodman and Louis Armstrong in every sense unique—as distinctive in their genre as "classical" musicians? Don't Fred Astaire and Michael Jackson merit a spot in the history of modern dance?

Ancient Sparta was a military state, ancient Israel a religious state, modern England an industrial state. In the 20th century, the United States became the world's first media state. It is not missiles and minute man which give us our essential power and leadership; it is our mastery of media.

The Media have become many things: the message, the massage, the money, and some would add, the monster. Our very atmosphere has become a mediatmosphere. The word and the world are wired for sound.

All this is a relatively new phenomenon, which we have only begun to analyze, survey, and understand. Fundamental laboratory experiments, surveys, and content analyses have taken place only in the last half century—many in the last decade. Early pioneers were Harold Lasswell, Carl Hovland, Paul Lazarsfeld, and Wilbur Schramm. But communications, like the popular humanities, is still an ill-defined discipline.

Better to draw from anthropology and the brilliant recent work done in such areas as mythology, linguistics, ethnology, and archeology. Culture, we now know, is not inherited—it is learned. Men and women make themselves by making cultures. In this sense, all museums are anthropology exhibits, and the historian is a retrospective anthropoligist.

Being more specific, we should consider the work of Joseph Campbell and Clifford Geertz. When Campbell died in 1986, after teaching almost 40 years at Sarah Lawrence College, he was widely known for his work in mythology, which he called "the song of the universe, the music of the spheres." But it was the airing of taped interviews with Bill Moyers after Campbell's death, and the publication of *The Power of Myth*, that turned Campbell into something of a celebrity, and the book into a best seller. Why did he receive such fame and attention posthumously? What explains the new popularity of mythology, and its translation into other forms and media? The Moyers-Campbell interviews took place at George Lucas' Skywalker Ranch. Lucas' popular *Star Wars* trilogy, Campbell said, "put the newest and most powerful spin" on the classic story of the hero.

Clifford Geertz has championed the anthropology of performance and the idea that virtually anything is a "text" that can be read—be it elite, folk, popular, working-class or whatever. He has set for himself the task of writing a natural history of signs and symbols—an ethnography of the vehicle of meaning.[1]

He points to the important contributions others have made to the task: Claude Levi-Strauss with his theory of binary opposites; Roland Barthes with semiotics; and Janice Radway with her focus on the act of reading. He warns that much of their work deals, however, with abstractions; he wants to study signs in their real setting, the local habitat..."the common world in which men look, name, listen and make." This is the same world we examine when studying popular culture. We too "seek out forms where the senses, and through the senses the emotions, can effectively translate them. Find the tenor of the setting in the sources of their spell."

Geertz' goals seem clear, his strategy plausible. We should join forces with him as work continues. It is not a new cryptography that we need, but a new way to diagnose that can determine the meaning of things for the life around them.

Starting on this *terra firma*, anthropologists have developed the culture concept. Though the early French visitor Alexis de Tocqueville never heard of it, he employed something much like it in his own analysis in our "land teeming with a motley multitude whose intellectual wants are to be supplied...and who put great stress on profits and fame." Two key ingredients, all agree of popular culture. Yet not the "motley multitude" at home, but the elitist abroad, captured and dominated American intellectual life. "We have listened too long to the courtly muses of Europe," Emerson complained in 1836; but few kicked the habit. Dryden's words were heeded and repeated. "Without the taste and manner of the Ancients, all is nothing but a blind and rash barbarity." Culture, Matthew Arnold insisted, was "the study and pursuit of perfection...of sweetness and light."

Not definitions from literature but metaphors from anthropology might serve us best as we find a framework and a method:

Culture is a giant wheel, spinning through space. As it turns we move through life; the spokes help us to turn, then impale us.

Culture is a giant clock, whose hands wait for no one. Time is always out of joint.

Culture is a cage, into which everyone is shoved, from which no one can escape.

Culture is a cup of clay, and we drink our lives from it.

Culture is a suitcase, containing all we are or have. If only we could find the key...or catch a falling star.

Culture is, in sum, the building blocks of the humanities—not the humanities, but the stardust from which they are made. Elitist, popular, or folk— all mix in the vast continuum of life. All—not one or two—make up the humanities—not of yesterday but of today and tomorrow. Today is prelude to tomorrow—tomorrow to the future.

Note

[1] A good summary may be found in Geertz' *Knowledge: Further Essays in Interpretive Anthropology* (New York: Basic Books, 1984).

The Traveller and the Humanities

Ray B. Browne, Glenn J. Browne
and Kevin O. Browne

"Travel...is a part of education." Francis Bacon

If all the world's a stage in the theater of life, then surely it is easy and rapid to travel from one edge of the stage to the other. From the eyes of the space capsule Columbia *the stage and the theater are tiny and fragile. Both in fact merge into one with no distinction between the players on the stage and the players in the audience. Not only can we not tell the players without a program but a program is virtually useless since everybody is in fact a player on the stage of life in the theater of the Earth. There are differences among the players, to be sure, but they are relatively minor. And there are similarities, samenesses, which are the Humanities. It is time—indeed the time clock ticks perilously close to the final minute of the final hour—that we recognize the Humanities in all people. One of the greatest agents of this recognition is, of course, the electronic media. Another, less instant but just as important because probably longer lasting, that agent that has probably been with us as long as* homo sapiens *has had legs, is the traveller. Ray Browne, Glenn Browne and Kevin Browne point out in the essay below that the traveller is the permanent and palpable medium of communication. As such he/she/it is what stays on the land and with the people of other sites. Potentially the traveller is the Humanities. We have met the Humanities, and they are us.*

Mankind apparently from the beginning has been driven by necessity or lured by curiosity to see the country that is over what the Bible calls "the everlasting hills" and what lies beyond the trees. "Over the hills and far away," is a folk concept that goes back in England to at least the 17th century; perhaps no one has better expressed the lure of the sea than poet John Masefield in his "Sea-Fever" (1902): "I must go down to the seas again, for the call of the running tide / Is a wild call and a clear call that may not be denied."

Wherever they have gone, people seem to have been driven to discover and cultivate the humanities. The humanities are those elements in the individual and in culture which respond to the basic human needs in all of us, the common threads in all individuals and all societies, the ties that bind us together as *homo sapiens*. The humanities are a people's inheritance, their history. They are also the totality of the present. The humanities are what the tribe's sages teach, and what everybody sees and practices on the streets and in his/her home. The present-day humanities are, as they have always been, the popular culture in everyday life—mass media, entertainments, diversions, heroes, icons, rituals, psychology, religion, patriotism, skepticism, the whole swirl of a nation's various mixes of attitudes and actions. Popular culture, serving the basic drive of the humanities, has always tried to democratize society, to make all people equal participants in life and in the culture it generates. In popular culture, the rule "one person—one equal participant" has tried to prevail. Robert Coles, psychologist and Pulitzer Prize winner, summed up the role of the humanities: "The humanities," he says, "belong to no one kind of person; they are part of the lives of ordinary people, who have their own various ways of struggling for coherence, for a compelling faith, for social vision, for an ethical position, for a sense of historical perspective," for a meaning—a *raison d'etre* in life. Leslie Fiedler pushes the concept one step further toward its logical conclusion because he believes that popular culture—which increasingly we are calling the "new humanities"— can achieve mankind's greatest challenge, that of bringing us all together into the community which must have existed before people became separated by class, education, interests and desires. The humanities are the present, and they shape the future. We create the humanities and they control us.

We live in them when we are stationary. When we travel our own humanities, like an air bubble, go with us. We impose our humanities—and our concept of our humanities—on the societies we visit, and in turn absorb some of those we meet. In mankind's travels from the beginning there has been an aesthetically pleasing but probably more important practical reason for understanding the lands and people visited—the need to get along, to learn from them, and perhaps to spread our own culture.

Two thousand years ago, for example, the Greek city states were mixing with other Mediterranean cultures, learning from them and spreading their own notions of democratic lifestyles. In the fifth century the Roman historian Tacitus wrote his *Germania*, a study of the beliefs and practices of the Germans the Romans had conquered. This history enlightened the Romans about the people in their far-flung empire and in familiarizing them and humanizing the savages, and to a certain extent humanized the conquerors. In this early comparative study in the humanities, at least the Romans learned something about their subjects.

Military activities paradoxically almost inevitably have positive results in the humanities in the long run. For example, long after the fall of the Roman Empire the Venetian traveller Marco Polo spent two decades (1275-1295) in the court of Kubla Khan in Cambuluc (present-day Beijing) as friend and confidant to the ruler. He went to that strange land entranced by the stories his father had brought back from an earlier visit. When he got there Marco Polo was so entranced by the culture that he would not leave. When he did return from China he got involved in a war between Venice and Genoa, was captured and thrown into a Genoese prison, where his cellmate was a sometimes writer named Rustichello, from Pisa. Rustichello was a master at writing romance stories. Polo somehow retrieved from Venice the notes from his visit to China and then dictated them to his cellmate, who wrote it all down, embellishing as he pleased. The collaboration of these two demonstrate the paradox of war. "If either Marco Polo or Rustichello had not fought in the wars against Genoa, we might have no record of Marco Polo's travels and might not even heard his name," says historian Daniel J. Boorstin (137-38). It's an evil war that blows nobody some good!

But they did both fight and write, and provided a written account of Polo's adventures that have been invaluable to historians and culturists ever since. As he recounted in the Prologue to his account, Polo aimed to inform the world through his marvelous journey to the land of exotic people: "Ye emperors, kings, dukes, marquises, earls, and knights, and all other people desirous of knowing the diversities of the races of mankind, as well as the diversities of kingdoms, provinces, and regions of all parts of the East, read through this book, and ye will find in it the greatest and most marvelous characteristics of the peoples, especially of Armenia, Persia, India, and Tartary, as they are severally related in the present work by Marco Polo, a wise and learned citizen of Venice, who states distinctly what things he saw and what things he heard from others... Who, wishing in his secret thoughts that the things he had seen and heard should be made public by the present work, for the benefit of those who could not see them with their own eyes..." Polo's purpose, at least partially, was to educate by presenting the people as they were and therefore to humanize *them*, and, since a book page has two sides to it, to assist in humanizing the readers. Thus Polo's book constituted a text in the humanities.

Military activities—at whatever the horrible cost—continue to serve a useful purpose in the humanities in the long run. Thus in our own day, the introduction of thousands (perhaps hundreds of thousands) of U.S. military personnel into Saudi Arabia in August 1990 will have noticeable effects on American culture and momentous and irreversible results on Saudi Arabian culture. Mixing the two very different civilizations will introduce many Western attitudes and habits into the East. For example, Saudi men are aghast at the role American women play in male society. When American army women work alongside men, give orders that men obey, dress without all the restrictions imposed on Saudi women, they are demonstrating to Saudi society many characteristics which, though the results may not be immediately visible, are bound to ricochet through Saudi society with powerful results. Even in America, regardless of the present-day animosities generated by events, a greater understanding and appreciation of Saudi society and culture will result. From total evil can come some good.

Turning from the East to the West, or the East *through* the West, Columbus recounted in five publications his discoveries of the New World; and others followed in his wake. Richard Hakluyt published his *Divers Voyages* (1582). Samuel Purchas published in his *Hakluytus Postumus* (1625) the material that Hakluyt had not included in his earlier thin volume. Thomas Hariot, who had been sent by Walter Raleigh to visit the New World in the expedition of 1585, published his observations which were translated into Latin, French and German and republished (1590) by Theodore De Bry with illustrations and being reprinted at least nineteen times by 1625 became a best-seller.

By the eighteenth century accounts of travels had become a near obsession. America was on every European's mind and, in England, the Far East—especially the sands and people of Araby—held an almost fatal attraction with many visitors and authors of travel books; some people who read about and visited the deserts, like Lawrence of Arabia, became sensations in folklore and popular culture.

The nineteenth century saw Europeans and Englishwomen and men, like Mrs. Frances Trollope, in her *Domestic Manner of the Americans* (1832), and Charles Dickens in his *American Notebooks* (1842), visit America and recount their impressions to an ever-curious British Citizenry and the exasperation of Americans. Travel literature always contains a latent or obvious political statement. Trollope and Dickens and their compatriots sharpened their pens and dipped them in condescension. Americans of the nineteenth and the first half of the twentieth centuries viewed the rest of the world through political glasses. They saw their land as what religious patriarch John Winthrop had called "the City on a Hill," God's Promised Land, a model for American and European political systems. Americans were somewhat uneasy as they experienced the condescension of the Old World, feeling both superior and inferior, secure and insecure, in their "City on a Hill." Fundamentally the American travel books sparkled with the demonstration of the superiority of the democratic traditions and institutions over those lingering cesspools of despotism and royalty in the rest of the world, and were, in the words of one scholar "triumphantly American, written by Americans exclusively for Americans" (Kagle 80). But, he might have added, instructive to foreigners also because they throbbed with what made Americans Americans and distinguished that tribe from other tribes around the world.

But Americans liked to revisit the land of their ancestors and brag about their new home. Henry Adams, Anglo-phobic historian, taught us to dislike the British. Henry James, sensitive pope of elite American letters, alerted us to recognize the seductiveness of the Old World citizens and the vulnerability of the New World naifs. And Mark Twain, the voice of American satirists, tickled us with his pictures of the clash between Americans and people in the rest of the world.

All books, from all nations, were informed deliberately or inadvertantly and to one degree or another by the humanities of the human beings of all lands, though sometimes the degree was miniscule.

The stereotype of the nineteenth century person on the road was that of insulated traveler. He or she was what today we might call the Savoy Hotel type, a slasher and burner, who went to a country for his own benefit, his own amusement, and remained essentially indifferent to the culture he was in except as he could benefit from it there or back in his own country. He went to observe and receive, not to give; to take away, not to leave something in return. He heeded local customs only insofar as they could satisfy his curiosity or benefit him, and looked down upon the people and their culture, remained isolated in his cultural bubble and returned from his travels influenced only to the degree that he remembered the strangeness of the country he had visited. To a large extent his trip was to a human zoo, and the bars separating him from the animals could be rattled by them but not climbed, and he was safe. He could learn much that demonstrated that his culture was superior.

Through the years that old traveller stereotype has climaxed in that of the tourist-recreationer. Though they differ in their extremities, the tourist and recreationer essentially stem from the same impulses. The tourist, though now he/she lives in a bed-and-breakfast hostel for economy, travels on local transportation, still is a stranger in a strange land. He gets his information from the guide books and converses with the natives when he buys from them or needs their assistance. Still he is at best a benign invader.

There are two sides of the tourist trade. Many countries are exploiting the tourist for quite unexpected and useful purposes. For example, many African countries which have been losing their wild animals at a devastating rate are persuading the peoples that there is more money to be made in using animals for sightseeing safaris than in killing them. So the people are coming to look upon tourists as renewable natural resources and are letting the tourists photograph the animals while the authorities themselves shoot the poachers who would destroy the tourist attractions. Even in Japan tourists are being used to save wild life. Japanese ecologists, for instance, are using tourists' fascination with watching whales to dull and counter the peoples' desire to eat the big animals.

Some countries count on the tourist dollars to support their way of life. Israel, for example, must have the money brought in by tourists in order to maintain their status quo. Other countries direct the flow of tourist dollars into benign channels in order to protect the way of life they value. The island of Bali, for instance, now accommodates some 800,000 tourists a year. But they are controlled by being channeled to facilities that can accommodate them without serious ecological and social impact on the small country. Realizing that Balinese society is fragile and vulnerable to the influx of millions of outsiders, yet needing the money that tourists bring, the Balinese authorities have constructed hotels and other living facilities for tourists only in the south of the island. There is only one high-rise hotel. After it was built and the authorities realized how it clashes with the Balinese city—and countryscape—a law was passed which prohibits the construction of any building taller than the cocoanut trees. This means that the hotels must remain low and close to the ground, not clashing with the traditional buildings and ways of life. Against this background the Balinese have adapted their folk customs and rituals to accommodate the desires of the tourists. In other words, they now play to the tourists but without sacrificing their customs. The tourists in turn are onlookers of the customs, and treat the local rituals and practices as guests should—that is, they observe but do not alter. With this kind of behavior the Balinese have found the tourists a source of needed money—the renewable natural asset, again—and have modified their culture slightly to make room for the visitors. Perhaps only time will tell whether the two drastically different cultures can exist intermingled one with the other.

Another twist to the tourist trade is found in Tara Tarija, Indonesia, where unique cliff graves and funeral ceremonies have been successfully marketed to thousands of mainly European tourists annually. The government has encouraged the maintenance of the Tarajans' traditional lifestyle and stem the tide of young Tarajans leaving for the cities by providing jobs and revenue in the tourist industry.

Negative results, however, are evident in Nepal. Thousands of trekkers have brought with them a money economy, upsetting the traditional social fabric, as well as contributing to the catastrophic deforestation of the region and leaving behind them considerable refuse, scarring the countryside and causing environmental degradation.

Apparently a momentous decision about tourists has been made or is about to be made in England, and the decision is negative. In the summer of 1990 the English by and large have decided that they have too much of a good thing. According to Fernand Auberjanais, European correspondent for the Toledo *Blade* (August 23, 1990), London tabloids shout at tourists: "Wish You Weren't Here," and "Tourists: Who Wants Them?" Apparently travellers from America and Europe are increasingly overwhelming the locals. From 1983 to 1988 the number of tourist-nights in London almost doubled. The most attractive tourist locations are packed. Blackpools' beach has 6.5 million visitors every year; the Albert Dock in Liverpool, 5.1 million; the British Museum, 4.7 million. The media are responsible for whipping up anti-tourist animosity. In an August issue of the Sunday Telegraph, Sir Alfred Sherman, former advisor to Prime Minister Thatcher, called tourism "one of the worst environmental pollutants." He contended that "England's national culture does not favor tourists. The English do not speak foreign languages, nor do they feel the need for foreigners' approval." Tourism, he feels, costs more than it is worth. Little wonder, then, that the English think more and more negatively about the expensive "Chunnel" that is being built under the English Channel to connect England and France with a fast rail service. England's non-tourist mood will only be further exacerbated. Plans are underway to manage tourists by proportioning them throughout the country, a certain number in London at a time, a certain number in Bath, and so forth. But even the bureaucratic Britons are discovering that tourists are one natural resource they can't manage. Tourists continue to run wild and exact a heavy toll in natural and human resources, seemingly a necessary evil.

The vacationer is less benign. He/she rushes in, enjoys the physical setting, feeds on the pleasures the physical and human settings offer, then leaves. He exploits the setting and the people. Though somewhat less vulgar in his actions than his stereotypical progenitor, the vacationer is still to a large extent the Big Game Hunter, who kills the game, collects the trophies and glory to be used back home, then departs, leaving the community somewhat the poorer for the visit in every way except financially. His degradation of the eco-system— the environment—can be staggering. It is estimated, for example, that vacationers wear away the height of the Alps four inches every year. What they do to the Himalayas, the Rockies, Antarctica, the Utopias, Shangri-las, paradises, and the other places they visit can only be guessed at, despite the increasing intervention of governments and other agencies which insist that vacationers leave the physical environment in no worse condition than they find it. Despite the fact that vacationers and tourists constitute generally the third most important part of any geographic area's economy and as such is felt to be indispensable, and although they are being more considerate of the environment they visit, the vacationer probably will continue to be the Grim Degrader of the physical world he visits.

Despite the truth of what has been said, various people visiting various lands have gone with different purposes and come away with different results. In the 17th century British philosopher-essayist Francis Bacon observed: "Travel, in the younger sort is a part of education; in the elder, a part of experience. He that travelleth into a country before he hath some entrance into the language, goeth to school, and not to travel." Bacon recognized that then as now one gets from travel what he puts into it and that result derives proportionately from whatever preparation he has made for the trip. Nowadays the lesson should be even more thoroughly learned. Today the traveller boards a plane and is in a totally different culture within hours. There is bound to be a jolt on the incoming traveller, and he has to adjust to survive. The difficulty of adjustment and survival depends upon the intellectual baggage, the emotional maturity, that he brings with him. And upon his attitude toward the culture and toward himself.

The jolt can be made easiest and safest for all if the traveller—or permanent resident, for that matter—has the cushion of the humanities to soften the impact, integrate him/her into the foreign society and teach him/her about the people among whom he is travelling. That is, for the outward reach of the meeting of the two cultures. The incoming traveller jolts the receiving society least if he understand the impacted culture and adapts himself to it rather than forcing it to adjust to him.

The benefits from the vacationer are at best problematic. Most are fiscally beneficial; most are culturally and environmentally questionable. For years the governor of the state of Oregon let it be known that the vacationer to his state would be merely tolerated, and was not invited to remain as a permanent resident. When the vacationer, seeing the joys of a section of the world he has not delighted in before, decides to stay, much destruction of the environment and eco system can result. In 1990, for example, the city of Seattle, Washington, is doing everything possible to discourage an invasion of transplanted Californians, who having destroyed their own environment now want to move to the relatively pristine surroundings of Seattle—and consequently ruin it. The trouble with a better environment is that once somebody discovers it and lets its superiority be known everybody else wants to move to it—with disastrous results. Popular culture is replete with examples of how documentaries have been made for television picturing some shangri-la, and once the location is revealed it is a shangri-la no longer. The only way to keep paradise unpolluted is to withhold its address.

At times the mere moving through a district can be ruinous. Northern Europeans are now all driving their cars through the mountain passes of Switzerland, on their way to Italy and the surrounding sunny climates. So many drive through the tiny country that their gas fumes, and other wastes are destroying the forests, the lakes, the pastures of Switzerland, and turning the country into a ruin. The Swiss government is doing everything it can, within the bounds of the European Common Market, to discourage the vacationer's passage. The people are becoming vacationer-resistant, causing long delays over passport problems, charging outrageous rates for fuel, letting it be known that the passage is not encouraged. But the pollution continues to kill the environment, causing the trees to die on the mountainsides with the resulting landslides from rain and snow.

All of Europe is, of course, gripped by the same problems that plague us in the U.S. Europeans approach them in different ways, and with differing degrees of success. West Germans attack the automobile problem by slowing traffic in the cities, but, so profoundly irresistible is their obsession with high speed, they make no effort to reduce automobile pollution that results from high speeds on the autobahns. So what they help on the one hand, they harm on the other.

There is, of course, the negative side of the meeting of two cultures, the impact on the traveller himself/herself. He/she can suffer least if one is deeply grounded in an understanding of the humanities of his own country and of himself, as well as of the humanities of the country he is visiting. If he is deeply enough grounded, he will walk on soil common to both, and to all others. Sometimes the humanities lie deep underground; generally, however, they are immediately obvious, though often, for one reason or another, ignored or despised.

The humanities are those elements in the individual and culture which respond to the basic human needs in all of us, the common threads in all individuals and all societies, the ties that bind us all. In the U.S. the humanities are the qualities of society that make us Americans and a part of the human race. They constitute the air we breathe, if you will, and are like the water that fish swim in. Often they are not noticed or understood until called to our attention, or we are deprived of them. The humanities are the culture of the past—our inheritance—and the culture of the present—and, of course, they shape the culture of the future.

Often restricted by some observers to the history, philosophy, literature—the elite aspects—of society, the humanities are far more. They include those elements of our society, for certain, but they include far more. The humanities are all forms of entertainment, business, communication, religion, what we do while we are awake, and what we dream of when asleep. They are working culture and leisure culture. In other words, the humanities are the popular culture of our society and others like ours; in developing nations the humanities are the folk and urban culture, the mixture of both and the result of all swirls of the those cultures. In less technologically developed nations, the folk cultures are the folk humanities and differ mainly from our own as a result of technological development. Their humanities differ from our own only in appearance, not substance and purpose. Their humanities are the collective essence of their civilization, their hopes and aspirations. Though the humanities are these essences, sometimes people fail to recognize and understand them. But if people understand their own they can more easily understand others. If we understand our own humanities than we can more easily comprehend those of other nations and peoples.

The preferred tourist then is a folklorist-anthropologist-popular culturist traveller, especially the last, one who understands the people he visits but who also studies all elements of the culture, its history, development, and the people on the land, their life styles, their relation to nature, nature to them, their spiritual affairs and, above all, those elements common to all peoples. The ideal traveller is the visitor who understands the day-to-day existence of the people he is visiting. Any understanding short of this full understanding leaves something to be desired. The proper understanding of the humanities is the key and the safeguard.

Deep-felt knowledge and appreciation of the humanities marks the difference between the Savoy Hotel tourist of old, who arrived in and never got out of his carriage-hotel-suite-limousine-badge of nationality. For example when Ronald Reagan visited the incomparably beautiful island of Bali he never left the resort compound of the Nusa Dua Beach Hotel. How could he understand the culture? Now, however, the humanities visitor lives in his bed-and-breakfast, rides public transportation and mingles with the natives. The traveler of old can be paralleled to a big game hunter who went to a country to rape and pillage, to gather his trophies at whatever cost, and to take away the treasures— the big game or the equivalent of the 19th century thefts of the Elgin Marbles from Greece. The humanities visitor today to one degree or another brings his camera, takes pictures of the flora and fauna, without disturbing it, makes a positive contribution to the local and eco and cultural systems and leaves more than he takes away. The ideal tourist of today parallels the short-term Peace Corps worker, who contributes more than he drains away, or at least leaves behind tangible results and goodwill. He is the positive picture of the good American.

The everyday life and culture of a people that the visitor penetrates has a long history of antecedence. In every instance the culture goes back to the beginning of time for the culture. The humanities are the human history and culture that have shaped these people through time and determined what they are today. It is a cliche of the traveller that the more one knows of this history, the more he understands and appreciates the present. The more he is a visitor to the culture rather than a traveller in the country the more he appreciates and is appreciated.

At times the culture that the ideal tourist seeks lies deep and might easily be overlooked or considered of no importance. Take for example the cliches and proverbs of a society, the wit of one, the wisdom of a people, as somebody called those shorthand expressions used by everybody and generally despised by the elite. The proverb "Early to bed and early to rise / Makes a man healthy, wealthy, and wise," from Franklin's *Poor Richard's Almanac* (1757), speaks the secret of success obtaining in his day, as did another of Poor Richard's pearls of wisdom: "God helps them that help themselves." To the elite of Franklin's day, as to ours, the proverbs may have been embarrassingly simple. But to the everyday American the expressions were pithy and meaningful. Seventeenth century British essayist-philosopher Francis Bacon summed up their importance: "The genius, wit, and spirit of a nation are discovered in its proverbs." The wit of one and the wisdom of many, proverbs of a nation are the people's first effort toward abstracting and synthesizing their ideas and culture. In order to understand a people fully, one must know their proverbs. The degree to which Franklin's proverbs no longer voice the philosophy of American culture is the degree to which that culture has changed. It is imperative that one understand the humanities suffusing both times in order to understand American culture.

Likewise one must know other forms of a nation's popular culture. "Give me the making of the songs of a nation," said seventeenth century British Andrew Fletcher, "and I care not who makes its laws." If songs are then so fundamental to the spirit, the origin and development of a people, it behooves all who would know the people to understand their songs. Further, as Fletcher might have recognized, the same people who make songs of a nation force the making of the laws, as history continually demonstrates. Laws are drawn up and executed to the tunes of the people. That is, the people, both the living and the dead, speak and get laws enacted. There is, for example, more to be learned of everyday Egyptian life during the time of the Pharoahs from the thousands of graves of the commoners surrounding the pyramids than from the resplendant tomb of King Tutankamen (c. 1350 BC). Tut did not build the pyramid that housed his corpse. Hundreds of thousands of hard working people died so that Tut might dream of a life after death. It is they who supply us with an understanding of the civilization of the Pharaoh, not he of them. To overlook this fact of history is seriously to misread the past.

It would also behoove the traveller to be familiar with and knowledgeable of all other aspects of the society he is visiting, the people's games, forms of recreation, their aims, ways of making a living, ways of dying—all aspects of the everyday life of a people. Art historian Alan Gowans insists, quite properly, that if a person knows fully any piece of art, or artifact, he can know the society that created and cherished it. James Deetz has observed that "In ways great and small, gravestones, grape pits, houses, refuse, cuts of meat, recipes, ceramics, furniture, and cutlery inform us" of the way cultures live and view life. In a similar vein, Robert Blair St. George has broadened the inventory: "houses, furniture, teacups, probate inventories, diaries, account books, newspapers and tax lists may all warrant investigation" if one is to understand the implications of even a single topic. "Everything," says French historian Fernand Braudel, "is connected." To understand the connections one must understand the humanities. Malcolm K. Shuman observes that though the "way is hazardous," one can learn much about the ancient Maya from observing their society of today. With the book of culture both past and present open before the traveller, he/she must read deeply and widely in order to appreciate the culture he is in to avoid being destructive.

What then is the role of the present-day traveller? He/she is a mixed blessing. At one time philosophers and political theorists felt that mere association between peoples and nations would make them friendly and safe. American revolutionary Tom Paine once wrote naively that commerce would bind nations together. Nations that trade don't fight, he felt. The glue of greed was too strong to fracture peaceful self gain. But history has tragically proved him wrong on that score. Greed, ambition, lust, ego, mental derangement override peaceful intercourse, as hundreds of examples have demonstrated.

The role of the tourist is being shaped into a positive force. The revenue derived from tourism is being channeled into the development and preservation of natural game preserves. In Kenya, for example, tourism has demonstrated to poachers and those governments that might control poachers that living animals are worth more than elephant tusks and rhino horns from dead animals. Indigenous peoples who feel that their ways of life are being threatened are being strengthened in their traditions by tourism, as such peoples are being encouraged to maintain their ways of life as attractions for tourists, and the worlds they live in. "Rain forest conservation for a profit," is the attitude of Amos Bien, who runs a tourist lodge in Costa Rica. "Nobody is going to cut down the rain forest...if they can make more money by not cutting it down." Such is what conservationists are beginning to call ecotourism, which ties in as an extension of the philosophy of the trail-blazing explorer of eco-awareness Jacques Cousteau and the Cousteau Society he founded: "to protect and preserve the quality of life for present and future generations" (*Vis-à-Vis* 38, 50). So far so good. But this ecotourism needs to develop into a kind of humanatourism in which ecotourism becomes an encyclopedia of the humanities, opening the chapter on a whole new attitude and motto of the history and contemporary account of the popular culture of a region and a people. The tourist might then develop into the traveller, with an agenda far more understanding, searching and appreciative of the land and people he explores.

Currently the earth's population is growing at the rate of three babies every second, twenty-four hours a day. As we approach a population of five billion, and of course eventually more, and people become more and more closely packed on the non-expanding spaceship of earth, a compressed population creates more and more problems. The evils of narrow-minded ethnicity, regionalicity and nationalicity, fueled by individual and group violence, long felt to have been moderated somewhat, are breaking out in fierce warfare not known for a hundred years, and religiocity threatens to surge to proportions not known since the Holy Wars. All these forces drive people more and more toward divisiveness. Through these forces, the traveller can be a positive and cohering force. Writer of crime fiction Ross MacDonald read the force of congestion clearly as he saw Americans lured to the West, then packed like lemmings against the Pacific Ocean and unable to go further toward the setting sun. The options were, like lemmings that jump into the Pacific, or like rats to back into the corner and devour one another—or like intelligent human beings to behave responsibly, recognize the setting and do something about it, to mitigate the forces that divide.

But this change can occur probably only as the tourist develops more fully into the human tourist or the traveller who becomes a positive integrating and cohering force. He/she can act as the human embodiment of the integrating force of the electronic media, the personification of the artifacts and abstractions pictured in the media, demonstrating that life among human beings does not necessarily have to be individualized and lonely, but can be communitarian and pleasurable.

But this can come about only as the traveller becomes more and more filled with the reaction to the humanities of his culture, of the cultures he is visiting, and of those of the world in general. The electronic media drive us toward what Marshall McLuhan called the global village. Perhaps the more proper term for this squeezing of all humanity into one global community is global ghetto because world poverty will for perhaps a thousand years doom mankind to grinding poverty. The world community will have deprivation as its common core as long as mankind overpopulates and abuses earth's natural resources. Regardless of its configuration and setting, the mass of humanity on the earth will be viable and endure only if the intercourse between individuals and nations is humanistic and charged with the understanding generated by the humanities.

Few human activities are more supercharged with potential and consequence than the role of the traveller of the future. Some people think that the traveller should in fact become the explorer, someone examining all the possibilities and developing the potentials of the earth, the eco-system and society at large. To be sure the explorer of the physical and scientific environment has succeeded to a certain extent in the past and now in the present seems poised finally to recognize his/her role vis-à-vis the physical and cultural environment and the potential of the human being to fit into these two environments. This exploration has undoubtedly only begun. But there is another, parallel, exploration that needs to be examined. People living together throughout history have had to try to determine how they could best adjust one to another and to society in general—to some degree, at least, the tension between the individual and the collective society. This exploration must be continued and intensified—because the need is greater now than it has ever been in the past. Indeed the need now is critical and explosive. It must be addressed and the problems solved.

The traveller as explorer can explore new fields and areas. The traveller *qua* traveller can be immediately effective, if he/she will be the cutting edge of movement toward a gentler, happier more peaceful global society. But a new realization is probably called for, and this is the opportunities offered by the electronic media if they are fully appreciated and understood.

TV is everyperson's university, and the documentary is the textbook. Television has taken the place of the bard, the storyteller of old. It transmits information, it comforts, it passes the time of day, it lulls to sleep. Television ignores political boundaries and walls. Sooner or later it penetrates jamming. Television, along with McDonald's hamburgers and rock 'n' roll, broke down the Berlin wall. Now that virtually every house in urban China has a TV antenna rising above its roof, the Bamboo curtain is bound to crack and crash. With every village in India cradling at least one TV set, momentous changes are bound to occur in the Indian countryside and village. The world is being TVized.

TV is the medium; the language is English. English is the most widely used language in the world; at least one person in every seven uses it with a certain amount of fluency. Half of the books in the world are in English, more than half of the international telephone calls. English is used in more than sixty percent of the world's radio programs, and the number approaches that in TV, with or without subtitles. English is the language used by all international air controllers; it seemed ironic that even during the coldest portions of the Cold War international air flights were brought down in Moscow in English, and the airliner was then forced to follow a vehicle on which was printed the English command: "Follow Me."

English is the unofficial language of the world, the *lingua franca*, and America, for better or worse, is the culture that is having, on TV and off— directly or indirectly—the greatest impact. Examples abound all around us. One of the more immediate—and perhaps far-reaching—examples of the impact of American culture is occurring in Saudi Arabia with the build-up of American military forces there to oppose Saddam Hussein, strong-man of Iraq. The Saudi men are nonplused, amazed and undoubtedly somewhat frightened to see American female members of the military working alongside men, giving them orders, acting with full equality with men. Through direct observation, this element of American culture is having effect on Saudi men. Imagine the impact when it is broadcast on local television so that Saudi females can see it. The positive effects of the evils of war are generally unexpected but deep and long-lasting. The wonders of education change the world, sometimes slowly, sometimes dramatically, but always inexorably.

In our culture, made comfortable by technological gadgets and promises of ever more efficient ones that create leisure and then promise to satisfy it, we do not fully use our television as a potential "university." In our day when we have all kinds of "universities"—universities without walls, universities of the air, universities on VCRs, and many others—we must realize that the electronic media are potentially the greatest opportunities for teaching and learning the world has ever known. "Television means the world in your home and in the homes of all people of the world," wrote Thomas Hutchinson in 1938 (Madson 113). "It is the greatest means of communication ever developed by the human mind. It should do more to develop friendly neighbors, and to bring understanding and peace on earth than any other single material force in the world today."

To utilize this great force properly and fully educators must give up their conventional approach to teaching, and to what constitutes knowledge, and realize that television can be an ally and friend if properly used, not an enemy. Television, like a book or any other medium of communication is precisely that, *a medium of communication*. What is aired through it depends on the people doing the airing. The signal and material can be weak and negative or strong and positive. The choice is the educators. To paraphrase Thomas Jefferson in a different time though in a similar context, all that educators have to do to see television as an educational tool wasted is to stand by and see other interests exploit and monopolize it. The medium may at the moment be looked upon as purely a means to sell goods, a "commercial" instead of an "educational" channel. So be it. Our capitalistic, free enterprise political system, grossly imperfect as it is, has not been proved so distasteful that we are prepared to scuttle it though we could obviously improve some of its nature. We find that active participation in all activities is helpful. Perhaps the tail needs to catch up with the dog. Indifference to or disdainful non-affiliation with the educational potentials of commercial television invites abuse of a great potential.

So the traveller of today does not necessarily have to hit the road in order to travel. Throughout history, many people have traveled in various ways. We should remember that the poet John Keats was "much...travell'd in the realms of gold," when he first looked at Chapman's translation of Homer.

Others have recognized the value of being the active instead of literary traveller. Henry David Thoreau bragged that he had "travelled a good deal in Concord," and Percy B. Shelley learned of the vanity of human assertions when in the poem "Ozymandias" he recounts that he "met a traveller from an antique land" who told his tale of "two vast and trunkless legs of stone" standing in the desert as mute testimony to the hollow boast of the tyrant about his immortality. But the better informed and possibly more richly opinioned traveller is he/she who travels the world over—through the media of the airplane, local transportation and possibly the spaceship, or television. Travel indeed can educate, especially if the traveller is accompanied by a mind and attitude opened and strengthened by the humanities. "I am a part of all that I have met," asserted Alfred Tennyson's Ulysses in the nineteenth century in the poem by the same name in which the poet ties the future to the mythology of the past. And, he might have added, "it is a part of me." This symbiosis should be the inevitable result of travel.

The humanities traveller knows enough to free himself/herself from the biases, prejudices and restrictions of her/his own culture, to rise above regionalicity, ethnicity, nationalicity and religiocity and to view the humanities as the bond common to us all. The global ghetto—or if we are lucky ultimately global suburbia—can be borne with less pain and more understanding—with less trauma and danger—if we realize that the popular culture of our world is the humanities of our time. We need to understand and appreciate that fact. That having been done, there can be a new potential in the cry in the wilderness of the world to give the real humanities a chance—all we can save is ourselves and our earth.

Works Cited

Bacon, Francis. *Of Travel*, 1625.

Boorstin, Daniel J. *The Discoverers*. New York: Random House, 1983.

Deetz, James. *In Small Things Forgotten: The Archeology of Early American Life*. Garden City, NY: Anchor , 1977.

Kagle, Steven E. *America: Exploration and Travel*. Bowling Green, OH: Popular Press, 1979.

St. George, Robert Blair. *Material Life in America: 1600-1860*. Boston: Northeastern, 1988.

Vis-à-Vis, The Magazine of United Airlines, July 1990.

Television and the Crisis
in the Humanities

Gary Burns

Precise knowledge and education are, no doubt, the greatest protectors against the sham of what people pass off for their own benefit as the valuable in the Humanities. Conservative canonists—for their own purposes—insist that what they peddle is the proper product. To sell their propaganda, they clothe their wares in quotes and pseudo-scholarship and wisdom and shout alarms in the night that crises are upon us and civilization is being trampled by the giant monster of movement and development. Nowadays the monster is television and the warped children it creates. Actually, as Burns demonstrates clearly and quietly in the following essay, the greatest danger to the fully developed growth of the Humanities is not the shrill half-truths of the canonists but the equally shrill half-truthful ignorance of the educationists who try to sell their ideas. As Burns develops, the profoundest threat to the Humanities comes not from television and its siblings but from the eternally endarkened canonists who in order to protect their little learning and transitory political and educational positions try to stifle open and free inquiry. To do so is to plant the seeds of contintued ignorance; for educators to cultivate such crops is to encourage ossification of culture.

Comes now *TV Guide* complaining that "54 percent of Americans know that Judge [Joseph] Wapner runs *The People's Court* but only 9 percent know that Justice William Rehnquist heads the Supreme Court." Lest readers miss the point of this supposedly shocking allegation (drawn from an unidentified survey), *TV Guide* solemnly concludes: "That's a sad commentary on the public's legal savvy."[1]

Of course, one could look at it another way and say that it is a sad commentary on the Supreme Court. The "legal savvy" of Americans has probably increased as a result of *The People's Court*—more people now know that small claims court exists and is available to anyone who wants to use it. On the other hand, the Supreme Court is remote, arcane, and (as a cynic might conclude) primarily concerned with disputes among people and groups rich enough to hire lawyers to pursue the matter that far.

This is not to say that *The People's Court* is a masterpiece of public service, entertainment, or art. Its appeal lies not in any kind of "legal savvy," however meager, but in the judge's personality and the lurid disputes he presides over. The problem with the *TV Guide* article is that it illogically implies some serious

149

deficiency in Americans' legal knowledge, which is operationally defined as familiarity with Rehnquist. Having set up this false crisis, the article pretends to blame TV (as if *TV Guide* ever *really* blames TV), but actually blames the audience. Then the article does a pseudo-about-face and says that the solution to the alleged problem is more TV, in the form of the new cable channel Court TV, which signed on July 1, 1991, with round-the-clock legal programming, including actual courtroom proceedings from around the country (as if this will increase the percentage of Americans who can name Rehnquist, much less increase their real legal knowledge).

I begin with this example because it treats television as a site of crisis. Americans should know Rehnquist (high culture), but instead they know Wapner (low culture). The audience has failed to reach a desirable level of cultural literacy. The culprits are audience members themselves, the inferior form of television they bring about through their viewing choices, and (by implication) the educational system whose job it really is to teach people about our revered legal institutions.

In both form and function, this line of reasoning bears strong resemblance to many of the recent, well publicized exposés of American education. The Wapner-Rehnquist comparison, while a minor part of the *TV Guide* article, is illustrative of a type of statistic widely used to sound alarm—a certain percentage of some surveyed group does not know some fact. A quarter of college seniors cannot "distinguish between the thoughts of Karl Marx and the United States Constitution." Forty-two percent "could not place the Civil War in the correct half-century." Fifty-eight percent "did not know Shakespeare wrote *The Tempest*." Seventy-five percent of Americans could not locate the Persian Gulf on a map. And so forth.[2]

In a similar vein, William Bennett, then head of the National Endowment for the Humanities, used smoking-gun statistics from the American Council on Education to support his 1984 call for reform in humanities instruction in higher education: "a student can obtain a bachelor's degree from 75 percent of all American colleges and universities without having studied European history; from 72 percent without having studied American literature or history; and from 86 percent without having studied the civilizations of classical Greece and Rome."[3] Bennett continues with numerous other statistics all in support of his thesis that humanities education is in a state of disarray.

Bennett's is only one voice in the strident chorus of conservative criticism aimed at higher education over the past several years. Other architects of the conservative critique include Allan Bloom, Dinesh D'Souza, Roger Kimball, Russell Kirk, Charles Sykes, Hilton Kramer, and current NEH head Lynne Cheney. This group is by no means monolithic, but there is enough agreement among them that we can give a fairly detailed and unproblematic account of what we might identify as the conservative position.

That position is that there is a crisis in the humanities or in liberal education (hence D'Souza's phrase "illiberal education"[4]). The principal evidence of the crisis is the various statistics, plus anecdotal evidence, about what students do not know. This student ignorance is the effect, and conservatives make a series of assumptions, largely unsupported, about what the causes are. They include: a hodgepodge curriculum; dilution of the canon of literary classics; substitution of popular culture for literature as an object of study in teaching and research; the rise of women's studies, ethnic studies, cultural studies, and other new fields; overspecialization and triviality in research (and a concomitant neglect of teaching); and overemphasis on cultural diversity, sensitivity, and multiculturalism on campus.

Above all, the conservatives blame professors. Sykes's book *ProfScam* depicts the professoriate as fraught with laziness, dishonesty, and selfishness. One of Bennett's main themes in *To Reclaim a Legacy* is that it is abandonment of the humanities by professors that has landed us in our current, sorry state.[5]

In particular, the conservatives blame radical professors for the alleged decline of the humanities. Kimball's "tenured radicals,"[6] ensconced in comfortable positions, have turned their backs on supposedly timeless and universal classics of literature in favor of a politicized curriculum. According to this view, politics (i.e., the politics of radical professors) is corrupting higher education, with results not only in curricular matters, but also in such phenomena as campus speech codes that institutionalize "political correctness" and a "new McCarthyism."[7]

What's wrong with this picture? Plenty, but in order to understand its appeal, we need to examine and acknowledge the many things the conservatives get right or almost right.

To begin with, let us admit that too many students are alarmingly ignorant when they enter college, and when they leave. A student should learn the location of the Persian Gulf in high school or earlier, along with the dates of the Civil War, who wrote *The Tempest*, and many other facts.

But statistics about ignorance of facts are hardly an index of the gravity of the problem university teachers face. Sykes, in a rare moment of moderation, admits that the accumulation of facts in one's brain amounts to a game of Trivial Pursuit and does not make one wise or educated.[8]

Yet the conservative position typically glosses over this point. The last one-fourth of E.D. Hirsch's book *Cultural Literacy*, a favorite among conservatives despite Kimball's later rebuke of Hirsch, is little more than Trivial Pursuit in book form.[9] The idea behind the book is that an educated person should know content—that is, facts. This requires rote memorization rather than the aimless "inquiry" into methods, skills, and concepts that conservatives imagine goes on in too many college classrooms.

As I said earlier, conservatives are correct to insist that students should learn facts. Where they are wrong is to emphasize this "cultural literacy" while overlooking actual literacy. The problem is not only that students do not know facts, but also that they cannot read or write.[10] As anecdotal evidence, I offer the following passage written within the past five years by a college senior in one of my classes. I use the passage with her permission. I am reproducing it, complete with mistakes, in exactly the form I received it:

In the era we are in today, Television is doing all it could to raise controversy, since that is how the culture seems to be going. Our society is controversial about A.I.D.S., children growing up to fast, and homosexuality. In relevance to these subjects, there are shows displaying these topics. One program from the show, *The Hogan Family*, Jason Bateman's best friend dies of A.I.D.S. Then of course there is the highly rated show *Bart Simpson*, a cartoon of an obnoxious, vulgar mouth kid admired by the younger generation.

The newest contraversial topic shown on television, is the Madonna video displaying homosexuality. It is not allowed to be shown on air, yet when *Nightline* aired it to show what it was like, thousands of viewers tuned in, and millions are talking about it. The idea that in today's society controversy is strong, therefore, the media tries to capture the audiences by having strong controversial topics on television.

This is by no means the worst writing a senior has ever submitted to me—in fact, it is fairly representative, and this student had actually shown some improvement after I gave her guidance and harsh grades on three earlier papers. Still, she is incoherent and close to illiterate. Elsewhere in the paper, she plagiarizes at length because she cannot write herself. Now, I can teach this student the location of the Persian Gulf, and I can even teach her how to spell it. What I cannot do is teach her in one semester how to read, write, and think. William Bennett's idea that everyone should read *Huckleberry Finn* is a splendid one, but this student cannot read a newspaper article, much less a serious book.

To blame professors for problems like this misses the mark. What this student needs is prolonged tutoring in remedial reading and English grammar. Of course, she will not get it, and she probably does not want it; but *these* are the subject areas that are especially in crisis, and they reflect problems in elementary and secondary education. We in higher education inherit the problems and handle them as best we can.

It is not enough to suggest, as Bennett does, that "we" raise college entrance requirements in the humanities.[11] This, according to Bennett, would have a ripple effect and cause high schools to raise their graduation requirements, or at least to increase their course offerings in the humanities. This is an unusual deviation from the conservative doctrine of local control over schools and is also pie-in-the-sky. Bennett seems to have the impression that the faculty is regularly polled about what admission requirements should be. In fifteen years in higher education, I have not once seen an issue of this sort come before the faculty. I was once involved in a decision to raise admission standards in a particular degree program, and the university administration overturned it. On another occasion, the campus faculty voted to raise graduation requirements, and the administration refused to implement the decision.

Admission and graduation requirements at all levels are very much subject to the whims of politicians and administrators. These whims lean strongly in the direction of vocational and professional training—for example, in June 1991 the Illinois legislature passed the Illinois Cooperative Work Study Program Act, which will (if signed by the Governor) promote and provide funding for cooperative education at the university level. This is a curricular matter, yet the faculty has nothing to do with it. If enacted, the new program, although probably well-intentioned, will certainly not have a positive impact on the humanities. It will, instead, increase the already overwhelming predominance of business and vocational concerns in student life.[12]

Bennett's conservatism will not allow him to venture into anything resembling a criticism of the business ethic. On the contrary: "To study the humanities in no way detracts from the career interests of students. Properly taught, they will enrich all."[13] Again the problem is professors, who are not teaching properly. Further:

Conventional wisdom attributes the steep drop in the number of students who major in the humanities to a concern for finding good-paying jobs after college. Although there is some truth in this, we believe that there is another, equally important reason—namely, that we in the academy have failed to bring the humanities to life and to insist on their value. From 1970 to 1982 the number of bachelor's degrees awarded in all fields *increased* by 11 percent from 846,110 to 952,998. But during the same period, degrees in English *dropped* not by a few percentage points, but by 57 percent, in philosophy by 41 percent, in history by 62 percent, and in modern languages by 50 percent.[14]

Let us apply a little good, old-fashioned humanistic logic to this paragraph. The uncredited statistics are quite scientific-sounding, but they do not prove what Bennett would like us to think they prove, which is that there is anything wrong with "conventional wisdom" about job-hunting. The statistics certainly do not support Bennett's assertion that "we in the academy have failed to bring the humanities to life and to insist on their value."

Who is "we"? Not Bennett, who gave up teaching to become an administrator and bureaucrat. Not Cheney, who left teaching to become a journalist and bureaucrat. Not Kimball, D'Souza, or Kramer, who are probably best described as gadflies with ties to conservative periodicals, foundations, and think-tanks.[15] Not Sykes, whose father was a professor but who is not a teacher himself.

These "untenured conservatives" have great reverence for Homer and Dante, but little respect for the teacher in the trenches, who must try to "bring the humanities to life," as Bennett puts it, in mass lectures to unruly crowds of poorly prepared and uninterested students. The students then grade the teacher, through evaluation-of-instruction forms, which help to determine whether the teacher will receive a 1% raise or a 1.5% raise. Low raises, poor pay and working conditions, deteriorating facilities, budget cuts, crowded classrooms, exploitation of teaching assistants and part-time faculty, low morale, and an anticipated severe shortage of qualified humanities faculty[16]—these are crises from the teacher's point of view, yet the conservatives have practically nothing to say about these issues. Similarly, from the student's perspective, the crisis lies primarily in such matters as high cost; declining availability of financial aid; balancing school, family, and career demands; and closed and canceled classes. On these matters, too, the conservatives are silent.[17]

In fact, the crisis rhetoric of conservatives has about it the ring both of Chicken Little and of Nero fiddling. Chicken Little, because life goes on at the university with very little day-to-day evidence of the sort of crisis the conservatives have announced. Students are disgracefully illiterate, but they were equally illiterate in 1975 when I started teaching, so what we have appears to me to be more a chronic problem than a crisis. Moreover, the idea of crisis is itself chronic—we can trace it back through Philip Coombs's *World Crisis in Education* (1985), the "Literacy Crisis" of the 1970s, Charles Silberman's *Crisis in the Classroom* (1970), Christopher Dawson's *Crisis of Western Education* (1961), Bernard Iddings Bell's *Crisis in Education* (1949), Walter Moberly's *Crisis in the University* (1949), and numerous other alarmist tracts. Here is how Jacques Barzun described recent college graduates in 1959:

...young men and women [who have] no knowledge that is precise and firm, no ability to do intellectual work with thoroughness and despatch. Though here are college graduates, many of them cannot read accurately or write clearly, cannot do fractions or percentages without travail and doubt, cannot utter their thoughts with fluency or force, can rarely show a handwriting that would pass for adult, let alone legible, cannot trust themselves to use the foreign language they have studied for eight years, and can no more range conversationally over a modest gamut of intellectual topics than they can address their peers consecutively on one of the subjects they have studied.[18]

The more things change, the more they remain the same.

The conservatives also resemble Nero fiddling because, as I have noted, they ignore real problems that have better claim to the word "crisis" than do such conservative worries as political correctness, radical professors, and the inability of students to quote Shakespeare. In addition, the left has a perspective of its own about a crisis in the humanities. As Patrick Brantlinger describes it, "[t]he conservative myth that 'theory'—structuralism, deconstruction, Marxism, feminism, psychoanalysis, and so on—has *caused* the crisis in the humanities needs to be turned around: theory is a response to crisis, not its cause."[19] Viewed in this way, crisis is the discovery of illegitimate authority. There are many dimensions of crisis, including economic crisis, political crisis, and failures of institutions to serve their ostensible functions and to provide for the needs of the population. These crises and failures impinge on the humanities as intellectual dilemmas and clashes.[20]

It is at this intellectual level, rather than at the more mundane level of teachers' and students' concerns, that the conservatives concentrate their attack. In "The Real Crisis in the Humanities," the concluding chapter in *Tenured Radicals*, Kimball focuses entirely on a 1989 Williams College panel discussion called "Crisis in the Humanities?". This particular conference, or any such conference, is so far removed from the everyday experiences of most humanities teachers and students that it seems a very unlikely setting for a crisis. But in Kimball's eyes it epitomizes a widespread intellectual subterfuge:

Here we had the most traditional of academic ceremonies, replete with academic regalia and communal singing of "My Country, 'Tis of Thee," providing the setting for a speech whose essential point was that the humanities can cut themselves off from both their foundation and their ideals and still be said to be thriving. What else are we to make of...the contemptuous reference to "the sanctity of the so-called canon"? Or the suggestion that "the referentiality of language" is something the humanities today could just as well do without? Or the idea that "new methods"—meaning deconstruction and its progeny— and new "subjects of inquiry"—meaning everything from pulp novels to rock videos— are fit subjects for humanistic inquiry?[21]

Recently conservative critics have been quite concerned with free speech issues—especially speech codes, political correctness, and instances in which conservatives have allegedly been punished for expressing their views. Here again I believe we should concede that the conservatives are correct to insist upon free speech. The problem is that, at least in one respect, they do not reciprocate. I refer particularly to Kimball's castigation of new methods and new subjects of inquiry. According to Kimball, the methods and subjects he disapproves of are not "fit subjects for humanistic inquiry." In making this assertion, he is seeking to deny the right of academic freedom to scholars who disagree with him. What is at stake in such a denial is not only the academic freedom of individuals, but also the very idea of a university as a place to study the universe. Kimball's position is also logically inconsistent in that by objecting to humanistic inquiry into rock videos, for example, he is himself, as a humanist, making a statement about rock videos. He would deny to others the right to study rock video, while reserving for himself the right to comment both about it and about anybody else's researches about it.

As someone who has conducted humanistic inquiry into music video, television, popular music, film, and other subjects Kimball despises, I object to his attempt to restrict what I am able to say and write. He has every right to disagree with any scholar's findings about music video or some other popular culture topic, but this is not his usual tactic. What he prefers to do is ridicule the subject matter so that it becomes unnecessary to make a substantive engagement with the author. It is not that he disagrees with something I have said in one of my studies—since the subject is unfit, the study ipso facto has no value and no right to exist. As Kimball says, quoting Nietzsche: "[W]e do not refute a disease. We resist it."[22] This tidy analogy, grounded in unreason and an inflammatory use of the word "disease," overlooks the fact that in order to resist a disease, it is helpful to research it and understand it.

The condemnation of media studies (and much else) is obviously an attempt to violate academic freedom, and therefore free speech, which the conservatives claim to support.[23] Sykes finesses this inconvenient fact by latching onto half of the American Association of University Professors' "Statement of Principles on Academic Freedom and Tenure," while ignoring the other half: "The AAUP drew a careful distinction between freedom of research, which was entitled to 'full freedom,' and classroom teaching, which required professional restraint."[24] Having noted this careful distinction, Sykes proceeds to ignore it. Despite the efforts of Accuracy in Academia, it is still difficult for conservatives to document lack of professional restraint in the classrooms of radical professors. Consequently, Sykes and Kimball focus instead on incoherent curricula, silly course titles, and what they consider absurd and politically irresponsible research projects. Their critiques of the titles of courses, conference papers, and articles are usually amusing, and when they offer substantive analyses of the contents of recent scholarship, their points are often well taken. But this does not excuse or justify the conservatives' true goal, which is to prevent research that does not conform to conservative ideas about proper subject matter, methods, and political outlook. Naturally, conservatives want their agenda upheld in the classroom and curriculum as well, but their critique of research should be seen for what it is. It is not an appeal for greater professional restraint by teachers. Rather, it is an attack against the full academic freedom claimed by AAUP for researchers.

Media studies and popular culture are particularly objectionable academic pursuits, in the eyes of conservatives. One of Kimball's most virulent attacks is against E. Ann Kaplan for her book *Rocking Around the Clock*, which is a study of MTV and music video.[25] Kimball does not demonstrate, or even state, that music video is bad—he assumes it. He does not allow for the possibility that some videos may be good, or even that the entire corpus of music video may, somewhere, contain something of value. Nor does he entertain the possibility that, despite its aesthetic inferiority, there is any value whatsoever in studying music video, or that some other music video scholarship besides Kaplan's might be worth looking at.

In his guerrilla-style critique of Kaplan, Kimball follows a pattern, also used by Sykes throughout *ProfScam*.[26] The pattern is this: Focus on the topic of research rather than on what the research says about the topic. In selecting research to ridicule, choose topics that can easily be portrayed as trivial (music video, TV commercials, everyday conversation, TV series, potholders, cheerleading) or sensational (masturbation, rape, phallic symbolism). Ridicule the title and subject of the study (or of a course in a college catalogue). And, sometimes, quote a few passages and make fun of them. The more ridiculous the passages, the better—and often they *are* quite ridiculous, especially when taken out of context. Interestingly, *TV Guide* was one of the pioneers of this technique in a 1988 article that poked fun at academic analyses of television.[27] It seems that anyone who wants to study television seriously needs to be prepared to withstand refutation-by-one-liner in books and magazines that reach millions of readers.

Kaplan was an attractive target for such an attack, both because of her prominent position in the humanities[28] and because of various flaws in her book. The passages selected for ridicule by Kimball use equivocation, jargon, and passive verbs to such an extent that Kaplan's meaning is often quite unclear. There is no point in trying to defend Kaplan against Kimball's substantive comments, because the comments are essentially correct. Those of us who write about popular culture should note these problems and try to avoid them in our own writing.

At the same time, we should reject Kimball's unwarranted position that music video is unworthy as an object of study. We should object not only to the position, but to the fact that Kimball arrives at it without logical argument (and in fact does so, erroneously, in the name of reason). His implied reasoning is that Kaplan's study is worthless, therefore the study of music video is worthless. In rejecting the study of music video, Kimball is refusing to take seriously the people who create videos, the people who watch them, and the people who study them. This is anti-democratic and irresponsible, not to mention mean-spirited in the case of the attack on Kaplan.

There are good videos, good studies of music video, and viewers who exercise aesthetic judgment in watching videos. That is not to say that music video should be part of the core curriculum at universities, or fulfill general education requirements. Music video is not part of the literary canon, nor should it be, nor is anyone saying it should be. But it is part of the humanities, and it should be studied by humanists and taught in specialized courses at universities, just as we study and teach obscure painters, writers, philosophers, theologians, composers, and even the obscure filmmakers whose work has inspired music video directors.

Of course, anyone who believes that music video is now one of the most-studied subjects in the humanities is wildly mistaken. On the contrary, it has received very little serious study, and outlets for publication are extremely limited—so, again, Kimball is Chicken Little. But even a few studies of music video are too many for the conservatives. In the conservative view, there is such a thing as a corrupting "media culture," which universities should exclude and combat.

New Criterion editor Hilton Kramer makes the point in conference proceedings published in *Partisan Review*:

[O]ur subject today is the impact of the media on the university. We know that the impact of the media as it now exists on the university has been a corrupting impact. We know that a good deal of what university teaching has to contend with is this culture of simplifications, caricatures and lies that students bring with them to the university, as if they were bringing a state of nature. For more and more students find it impossible to distinguish between media culture and outside life, what might be called "real life," because there has been so little, in their education and in their upbringing before coming to the university, that encouraged them to make the requisite distinction between culture and life itself. Such distinctions are lacking not only in the students, who are in many respects the involuntary victims of the media culture, but also in the faculty and the administration, who are more and more inclined to countenance and indeed initiate the substitution of media artifacts, media studies, media propaganda for the traditional objects of study. Indeed, they have allowed media culture to supplant humanistic culture as the basic standard of discussion.[29]

Leaving aside the question of proof, which is so often absent in conservative polemics, we find again, at the heart of the argument, the conservative distaste for media studies. Elsewhere in his remarks, Kramer makes it clear that newspapers and magazines are included in what he means by "the media"—so, in the end, apparently it is only permissible to study books (the Great Books, of course), live performing arts, and museum art. In case his position is not clear enough in the preceding passage, we may refer to an article in *New Criterion* in which Kramer states that "all forms of popular culture should be banned from courses in the arts and the humanities." This includes films, "either as objects of study or as aids to study."[30] It is safe to assume that Kramer would include television in his ban, since it is, of course, "media culture," which consists of "simplifications, caricatures and lies" (in Kramer's own simplification and caricature).

What is the "requisite distinction between culture and life itself"? Indeed, what is "life itself," and by what authority does Kramer claim to know? Kramer's life is, no doubt, quite different from that of the average student or faculty member. What is "humanistic culture," and how is it so different from "media culture," and how are these related to the "culture" that students cannot distinguish from "life itself"? Kramer does not say, but later in his remarks he provides a clue that suggests a possible interpretation of the "distinction between culture and life itself."

In a response to a "point about the ideological character of television being the result of an economically determined program," Kramer says:

Yes, in some general way that's true. Television is a business and it's in business to make a profit. But that doesn't really address the question of what shapes its ideological content and why, from one period to another. After all, the television networks in the fifties were just as concerned with making a profit as they are in 1990, but the shift from what might loosely be called "family values" to what might loosely be called "uncontingent self-fulfillment" which dominates television today—that is, the shift to an emphasis on total autonomy of self—this is not economically determined. That's determined by the political and cultural values television shares with the elite culture of the moment—what I call the intellectual academic elite culture.[31]

It is difficult to imagine a more ill-informed view of television. First, it is not categorically true that television is a profit-oriented business enterprise. PBS is not. The BBC is not. Video art is not. Public access is not. Religious TV stations such as KNLC, St. Louis, are not. To ignore the variety of television is a grave intellectual error.

Second, it is nevertheless true that the type of TV that *is* in business to make a profit (i.e., commercial TV) is more responsive to the "economically determined program" of capitalism than to any other force in society. Todd Gitlin's *Inside Prime Time*, the most thorough recent study of the American TV industry, demonstrates this convincingly.[32] This point is so undeniable that Kramer must admit it "in some general way" before moving on to his own muddled explanation.

Third, Kramer's characterization of the ideological content of both 1950s and 1990 TV is simplistic and naive, at best. There is also a logical inconsistency in his implicit nostalgia for 1950s TV, both because 1950s TV was part of "media culture" then, and because it still is, in the form of reruns.

Fourth, even if Kramer were right in his summary view of the change in TV's ideological content from the 1950s to 1990, he would still be wrong about the cause of change. That cause is primarily economic, rooted in the economic interests of advertisers, networks, stations, and other participants in the industry. For verification of that, one needs only to look at any good book on the history of television. A particularly instructive source is *The Sponsor*, written by Erik Barnouw, the foremost historian of American broadcasting.[33]

Fifth, Kramer's sentence about "the intellectual academic elite culture" seems to reverse his earlier position. In the previously quoted passage from *Partisan Review*, Kramer refers to the corrupting impact of "media culture" on the university. Now he blames the "political and cultural values" of "the intellectual academic elite culture" (presumably the university) for the shortcomings of television. It appears he would like to have it both ways, and perhaps his position actually is that there is a reciprocal influence—but a more plausible interpretation is that he will resort to any logical contortion necessary to keep from criticizing the commercial, "free" (and conservative) system of television. To a conservative, this system is desirable because it supports capitalism as we know it, but its content is "media culture" that must be kept out of the university and separate from "real life."

Kramer's mistaken understanding of television underscores the need for more, not less, media studies. Otherwise, how will we know the history of television? How will we have the knowledge to make intelligent responses to nonsensical polemics? (The *Partisan Review* panel participants clearly did not have sufficient knowledge.) Especially, how will we be able to evaluate, sensibly, the true contribution of television and other media to the humanities? Rather than exclude media studies, and the media themselves, from the humanities, we should include them wholeheartedly, which, conservative fears notwithstanding, has still not been done.

It is irresponsible to prate about "media culture" as if nothing worthwhile has ever appeared, or could ever appear, on television. Such a position is inconsistent with what the humanities stand for. The *Oxford English Dictionary* defines the humanities as "[l]earning or literature concerned with human culture."[34] This definition certainly encompasses television, which is human culture, and media studies, which is learning and literature concerned with it. If it still seems unnatural to think of television as part of the humanities, it is because of deficiencies not only in television itself, but also in our understanding of it and our aspirations for it.

At the 1939 New York World's Fair demonstration of television, RCA President David Sarnoff said:

Now we add sight to sound. It is with a feeling of humbleness that I come to this moment of announcing the birth, in this country, of a new art so important in its implication that it is bound to affect all society. It is an art which shines like a torch in the troubled world.[35]

Today, not even an NBC executive would claim that television is a torch for the troubled world. It could have been, and it could still be, but it is not. If this is not a crisis in the humanities, it is at least a tragedy.

In his book *Theory of the Film*, Béla Balázs said:

[A]bout fifty...years ago a completely new art [film] was born. Did the academies set up research groups? Did they observe, hour by hour and keeping precise records, how this embryo developed and in its development revealed the laws governing its vital process?

The scholars and academies let this opportunity pass, although for many centuries it was the first chance to observe, with the naked eye so to speak, one of the rarest phenomena of the history of culture: the emergence of a new form of artistic expression, the only one born in our time...[36]

We have duplicated this mistake with television, and if the conservatives have their way we will continue to do so. If this is not a crisis in the humanities, it is at least a scholarly oversight from which future generations, if not we ourselves, will suffer.

In his book *The Media Monopoly*, Ben Bagdikian demonstrates that "despite more than 25,000 outlets in the United States, twenty-three corporations control most of the business in daily newspapers, magazines, television, books, and motion pictures."[37] Five or six giant corporations dominate mass communication internationally (these include Rupert Murdoch's arch-conservative News Corporation Ltd., which owns *TV Guide*).[38] The largest media companies are increasing their integration and market shares at a rapid rate, with alarming effects on media content. If this is not a crisis in the humanities, it soon will be.

Meanwhile, it is indeed a problem, perhaps even a crisis, that many Americans are ignorant of *The Tempest*, the Civil War, the Persian Gulf, the Constitution, and Justice Rehnquist. But if humanists continue to ostracize, scorn, and ignore both media studies and the media themselves, the result will not be a return to the good old days when people read Homer and listened to Bach, but an even darker veil of ignorance, fostered for economic and political purposes by the very media that some humanists do not wish to understand. If the humanities have no use for the media, the globally monopolized media are certainly not going to have any use for the humanities—and it is the humanities, and culture itself, that will suffer the most in the ensuing Dark Age.

Notes

The author thanks Doug Davis, Arthur P. Doederlein, George Lipsitz, and Janet Novak for providing helpful materials.

[1]Neil Hickey, "Can TV Do Justice to Real-Life Courtroom Dramas?", *TV Guide* 29 June 1991: 8-9, quote on 9.

[2]First three statistics: Charles J. Sykes, *The Hollow Men: Politics and Corruption in Higher Education* (Washington, DC: Regnery Gateway, 1990), 14. Sykes is somewhat inaccurately citing Lynne V. Cheney, *50 Hours: A Core Curriculum for College Students* (Washington, DC: National Endowment for the Humanities, 1989). Cheney, in turn (11), cites *A Survey of College Seniors: Knowledge of History and Literature*, conducted for the National Endowment for the Humanities (Princeton, NJ: Gallup Organization, 1989) 33-56. Persian Gulf statistic: National Geographic Society/Gallup survey, reported in Philip Dine, "Geography Ignorance 'Shocking,' " *St. Louis Post-Dispatch* 31 July 1988: 1A, 9A. As of 1991, the latter survey is being used in direct mail solicitations to sell the National Geographic Society book *Exploring Your World: The Adventure of Geography*.

[3]William J. Bennett, *To Reclaim a Legacy: A Report on the Humanities in Higher Education* (Washington, DC: National Endowment for the Humanities, 1984), 13.

[4]Dinesh D'Souza, *Illiberal Education: The Politics of Race and Sex on Campus* (New York: Free P, 1991).

[5]Charles J. Sykes, *ProfScam: Professors and the Demise of Higher Education* (Washington, DC: Regnery Gateway, 1988); and Bennett, *To Reclaim a Legacy* 15-17.

[6]Roger Kimball, *Tenured Radicals: How Politics Has Corrupted Our Higher Education*, paperback ed. (New York: Harper Collins, 1990).

[7]For a summary, see Laura Fraser, "The Tyranny of the Media Correct: The Assault on 'the New McCarthyism,'" *Extra!* May/June 1991: 6-8. On the politics-corruption connection, note the subtitles of Kimball's *Tenured Radicals* and Sykes's *The Hollow Men*.

[8]Sykes, *The Hollow Men*, 14. See also Michael C. Berthold, "*Jeopardy!*, Cultural Literacy, and the Discourse of Trivia," *Journal of American Culture* 13.1 (Spring 1990): 11-17.

[9]E.D. Hirsch, Jr., *Cultural Literacy: What Every American Needs to Know* (Boston: Houghton Mifflin, 1987). The follow-up volume is entirely in the Trivial Pursuit mode (E.D. Hirsch, Jr., Joseph F. Kett, and James Trefil, *The Dictionary of Cultural Literacy* [Boston: Houghton Mifflin, 1988]). For Kimball's criticism of Hirsch, see *Tenured Radicals* 7-10, 172-74.

[10]On the dimensions of this problem, see Jonathan Kozol, *Illiterate America* (Garden City, NY: Anchor P/Doubleday, 1985).

[11]Bennett, *To Reclaim a Legacy* 21-22.

[12]For an account of the intellectual decline brought about by the policy of "career education" (former Education Commissioner Sidney Marland's euphemism for vocational

education), see Ira Shor, *Culture Wars: School and Society in the Conservative Restoration 1969-1984* (Boston: Routledge & Kegan Paul, 1986) esp. 30-58.

[13]Bennett, *To Reclaim a Legacy* 15.

[14]Bennett, 13-14.

[15]See Kimball, *Tenured Radicals* ix; and D'Souza, *Illiberal Education* ix. See also George Lipsitz, "Listening to Learn and Learning to Listen: Popular Culture, Cultural Theory, and American Studies," *American Quarterly* 42 (Dec. 1990): 615-36, esp. 632, 636; Lawrence Soley, "Right Thinking Conservative Think Tanks," *Dissent* 38 (Summer 1991): 418-20; and Jon Wiener, "The Olin Money Tree: Dollars for Neocon Scholars," *Nation* 1 Jan. 1990: 12-14. Kramer is editor of the conservative journal *New Criterion*. Kimball is managing editor.

[16]"The Academic Labor Market: A Look Into the 1990s," *University Affairs* June-July 1990: 3-4.

[17]On the Reagan administration's role in financial aid cutbacks, see Svi Shapiro, *Between Capitalism and Democracy: Educational Policy and the Crisis of the Welfare State* (New York: Bergin & Garvey, 1990) 117.

[18]Jacques Barzun, *The House of Intellect* (New York: Harper & Brothers, 1959) 98-99. Barzun is an excellent source on the history of "Intellect" and the lack thereof, through the late 1950s. A good history of the more recent "crises" in education is Shor, *Culture Wars*. The other books mentioned are Philip H. Coombs, *The World Crisis in Education: The View from the Eighties* (New York: Oxford UP, 1985); Charles E. Silberman, *Crisis in the Classroom: The Remaking of American Education* (New York: Random House, 1970); Christopher Dawson, *The Crisis of Western Education* (New York: Sheed and Ward, 1961); Bernard Iddings Bell, *Crisis in Education: A Challenge to American Complacency* (New York: Whittlesey House, 1949); and Walter Moberly, *The Crisis in the University* (London: SCM P, 1949).

[19]Patrick Brantlinger, *Crusoe's Footprints: Cultural Studies in Britain and America* (New York: Routledge, 1990) 10.

[20]Brantlinger, 1-33.

[21]Kimball, *Tenured Radicals* 187-88.

[22]Kimball, 204.

[23]To an extent, the conservatives' concentration upon free-speech issues appears to be part of a larger plan—an organized, carefully conceived campaign to "attempt to steal [the] high ground away from the left." See Sara Diamond, "Readin', Writin' and Repressin'," *Z Magazine* Feb. 1991: 45-48, quote on 46.

[24]Sykes, *The Hollow Men* 34.

[25]E. Ann Kaplan, *Rocking Around the Clock: Music Television, Postmodernism, and Consumer Culture* (New York: Methuen, 1987); Kimball, *Tenured Radicals* 42-45.

[26]See especially chapters 6 and 7 in Sykes, *ProfScam* 101-14. Sykes also criticizes a music video course at California State University, Los Angeles (*ProfScam* 81).

[27]Merrill Panitt, "If Tom Selleck Is a 'Libidinal Spectacle'...Then *Miami Vice* Is a 'Confluence of Commodities,'" *TV Guide* 5 Nov. 1988: 13-14.

[28]Kaplan, a well known film scholar, is professor of English and director of the Humanities Institute at the State University of New York at Stony Brook.

[29]Hilton Kramer, remarks in "The Impact of the Media," panel discussion proceedings, *Partisan Review* 58 (Spring 1991): 227-48, quote on 229-30.

[30]Hilton Kramer, "Studying the Arts and the Humanities: What Can Be Done," *New Criterion* Feb. 1989: 1-6, quotes on 4.

[31]Kramer, "Impact of the Media" 233-34.

[32]Todd Gitlin, *Inside Prime Time* (New York: Pantheon, 1983).

[33]Erik Barnouw, *The Sponsor: Notes on a Modern Potentate* (Oxford and New York: Oxford UP, 1978).

[34]*The Oxford English Dictionary* 2nd ed. (Oxford: Clarendon P, 1989) 7: 476. The definition actually appears under the singular form, "humanity."

[35]David Sarnoff, quoted in Harry Castleman and Walter J. Podrazik, *Watching TV: Four Decades of American Television* (New York: McGraw-Hill, 1982) 10.

[36]Béla Balázs, *Theory of the Film: Character and Growth of a New Art* trans. Edith Bone (New York: Dover Publications, 1970) 22.

[37]Ben H. Bagdikian, *The Media Monopoly* 3rd ed. (Boston: Beacon P, 1990) 4. See also Ben H. Bagdikian, "Cornering Hearts and Minds: The Lords of the Global Village," *Nation* 12 June 1989: 805-20.

[38]Upon buying *TV Guide* in 1988, Murdoch declared the magazine "too cerebral" and promptly steered it to new depths of fatuousness, lowering the level of public discourse about television to an all-time nadir. See Katharine Seelye, "TV Guide: The Shake-Up," *Columbia Journalism Review* Nov./Dec. 1989: 41-45.

Can the Humanities Cross the Pacific?

Marshall W. Fishwick

From the eye of the space capsule Columbia *there is no East or West though there is, of course, a Pacific Ocean. But in the eye of the Capsule or of God the body of water must seem of little consequence. In the history and present and future state of Humankind, must it not be consequential only to the same magnitude? Since most examples of humankind are characterized by two legs, two arms and hands and one only half developed brain, is it not sad indeed to have to even ask the question are the Humanities a human rather than Eurocentric assertion of what distinguishes us, though perhaps slightly, from other animals of the planet Earth? Marshall Fishwick thinks so. And his answer to the question of whether the Western Humanities are also Eastern, and Middle-Eastern is ultimately an affirmative resounding Yes. At the present time wearing apparel differ, transportations differ, means and forms of entertainment differ. But, for better or worse, eventually people around the world will watch the same television, attend the same movies, travel on the same means of transportation, and eat the same fast food. Nobody may admit he or she likes it, but Modernity is with us. Since we are not able to reverse it, we might as well make the most of it.*

Since no man (woman, country, continent) is an island, and the Humanities involve us all, the answer to my question of whether the humanities can cross the Pacific Ocean seems obvious: of course.

Don't be too sure. Ask another question: why *haven't* they? How many of us have really mastered a culture East of Suez?

"Humanities," as we move into the 21st century, have for generations involved the Mediterranean world (especially Greece and Rome), and the spread of Mediterranean culture to Europe, North America, and the European empires. All the rest of the world (non-white, non-Christian) was "heathen." Marco Polo glimpsed it, Rudyard Kipling romanticized it—assuring us that East is East, and West is West, and so much for that.

For Americans, the West was our mythic frontier. Moving West was our destiny, our salvation. It was the great heroic story of the New World, and Frederick Jackson Turner devised the Frontier Thesis which has become the foundation on which American history and thinking are built. The West meant free land and open space: a "safety valve" for dissent, and ultimately to America's political system. Turner died in 1932, but his Thesis, like Old Man River, just kept rolling along.[1]

Yet the actual frontier was closing long before Turner's death. The 1890 census showed that Western settlements "lie so scattered over the region that they can no longer be called frontier." That didn't stop novelists, playwrights, and movie makers from extolling "the Wild West." Eventually the American Western became our chief contribution to world mythology.

With the coming of the Space Age, some argued that the Frontier was in outer space; but I suggest that, as we enter the 90s, we put aside that notion and seek it elsewhere—to the far west of America's Far West—across the vast Pacific Ocean to what we have long called the Far East.

The Pacific Rim is our New Frontier.

This Rim (or Basin, or Community) embraces the Asian Pacific, coinciding roughly with the western rim of the Pacific Ocean. Because of their unique importance, Japan and China spring first to mind. One then thinks quickly of the Newly Industrialized Countries (NICs): South Korea, Taiwan, Hong Kong, Singapore; of the Association for Southeast Asian Nations (ASEAN): Indonesia, the Philippines, Thailand, Malaysia, Brunei, and (again) Singapore; the far-flung islands of Oceania; and of the land controlled either by the U.S.S.R. or Socialist partners (Vietnam, North Korea, and Cambodia). Australia and New Zealand are somewhat removed from Asia by their location and Western orientation.[2]

The growth and changes in this part of the world since World War II have been dramatic and revolutionary. Pacific Rim economic growth has far outdistanced the rest of the world, leading to gigantic trade deficits and talk of protectionism. Nothing seems to able to stop the "miracle" of the Rim. Will Europe be dwarfed, and the United States bought? This in turn affects many other aspects of world opinions and relationships. Suddenly all eyes have turned East, where the drama of our expanding world is writ large.

As the 1980s ended more and more representative American groups, in business, art, education, and communications were loosening their link to Mother Country. Globalization is clearly the strategy of choice for the 1990s—one heralded by the May, 1989 issue of *The Harvard Business Review* as "a main road to industrial prowess." "We need our Far Eastern customers, and we cannot alienate them," said Robert H. Galvin, chairman of Motorola, Inc. "We must treat our employees all over the world equally."

The "economic miracle of East Asia" tells us about the state of western democracy, philosophy, and popular culture. It's extremely important, Peter Berger states, to know what makes the Pacific Rim countries tick, "not only to understand them, but also to understand ourselves. Looking at them, we can see much more clearly what our own society is and is not."[3]

One important conclusion is that the link between individualism and capitalism isn't as necessary as most of us thought. Can this be explained as a modification of Confucian morality? If so, how has this modification affected other aspects of the culture?

"Look at what's happening now in South Korea," Peter Berger continues. Korea is very much of a communalistic culture; yet is is moving toward democracy by popular will. So opting for democracy, as for capitalism, doesn't necessarily mean opting for our individualistic culture.

If the Pacific Rim Community has great promise, it also has great tensions. There is Vietnam, scene of America's debacle in the '70s, and Cambodia, where war still rages. How can the Japanese forget Hiroshima and the atomic bomb? Further south, in Oceania, there are ethnic tensions in New Caledonia. The new government elected in Fiji in April, 1987, was overthrown in May. Papuan separatism plagues West Irian. Insurgents oppose Indonesian rule in East Timor. Further north, in the Philippines, the victory of Corazon Aquino has not quelled the revolt of the New People's Army and Muslims, and the future seems uncertain. The long-term question of reuniting Taiwan with Mainland China is still unresolved. Highly visible and recurring trade tensions between the U.S. and Japan have heightened, and spread to other Asia-Pacific countries. The 1986 Jenkins bill (vetoed by President Reagan) would have restricted textile imports from virtually every Asian country; that idea still has strong Congressional support. President Bush's announcement, in April, 1989, that America's new FSX fighter jet would be built in Japan raised a storm of protest. The debate over the reunification of the Korean peninsula, and America's military presence in South Korea, continues. Students are crushed in a shocking Chinese reaction to demonstrations. Everywhere the growth of ethnic and religious identity introduces explosive new issues and pitfalls.[4]

I shall not attempt here to analyze these complex and far-ranging matters. Instead, I shall ask if, how, and when we shall find common ground and understanding on a global scale; if East and West can hope to meet; and if popular culture, subject of my special concern, can help.

In his famous poem "The Ballad of East and West," Rudyard Kipling gave a much-quoted answer:

> Oh, East is East, and West is West, and
> never the twain shall meet,
> Till Earth and sky stand presently at
> God's great Judgment seat...

If many thinkers, Eastern and Western, are correct, Kipling might be wrong. Underneath the incredible diversity there may be unity—a common culture, too long obscured by aggression and conflict. A belief in the unity of all being runs throughout much Oriental thinking and religion. Our separate selves, according to Buddhism, Hinduism, and their offshoots, are not ultimately real. Philosophical Hinduism and Mahayana Buddhism reject dualism. For them there is no difference between myself and yourself and this river and that mountain. We are all one and the conflict between us is therefore illusary.

While such beliefs are diametrically opposed to utilitarian individualism, in which the individual is the ultimate ontological reality, there are elements in the Christian tradition to which they are not entirely opposed. Christian theology also felt the unity of Being and the necessity to love beings. The New Testament speaks of the church as one body of which we are all members. But Christianity has tended to maintain the ultimate dualism of creator and creation which the Oriental religions would obliterate. Christian mystics have made statements expressing the ultimate unity of God and man and, in mediated form, their unity through Christ. Yet the goal of unity among the major religions eludes us; indeed, it seems further away now than a few years ago.

Perhaps it will not be religion, but secularism, science, and media that will bring us together. We may be moving into an age when real power will not be primarily religious or even military; real power will be *information*. We are perfecting communication systems where virtually all the media will be computerized and electronic. If we accept the notion that these need to be regulated both within countries and at national borders, we will hamper real unity.

Surely we should not limit people's access to knowledge, any more than we should deny them access to water or electricity. At home and abroad, we must not permit underdeveloped wastelands of communication. Our goal should be competitive world-wide information flow, with room for experimentation and dissent. Both self-criticism and mutual criticism are crucial. These are not only technical but social and ethical problems. Nothing less than human freedom and growth is at stake.

Many nations in the Third world already worry about media imperialism and exploitation; and wonder if technology won't create a new elite, no more aware of "the people" than was the old one. This thought prompted (at a 1981 UNESCO meeting in Paris) a proposal for a New World Information Order, whose motto would be "the free and balanced flow of information." So far, the proposal has not changed the flow of news significantly. *Communication* seems to be coming to the linking of computers, fiber optics, satellites and other newly-emerging items that allow us to talk back to our information systems and bring the world into our home or study. This might increase the information clutter (garbage in, garbage out), fragment audiences, reduce the quality of programming and trivialize the uses of technology.

In earlier times when values, systems and status tended to be predetermined, we were often isolated against an awareness of process and the consistency of change. No one can be so isolated now. Our awareness of process is reflected in our private and public lives. Like our government, all of us must live (like it or not) on the cutting edge of New Frontiers.

Lancelot Whyte sums it up in *The Next Development of Man*:

Man shares the special form of the universal formative process which is common to all organisms. While life is maintained, the component processes of man never attain the relative isolation and static perfection of inorganic process.

East and West *have* met. Both enter the Age of Zations: urbanization, mechanization, systematization, specialization, sychronization. The realization creates a new dimension in modern living, as human knowledge accumulates faster than the ability to assimilate it. Scholars estimate that we are now doubling our available knowledge every ten years.

Many concepts link up with *common*. A common carrier (bus or train) is obligated to transport all who solicit the service. The common denominator works with all numbers in the equation; common law applies to us all; the House of Commons, like the Book of Common Prayer, cuts through class privileges. A common right is the property of every citizen, "Do me the common right," Shakespeare has a character say in *Measure for Measure*, "to let me see them."

Standing outside, but integrally connected to common is community; Beings of any shape, size, or color who live together, sharing a common heritage. Such a congealing is part of our nature: man, Aristotle pointed out centuries ago, is a social animal. We come together not just to do things, but to be together.

What holds us together is our popular culture—people's culture, our common heritage. Though only recently instituted in colleges and universities, exploring popular culture holds fresh promise for the greatest adventure of the twentieth century: the exploration of the world's enormous diversity. Immigration, ethnic, and Third World studies are part of this pursuit. Popular culture study is enriched by these movements. It also has something to offer them: a comprehensive interface by which these new fields of interest can be incorporated to bring the international scene into focus.

The nations of the world have long known each other by their elite productions. Now that the "international style" is upon us through the network of global mass media, we need other approaches, other materials that go beyond mass media. We need to understand that tradition works hand in hand with modernity in the rich mix of people, places and perceptions.

How does one study such things? Where shall we begin? These are only points of entry—this scheme covering twenty topics or areas of popular culture:

1. National Integration and Popular Culture
2. Language and Ethnicity
3. History and Mythology
4. Tradition and Hierarchy
5. Theatre, Outdoor Events, and Holidays
6. Film and Photography
7. Television, Video
8. Radio, Phonograph, Audio
9. Lifestyles—Food Habits, Clothes, etc.
10. Popular Literature (oral and written)
11. Sports and Recreation
12. Music, Jazz, Rock, etc.
13. Painting, Design, Sculpture
14. Architecture, Public and Private
15. Religion—Godmen and Godwomen—Pilgrimages
16. Advertising and Propaganda
17. Gender and Race
18. Cultural Geography and Geopolitics
19. Oral Tales and Folklore
20. Rituals and Rites of Passage

By the very nature of these topics, they require first-hand observation, contacts, and experiences. We can never really penetrate the lives and experiences of other people by sitting in libraries or at computer terminals. Nothing takes the place of first-hand experience and observation. Peasant and primitive societies have very complex rituals and symbols. There is much that is first rate in the so-called Third World.

And there is much we miss, or misinterpret on quick hectic visits. In *Waterbuffalo Theology*, Kosuke Koyama says that before going to rural Thailand he thought that Buddhism was dying in the face of science and modernity. After three years in the field he completely reversed his opinion—he had actually seen how Buddhism works.

Bearing all this in mind, Dr. Richard Gid Powers and I founded in 1980 a new journal called *International Popular Culture*. It was born out of the curiosity about the effect of modern communities on human cultures. The magazine has been created out of a sense of the perils as well as the promise of internationalism, a concern for the survival of national cultures besieged by international entertainment and lifestyles. The international exchange of ideas, entertainment and goods had made it true (in a new and unexpected way) that nothing human is any longer completely foreign to anyone, anywhere. Can human cultures survive when the distinction between national and foreign is dissolved? What happens when nations import more and more of their culture from abroad? When the content of consciousness is foreign, will the patterns of consciousness, attitudes and values, also become foreign? When nothing is foreign, is anything native? Does man everywhere become a stranger in his own land? Or does the internationalization of culture have precisely the opposite effect? Does the impact of international culture make a country more conscious of its own national identity, forcing a re-examination and re-invigorization of its own cultural roots.

Few fields hold such possibilities for international research and comparisons as does popular culture. Dramatic changes in media technology have quickly expanded the field. High or elite culture speaks primarily to the well-educated minority. They were basically print-oriented, so that the electronic revolution did not mean a radical change. But for popular or vernacular culture, the spectacular substantive increase in communications efficiency had an equally spectacular substantive effect. The natural, organic spontaneous part of vernacular culture continued to be local in orientation and became known primarily as folk culture. But artists and entrepreneurs who consciously created cultural products in order to meet a market demand, found themselves faced with extraordinary opportunities. Railroads, telegraphs, automobiles, telephones, record players, radios, movies, television, and airplanes increasingly made it a relatively simple matter to market and sell mass entertainment on an international level. Thus, popular culture became distinct from folk culture as the former became an international phenomenon that transcended the nation-state.

No country benefitted more from all this than the United States. The power of popular culture penetrated where economic and military power failed. If Sparta was a military state, and Iran a religious state, the United States might be called a media state, beaming its message to the whole world. American music—first jazz, then Rock and Roll, and recently Country; American television shows—"I Love Lucy," "Falcon Crest," and "Dallas"; youth dress-blue jeans, sweatshirts, and printed T-shirts; food and drink—hamburgers, cola, and wine coolers; can be found in most parts of the world. Only a few isolated enclaves have resisted this onslaught. In the Soviet Union, teenagers offer tourists large sums of money to buy the jeans they are wearing. A Disneyland amusement park opened recently in Japan, and is extremely successful. France will also have one. The Indian film industry makes hundreds of movies in Hindi with Indian actors and actresses who are placed in stories appropriate to America but totally removed from traditional Asia. Popular culture has developed far more of an international market than has high culture. Ballet and classical music were restricted primarily to western civilization: they made few inroads in the Third World. The popular culture which originated in the United States probably has had maximum effect on western civilization, but, nevertheless, its effects on non-western societies have been profound.

Thus one might hope that scholars specializing in aspects of American popular culture would compare and contrast their conclusions with those of scholars examining similar phenomena in other societies.

There are many questions to be answered, problems to be explored. Why do similar artifacts and activities have different meanings in different cultures? If American western movies are popular because we recently had vast open spaces and a frontier, why are they so popular in Italy and Japan? Why do Scandinavians relate so quickly to jazz? Arabs to Coca Cola? Why have dozens of European and Asian countries fallen in love with American basketball but only a few with baseball? Asking and answering questions such as these will help students of popular culture separate the particular from the general and will help them identify more precisely the relationships between surface behavior and underlying meaning.

Too often Asian history—like that of the rest of the world—has been written from the top down. We learn the names of the dynasties, emperors, pagodas, and temples, but know nothing about he untold thousands who labored and died creating them.

A primary goal of popular culture is to include every epoch, people, and class—to be free of racial, gender, and political bias. Everyone has a place in the story of humankind. Popular Culture is an aspect of democracy.

In American culture there is an increasing realization that Western culture without its strong Asian and Middle-Eastern elements would be unrecognizable. The travels of Marco Polo to the Far East and the European discovery of Chinese and Middle-Eastern arts and technics were what opened eyes to the Greco-Roman heritage by stirring interest in other cultures.

We are beginning to understand how much we can learn from the Pacific Community. In China, Korea, and Japan, Zen philosophy provides a clue to the difference between a unified culture vision and the battle of elite vs. popular we experience in the West. This battle rages in the secular world as matter of good vs. bad taste, and within our religions, as the "sacred vs. profane"—the battle of good and evil. Zen offers the idea of the sacredness of all—the simple stone equal with the splendid jewel. Artistic care is given to the "ordinary" matters—the popular is also the profound.

In this way the East's cultural view is predisposed toward popular culture while the West has centuries of dualistic thinking to overcome in order to embrace everything people do as being worthy of attention, of interest, of appreciation; to accept everything human. What a discovery to find that such culture exists, and can bring new insight to the West.

Few countries seem as ready to provide new insights as South Korea. The last of the "hermetic kingdoms," her doors were not opened to the world until later in the 19th century. The year 1982 marked the centennial of diplomatic relations between Korea and the United States, but ties have become closer with every passing year. The interests of four major power—The U.S., U.S.S.R., China, and Japan—converge on this ancient and beautiful peninsula. Meanwhile, a series of economic and cultural successes, culminated by the 1988 Summer Olympic Games in Seoul, have given South Korea an ever larger role in world affairs.

There are many unique features in Korean culture that might be explored— the martial arts of taekwondo, for example, or Korean wrestling (ssirum). There are special holidays (Tano and Ch'usok, for example) and Han-gul Day, October 9, commemorating the promulgating of the Korean alphabet by King Sejon in 1446.

Because of the importance of cartoons and comics, we should explore that aspect of Korean popular culture. Kim Hong-do, a famous 18th century artist, is said to have been the originator of the Korean cartoon; the first group of professional cartoonists emerged in the mid-1920s. At that time, "Bong-i" and "Kim-boyl-jang-i" were carried in the monthly magazine, *Yadam*, as the first completely plotted cartoons. They were followed shortly after by the first newspaper comic strips—"Mongtongkuri" ("The Fool"), by No Shimsun in the daily *Cosun Ilbo,* and the works of Woongcho in the monthlies, *Shindonga* and *Jokwang.*

World War II provided the impetus for comic book development in Korea. Kim-Yong-whan, whose character is "Kojubu" ("Mr. Nosey"), took the lead in drawing completely composed cartoons, followed by Kim Song-whan ("Old Man Gobaoo"), Shin Dong-hun ("Notol Jusa" or "Mr. Guffaw"), and Ahn Eui-sup ("Dookobi" or "Mr. Toad"), Chung Woon-kyong ("Aunt Walsoon"), Lee Sang-ho ("Galbissi" and "Mr. Skinny") and Kil Chang-dok ("Jadang-i" or "Clever Boy"). Some of the strips and books continued throughout the Korean War, the longest-lived of the strips being "Old Man Gobaoo."

Comic art is very popular in Korea. In fact, the boom in magazines—with about 800 titles—has been a godsend for cartoonists. The number of comic strip fans increased considerably during the 1970s, and more than one half of all newspaper readers turn to the comic strips first. Many of these strip satirize problems of a nation going through rapid industrialization, i.e., issues of pollution, inflation or terrorism. Although children's comic books are relatively old in Korea, it was not until 1977, that adult versions appeared. That market has continued to expand through the '80s, and today Korean cartoons and comics are among the best in the world. They deserve careful scrutiny and analysis.

What sort of cooperation and collaboration might we seek in the Global Village? There are many possible answers. One good example turned up on a recent lecture tour of Egypt—the Adham Center for Television Journalism in Cairo.

The Center's goal is to introduce into Egypt international standards for TV News field reporting, writing, and video tape editing. The Center teaches students how to use the electronic camera, how then to write a news story as "script" for pictures, interviews with natural sound-on-tape they have secured, how to read their story as a narration "voiced-over" picture, and how to edit that picture to the narrative sound track. There are courses in Broadcast Journalism, TV News Production, Introductory and Advanced TV and News

Reporting and Writing. These courses are offered along parallel lines as a senior-level undergraduate concentration for Mass Communication majors, as well as on the graduate level. Perhaps this format, with suitable variations, can be set up throughout the Middle East, Africa, and Asia. Then a vast source of information and understanding should result.

We watch, we wait. Nothing is more foolish than assuming we know what the future will bring. The stunning drama in China during the summer of 1989 showed how quickly events change the course of a nation, perhaps the world. Words of the American Patriot Patrick Henry, spoken in Richmond in 1775, echoed through the streets of Beijing—"liberty or death." Who can see what lies ahead?

What we can see is how much has happened, in the United States and the world, since Frederick Jackson Turner put forth his Frontier Thesis. Nearing the 21st century, we may well ask William Butler Yeat's question in "The Second Coming":

> And what rough beast, its hour come round at last,
> Slouches to Bethlehem to be born?"

Notes

[1]For a complete list of Turner's writings—plus dissertations and writings about Turner—see Vernon E. Mattson and William E. Marion, *Frederick Jackson Turner: A Reference Guide* (Boston: G.K. Hall, 1985). Turner's disciples and dissenters have created a small library in itself, of which three volumes are especially relevant here: Robin Winks' *The Myth of the American Frontier* (Leicester: Leicester UP, 1971); Jerome O. Steffen's, *Comparative Frontiers: A Proposal for the American West* (Norman: U of Oklahoma P, 1981); and Margaret Walsh's *The American Frontier Revisited* (Atlantic Highlands: Humanities P, 1981).

[2]*The Pacific Rim and the Western World* (Praeger, 1987), edited by Philip West and Frans A.M. Alting von Geusau, provides an up-to-date series of strategic, economic and cultural perspectives. *Pacific Basin and Oceania*, edited by Gerald Fry and Rufino Mauricio in the "World Bibliographical Series" (Clio P, 1987) is the most comprehensive bibliography to date, annotating 1,178 books covering a multitude of subjects and places. *The Emerging Pacific Community: A Regional Perspective*, edited by Robert L. Downen and Bruce J. Dickson (Westview P, 1984) examines the advantages and disadvantages of this concept.

[3]Berger's essay is included in Bill Moyers's *The World of Ideas* (New York: Basic Books, 1969).

[4]For more details, see the 1987 *Asia-Pacific Report*, edited by Charles E. Morrison, and issued by the East-West Center (U of Hawaii P, Honolulu, 1988).

Epilogue

Marshall W. Fishwick

The humanities in our time are in deep trouble. They are in a state of enforced retreat inside Academia and they are marginalized in the wider society. In this book we have attempted not only to suggest why it is so, but how we may alter this retreat. In our bold and bloody epoch this is no easy task—but it is crucial to our survival and well-being.

Ours is the age of the "quickie," which the dictionary defines as "anything hastily produced or contrived by slapdash execution for quick availability." We thrive on instant issues, instant coffee, posters and protesters unlimited. The humanities must show us the eternal in the instant, the meaning in the chaos. If the world alters as we walk on it, they must be as constant as the northern star.

In the Middle Ages the term "humanities" was simply the plural of "humanity," used to designate a subject taught in the universities (such as grammar, rhetoric, or logic). The Renaissance extended "humanities" to signify love of the past, the elevation of human beings, and the spirit of free inquiry. Somehow we have lost this high vision and direction. Behaviorists, positivists, and quantifiers have become anti-humanists. Such movements as existentialism, post-structuralism, and post-modernism have splintered, not united, humanists. They have put us out of touch with reality.

We are molded and modeled by the media: not only what we see, think, eat, and believe, but even the way we dress. Names of people we never say— Calvin Klein, Bill Blass, Ralph Lauren, Gucci, Pucci—give the affluent the same look worldwide...even the same smell. As early as 1973, Ted Carpenter documented the enormous effect of electronic media on traditional societies, in *Oh What A Blow That Phantom Gave Me*; scores of studies since then show how unreality is converted into reality around the globe. Not our bombs but our films are conquering the world.

In the struggle to free Eastern Europe in 1989 and 1990, the bitterest fighting often took place around national television facilities. Those who controlled the tube would control the people. As Jacques Ellul puts it in *Political Illusion*: "To exercise effective control over the state means to be fully available." TV is available.

If power corrupts and absolute power corrupts absolutely, might we be entering a period of electronic tyranny? This is the kind of question humanists should be asking.

172

Once historians wrote about the Hundred Years' War. Now wars are over (as in the Persian Gulf) in a hundred days or hours. But how can we interpret and understand lightning changes in time and space? Let humanities attack that question too.

We live in plural present, with new questions about gender, race, and ethnicity which demand answers. We are travellers passing through all too quickly, and we want our short visit to be full of meaning. The job of the humanities is to supply it.

When we set out to modernize the humanities—as the contributors to this volume suggest—we neither ignore nor underestimate the past. Our future rests in our past: in prehistoric memories, eternal truths, unending struggles. As we move forward to the end not only of a century but a millennium, we see old barriers and platitudes crumble. Some may say we approach Armageddon. We say a new renaissance is at hand, or opportunity for a renaissance.

Many perils await us. The same rocket boosters that carry probes to other planets could carry scud missiles and nuclear bombs to other nations. One road promises discovery, the other destruction. On the one road, a more powerful humanities than we have yet imagined could emerge. All the elements of a new mythology are at our finger tips. Now it is up to us.

Contributors

Glenn J. Browne earning a Ph.D. in Decision Sciences, is co-editor of *Laws of Our Fathers: Popular Culture and The U.S. Constitution* (1986).

Kevin O. Browne a practicing psychologist, is earning a Ph.D. in psychological anthropology.

Ray B. Browne is Distinguished University Professor of Popular Culture and Chairman of the Popular Culture Department, Bowling Green State University. He was founder and is Secretary-Treasurer of the Popular Culture and American Culture Associations, founder and editor of *Journal of Popular Culture* and *Journal of American Culture*. He is an intrepid traveller, is author and editor of more than forty-five books on various aspects of American and popular culture.

William E. Brigman is at the University of Houston-Downtown, Houston, TX.

Gary Burns is Associate Professor of Communication Studies at Northern Illinois University, DeKalb, IL.

Jack Estes is a Professor of Humanities and Social Sciences at Peninsula College, Port Angeles, WA.

Marshall W. Fishwick is Professor of Humanities and Communication Studies at Virginia Polytechnic Institute and State University. Co-editor of *International Popular Culture*, he has held Fulbright grants to four European and four Asian countries, and is currently at work on a book entitled *The Puzzle of Popularity*.

Jon Huer, Associate Professor of Sociology at the University of North Carolina, Wilmington, received his Ph.D. from the University of California, Los Angeles in 1974 (Sociology). He has been teaching and writing in the areas of American culture and institutions. Among his numerous books and articles, *Art, Beauty and Pornography* (1987) and *The Great Art Hoax* (1990) deal with art and the art market more extensively than expressed in this article.

Susan B. Laubach is Vice President at Alex, Brown and Sons. She is a governing trustee on the Maryland State Council of Economic Education and the National Board of the Joint Council of Economic Education. She is currently pursuing her doctoral degree at the University of Virginia.

Michael T. Marsden is a Professor in the Department of Popular Culture and Associate Dean of the College of Arts and Sciences at Bowling Green State University. He is also Co-Editor of the *Journal of Popular Film and Television*.

A.D. Olmsted is Associate Professor of Sociology at The University of Calgary, Calgary, Alberta, Canada.

Rodney Douglas Parker is assistant professor of Architecture in the College of Architecture and Urban Planning at the University of Michigan. His doctoral dissertation at the University of California, Berkeley, was on rhetoric and architectural theory, and since then he has studied the application of both rhetorical and phenomenological theory to architectural aesthetics and interpretation.

Michael Pettengell teaches Popular Culture at Mankato State University, MN.

Joyce Pettis teaches English at North Carolina State University, Raleigh, NC. She is associate editor of *Obsidian II: Black Literature in Review*.

Fred E.H. Schroeder is Executive Secretary-Treasurer of the National Association for Humanities Education and edits their journal, *Interdisciplinary Humanities* from his office at the University of Minnesota, Duluth.

James Seaton is a Professor of English at Michigan State University. Co-editor of *Beyond Cheering and Bashing*, a collection on essays on Allan Bloom forthcoming from the Popular Press and the author of *A Reading of Vergil's Georgics*, he is currently working on a book on American cultural criticism.

Joseph Witek is an assistant professor of English at Stetson University. He is the author of *Comic Books as History: The Narrative Art of Jack Jackson, Art Spiegelman, and Harvey Pekar* (University Press of Mississippi). He is presently working on a narrative study of the comic book form.